Working with DOS

SECOND EDITION

Mark Allen
and
Jean Gonzalez

Prentice Hall
Englewood Cliffs, New Jersey 07632

Library of Congress Cataloging in Publication Data

Allen, Mark
  Working with DOS/Mark Allen Jean Gonzalez.—2nd ed.
    p. cm
  Includes index.
  ISBN 0-13-963828 (pbk.: w/3 1/2-inch diskette).—ISBN 0-13-963844-X (pbk.: w/5 1/4-inch diskette)
  1. Operating Systems (Computers)   2. Microcomputers—Programming.
  I. Gonzalez, Jean   II. Title
QA76.76.Q63A45 1991   91-20080
  005.4'469—dc20   CIP

Prepress buyer: *Ilene Levy*
Manufacturing buyer: *Ed O'Dougherty*
Acquisitions editor: *Elizabeth Kendall*
Marketing manager: *Robert Kern*
Editorial assistant: *Jane Baumann*
Editorial/productions supervision: *BMR, Corte Madera, California*
Copy editing: *Christopher Bernard*
Electronic composition: *Rad Proctor*
Illustrations: *Kit Croucher*
Index: *Susan DeRenne Coerr*
Interior design: *Samuel Jennings*
Project management: *Lisa Labrecque*
Proofreading: *Christopher Bernard*

 ©1992 by Prentice-Hall
A Simon & Schuster Company
Englewood Cliffs, New Jersey 07632

Printed in the United Stated of America

10 9 8 7 6 5 4 3 2 1

ISBN 0-13-963828-8

ISBN 0-13-963844-X

Prentice-Hall International (UK) Limited, *London*
Prentice-Hall of Australia Pty. Limited, *Sydney*
Prentice-Hall Canada Inc., *Toronto*
Prentice-Hall Hispanoamericana, S.A., *Mexico*
Prentice-Hall of India Private Limited, *New Delhi*
Prentice-Hall of Japan, Inc., *Tokyo*
Simon & Schuster Asia Pte. Ltd., *Singapore*
Editora Prentice-Hall do Brasil, Ltda., *Rio de Janeiro*

Contents

8 EDLIN—The DOS Editor 259

9 Sorting, Locating, and Redirecting Input/Output 283

Preface

This book was designed for use in an introductory DOS course. It can be used for those who have no prior computer experience. While the book is intended especially for users of applications programs, it can also be used as an introduction to DOS for beginning programmers.

Outstanding Features
Working with DOS, 2nd Edition, has a number of outstanding features that set it apart from other DOS books. Among them are the following:

1. An overview of general concepts.

2. Learning and performance objectives.

3. Step-by-step guided instruction.

4. Review exercises that reinforce the step-by-step guided instruction.

5. A prepared disk that contains a number of files that enable users to experience the power of DOS.

6. Realistic exercises that use word processing, spreadsheet,and database demonstration files.

7. Summary points that summarize the important concepts in each chapter.

8. Application exercises to be done at the computer that require users to demonstrate their ability to apply what they have learned.

9. Comprehension questions to test understanding of concepts.

10. Completion and matching exercises for general recall.

Where It Can Be Used
The design of the book makes it ideal for use in a number of different instructional settings. It can be used as a textbook for a lecture/laboratory course, as a self-paced laboratory DOS course, as a supplement within a number of different courses, or for independent learning.

Highlights of Each Chapter

Unlike other DOS books, this book explains the importance of learning various DOS commands and whenever possible illustrates important DOS concepts through practical examples.

The Introduction presents an unintimidating overview of computers for those who do not have a computer background.

Chapter One explains how to get started in floppy-disk, hard-disk, and LAN environments. This chapter includes starting a computer, setting the date and time, determining the version of DOS being used.

Chapter Two explains how to prepare floppy disks for use in either a floppy-disk or hard-disk environment. It distinguishes between formatting high- and low-density disks. It also describes how to use the DOS CHKDSK and VOL commands.

Chapter Three explains how files are created and displayed, shows how to use COPY CON to create files, how to display files on the screen and on the printer, how to find out if a file is on a disk without listing the entire directory, and how to display a list of selected files from a directory and send the list to the printer.

Chapter Four differentiates between DISKCOPY and COPY. It shows how to copy, rename, and delete files. It also explains how to change the attributes of a file using the DOS ATTRIB command.

Chapter Five explains what subdirectories are and shows how to plan a tree structure, create, move between, copy to and from, erase and rename files, remove subdirectories, and find out the files that exist in each subdirectory. It includes the use of the DOS commands TREE and XCOPY. It also briefly explains the use of several commercially available software packages that perform the same tasks more easily.

Chapter Six explains more about hard disks. It explains the DOS commands FDISK, APPEND, BACKUP, and RESTORE. There is also a brief explanation on CONFIG.SYS and AUTOEXEC.BAT files.

Chapter Seven explains in detail how to create various batch files, including batch files to help you copy files, erase files, and display the contents of subdirectories.

Chapter Eight explains what an editor is and shows how to use EDLIN.

Chapter Nine explains what filters and pipes are and shows how to use the MORE, SORT, and FIND commands.

How to Use This Book

To use this book, you will need to have three blank disks and the EXERCISES disk that accompanies this book. One of the blank disks will be used to make a backup of the EXERCISES disk. One of the exercises provides instruction for performing this activity.

About the EXERCISES Disk

The EXERCISES disk that accompanies this book contains a number of prepared files that you will use when completing the exercises and learning about DOS. The disk contains some applications software demonstration screens that will help beginners understand what applications software is. It also contains items such as a menu called up when you use batch files, and batch files that contain review questions.

Instructor's Manual

An instructor's manual is available. It contains answers to all of the questions, a comprehensive test, and printouts of all of the screens on the EXERCISES disk.

Acknowledgments

This book was written and developed from a combination of user experience, teaching notes, lab exercises and feedback from colleagues, instructors, and a number of consultants. Many thanks go to a number of reviewers for suggestions and comments on the book: Jack Atkins, Greenville Technical College; Darrell Couch, Florida State University; Delta R. Green, National School of Technology; Lewis E. Hall, Riverside Community College; Victor D. Lopez, Plaza College for Business; Judith Read Smith, Portland Community College; Marjorie J. Sorenson, Golden West Community College. And, finally, thank you to the editors at Prentice Hall, Liz Kendall, Sue Jacob, Catherine Rossback, and Dennis Hogan, and to Susan Nelle at BMR.

Mark Allen
Jean Gonzalez

Introduction

Overview
of Computers

When you have completed the introduction, you will be able to

Learning Objectives:

1. Identify the parts of a computer.
2. Distinguish between temporary and permanent storage of information.
3. Distinguish between floppy disks and hard disks.
4. Explain how disk drives are named.
5. Describe several types of disk drives.
6. Identify the different categories of monitors.
7. Identify the various keys on a PC keyboard.
8. Identify the different types of printers.
9. Explain what a modem is.
10. Explain what software is.
11. Distinguish between application and system software.
12. Explain the meaning of the term DOS.
13. Explain why there are various versions of DOS.
14. Explain how DOS works.

What You Should Know

This book is about DOS—an operating system used for communicating with personal computers. With a knowledge of DOS, you will be able to take control of your personal computer—commanding DOS to help you use your computer for writing letters and reports, preparing budgets and forecasts, invoicing, playing games, and other activities. Before learning what DOS is, why it is necessary, and how it works, you need to be familiar with the equipment on which DOS is used. This chapter briefly describes the parts of the computer system, defines some terms and concepts, and gives you an overview of the equipment that DOS will help you control.

The Computer System

Computers can be used to tutor a learner, act as an opponent in a chess game, reconcile a checkbook, write a letter, project how much money will be earned if a set amount is deposited each month, design an automobile or building, and much more. All these activities can be performed on equipment known as hardware.

Although the equipment can be the same for a variety of activities, each activity requires a different set of instructions. The equipment can only do what it has been instructed to do; therefore, the instructions are what change, not the equipment. These instructions are often referred to as software programs, software packages, or simply software. There are two broad categories of software: applications software and systems software. In this chapter, you will learn about what hardware is, what software is, the kinds of applications software available for use, and how a system software like DOS manages the equipment and enhances the use of applications software. The computer system therefore is both the hardware and software that are needed for performing computer activities.

In many businesses, computers may be linked together to form a local area network (LAN). LANs are commonly used to make it possible for a number of users to access or share the same information. You will learn that using DOS on a computer in a LAN environment is not much different from using DOS on a single computer.

Hardware

The most common pieces of hardware in a computer system are shown in Figure 0.1.

Figure 0.1

Hardware found in a typical computer system.

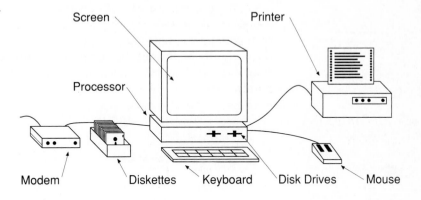

Computers perform three distinct functions: input, processing, and output. Figure 0.1 shows you the pieces of hardware that perform each of these functions. Processing is the ability to change or manipulate data to produce information. This function is performed by the processing unit located within the system unit. In order to process data into information, the computer must first obtain the data from somewhere. Data consist of words, numbers, characters, symbols, or commands that must be entered into the computer by means of a keyboard or other input device (scanner, disk drive, modem, mouse, or touch-sensitive screen). The function of supplying the computer with data is called *input*. Once the data have been changed into information (data in usable form) with the processing unit, they need to be displayed, stored, and/or printed out. The function of displaying, storing, or printing the finalized product is called *output*.

The configuration of the computer in Figure 0.1 is that of the Personal Computer (PC) developed by International Business Machines (IBM) in 1982. Computers that have appeared since then are often enhanced versions of the Personal Computer, made by either IBM or one of its competitors. These computers make up what is known as the "family" of PCs. The computers in the family are categorized from least powerful to most powerful depending on the hardware they use for processing and storage.

Processing and Temporary Storage

Since processing and storage provide the key for determining the computer's power and capabilities, let's look at the hardware used for these purposes.

Central Processing Unit. The processing unit of the personal computer is housed in the same unit (system unit) that contains the disk drives in Figure 0.1. The processing unit contains a microprocessor chip also known as the *central processing unit* (CPU) and a number of temporary storage or internal storage chips. The microprocessor chip determines how fast the computer will process instructions and data; in other words, it affects how fast data will be manipulated within the computer. Figure 0.2 shows a comparison of the various microprocessor chips with representative computers using each chip, and allows you to see how each chip affects a computer's performance.

Figure 0.2

A comparison of the various microprocessor chips used in the PC family of computers.

Chip	Word Size	Size of Word Path for Input/Output	Computer Model	Speed in Megaherz (MHz)
8088	16-bit	8-bit path	IBM-PC, XT	4.77
			IBM PS/2 Models 25, 30	8
8086	16-bit	16-bit path	Tandy 1000 RL	9.54
80C86	16-bit	16-bit path	Toshiba 1000 SE *	9.54
80286	32-bit	16-bit path	IBM PS/2 Model 25-286	10
			IBM PS/2 Model 30-286	10
			IBM PS/2 Model 50 Z	10
			Tandy 1000 RL/2	10
			Tandy 2500 XL/2	16
			Compaq DeskPro 286	16
			Toshiba 1000 XE, 1600 *	12
80386SX	32-bit	16-bit path	IBM PS/2 Model 55SX, 65SX	10
			Tandy 4020 SX	20
			Compaq DeskPro 286	16–20
			Compaq LTE 286 *	16–20
80386	32-bit	32-bit path	IBM PS/2 Model 70	16–25
			IBM PS/2 Model 80	20–25
			Tandy 4016 DX	16
			Tandy 4025 LX	25
			Tandy 4033 LX	33
			Compaq DeskPro 386/20	20
			Compaq DeskPro 386-25	25
			Compaq LTE 386/20 *	20
			Toshiba 3200 *	16
			Toshiba 5200 *	20
80486	32-bit	32-bit path	IBM PS/2 Model 70	25
			IBM PS/2 Model 90	25–33
			Compaq DeskPro 486	25–33

* = Portable computer

The 8088 was the most common chip found on IBM PCs and compatibles during the 1980s. As the need for processing power increased, the 8088 chip became obsolete. It was replaced by the 80286 chip. The 80286 chip could handle approximately eight times as much information as the 8088. It too was replaced by the 80386 and 80386SX. These chips have also been superseded by the 80486.

The 386, 386SX, and 486 chips are all based on the same technology—which means that they are not significantly different. The 486 is actually a combination of 80386 and 80387 in one chip.

The 8087, 80287, and 80387 chips are co-processors. These chips work with the CPU to do heavy arithmetic calculations. For this reason, they are also called math co-processors. Math co-processors are usually an add-on item.

The 80386 and 80486 chips are also rated in speed ranging from 25 MHz to 33 MHz. They are manufactured the same way; however, each chip is tested after manufacture and is categorized as one speed or another.

Our current level of chip development has allowed processing speed to double every six to eighteen months while the cost of these new chips has decreased. The result is that computer users are able to process large amounts of information in a fraction of the time it used to take and at a lower cost.

A *word* is the unit of data that is processed at one time. It does not correspond to a word in English. The size of the word influences how fast data are processed. A larger word means that more data can be processed at a time. Notice that the size of a word and the size of a word path for input/output may differ. The size of a word path for input/output determines how fast data move from an input device such as a keyboard to the processing unit or from the processing unit to an output device such as a printer.

A *megahertz* is the unit for measuring how fast the clock runs that processes data and instructions. A megahertz is one million cycles per second. The faster the clock runs, the more powerful the computer is because it can process data faster.

An easy way to visualize processing power with regard to clock speed and bit-path size is to think of a freeway. If you have an eight-lane highway with traffic moving at 47 miles per hour, it would be analogous to an 8088 chip where eight lanes equals the bit path and 47 miles per hour equals a clock speed of 4.77 megahertz. To increase the number of cars—that is, the flow of traffic—you can change either how fast the cars are allowed to move (47 mph) or increase the number of lanes (8). If you increase the number of lanes to 16, you double the flow of traffic. Likewise, if you increase the speed to 80 miles per hour, you increase the flow of traffic proportionately. A sixteen-lane highway with traffic moving at 80 mph is analogous to the 80286 chip. The 80386 chip at 33 megahertz is analogous to a thirty-three lane highway with traffic moving at 300 miles per hour.

Memory. The other factor that determines a computer's power is its ability to store data while you are working on them. For example, if you are creating or revising a document, the document must be held within the computer's memory while you are manipulating the text. In microcomputers, the hardware used to provide a temporary save area in the computer is called a *memory chip*. The name given to this type of short-term memory is RAM, *random access memory*. RAM can be compared to a blackboard in that you can write to RAM, read what is in RAM, change what has been placed in RAM, and erase all or part of what has been written into RAM.

You can also think of RAM memory, the memory, or storage space inside the computer, as similar to memory belonging to an individual. As an individual, you store miscellaneous data in your memory for a limited time period, until you no longer need them or forget them.

RAM memory also has a limited storage capacity. The amount of storage depends on the number of memory chips present in your computer. Standard memory sizes increased from 64k to 640k bytes (characters) during the 1980s. The letter k stands for kilo, meaning "thousand." In other words, a computer that had a storage capacity of 640k bytes allowed you to store internally approximately 640 thousand characters or 200 pages of text. Although this sounds like a lot of memory, it does not nearly satisfy the requirements of many of today's computer applications, such as scientific analysis, complex color computer drawings, and video presentations. For a long time, the computer industry was frozen at the 640k RAM barrier. Until the release of chips like the 80286 and 80386, chips could not handle more than 640k of text in RAM. Now, with the 80386 and 80486 chips, it is possible to handle 16 megabytes (million bytes) or more of information or approximately 5,000 pages or more of text in memory.

If your computer has more than 640k of RAM, it has what is called expanded memory—memory between 640k and 1 megabyte. Expanded memory is primarily used for video redraw and other hardware requirements; it is also known as shadow RAM. If your computer has beyond 1 megabyte, it has extended memory. Extended memory currently ranges from between 1 megabyte and 16 megabytes. In theory, advanced chips like the 80386 and 80486 can handle up to 4 billion bytes of memory. However, computer applications have yet to be able to take advantage of such large amounts of memory.

The computer you use must have enough memory and a fast enough chip to process the workload you will be generating. For example, if you are using your computer to write papers, an 8088 chip and 640k of RAM may be sufficient. However, if you are going to try to produce graphics, you will probably need at least an 80386 chip and two to four megabytes of RAM.

RAM stores data as long as the computer is running. When it is turned off, the data are lost. For this reason, you need to be able to store data permanently.

Permanent or Disk Storage

In an office, when you want to keep data or information permanently, you file it away. In a computer, when you wish to store data permanently, you need to transfer the data to a magnetic disk (the most common form of permanent storage) or another means of permanent storage such as magnetic tape or optical disk. Disk storage is comparable to a filing cabinet where data and information are stored. (See Figure 0.3.)

Figure 0.3

RAM memory can be compared to a person's memory—it is temporary memory. Disk storage can be compared to a file cabinet where information is stored permanently.

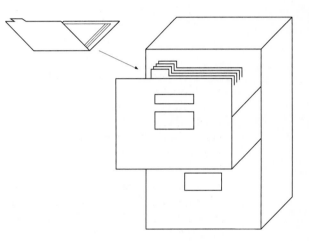

Disks may be floppy disks (also called *diskettes*) or hard (fixed) disks. Disks that are called *floppy disks* (or diskettes) are thin, light-weight, and flexible. They are sealed in plastic jackets to protect their recording surfaces. They are available in two sizes: 3 1/2 inches and 5 1/4 inches. In this book, we use the terms disk and diskette interchangeably.

Hard disks for most personal computers are called Winchester disks. Winchester disks are comprised of one or more rigid disks called *platters*. These disks are contained within an airtight unit and are normally permanently mounted within the computer. For this reason, they are also known as *fixed disks*.

Some newer types of permanent storage devices are optical and removable cartridge drives. Optical drives use disks that are similar to compact laser audio disks and store approximately 600 megabytes on each disk. Optical drives are currently slow to write information to but can retrieve information relatively fast. Optical drives are commonly used to store large amounts of data.

Removable cartridge drives are made from the same material as standard Winchester drives. The advantage of using a removable cartridge drive is twofold: (1) it can be transported easily between computers like a floppy disk; and (2) it provides a relatively low-cost, high-volume storage alternative. Removable cartridge disks store approximately 45 megabytes of information per cartridge. (See Figure 0.4.)

Figure 0.4

The three most common types of disks used are the 5 1/4-inch and 3 1/2-inch floppy diskettes and the Winchester hard disk.

(a) 5 1/4 inch diskette

Write-protect notch

Jacket

Hub opening

Disk

Read-write opening

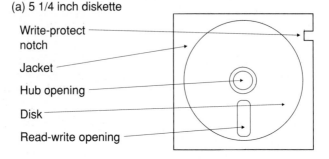

(b) 3 1/2 inch diskette

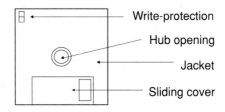

Write-protection

Hub opening

Jacket

Sliding cover

(c) Hard or fixed disk without its cover

Disk surfaces

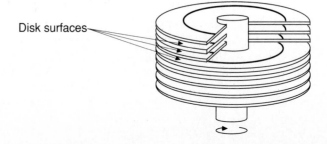

Disk Drives

The way that data are transferred to and from floppy or hard disks into RAM is by means of a disk drive. The disk drive is comprised of a motor that spins the disk(s) and one or more read/write heads, which copy data to the disk from RAM or read data from the disk surface into RAM.

The amount of data that can be stored on a disk depends on both the disk type and the disk-drive technology. For example, the original 5 1/4-inch floppy drive used a double-sided disk that could hold 360,000 characters of information. As with all computer hardware, disk drives have evolved. The 5 1/4-inch floppy disk was redesigned to store 1.2 megabytes (million characters). These are called high-capacity drives. The floppies themselves are called high-density floppies.

With the release of IBM's personal series two (PS/2), a new floppy disk format was introduced. This new format encased the disk in a semi-hard case to protect it from damage. The size of the disk was reduced to 3 1/2 inches in diameter. Originally, this disk stored 720k (thousand characters) of information. Its current storage capacity is 1.44 million characters. The 3 1/2-inch drives are also faster in storing and retrieving data.

Both the 5 1/4-inch high-capacity drives and the 720k 3 1/2-inch drives are becoming obsolete. Most computer systems in today's market contain either or both 360k 5 1/4-inch and 1.44 megabyte 3 1/2-inch drives. The reason that 360k 5 1/4-inch floppies are being used instead of the high-capacity floppies is due to the need to remain compatible with older computer systems. When high-capacity drives are needed, most people prefer the 1.44 megabyte 3 1/2-inch drives.

Disk drives are identified by a letter followed by a colon—for example, A:, B:, C:, D:. Using the PC in Figure 0.1 as an example, the disk drive on the left is considered A:; the one on the right is considered B:. If one hard disk is added, it is C:; a second hard disk is D:. Hard disks are sometimes divided into two separate storage areas. Although the drive may be one physical unit, the computer perceives the separate storage areas as individual drives. In this case, the one hard drive can be both C: and D:.

If a system is using only one floppy disk drive, that floppy disk drive can be considered to be two drives: A: and B:.

Arrangements of Floppy Disk Drives.   Floppy disk drives are also categorized as full height or half height. *Full height* and *half height* refer to the physical size of the drive. The original (full height) drives were approximately four inches tall; half-height drives are only two inches tall. Floppy disk drives can be mounted either horizontally or vertically.

When horizontal half-height drives are used, A: is usually the drive on top, B: is the lower drive. Half-height drives occupy less space than a full-height drive: two half-height drives can fit in the same space as a full-height drive. The half-height drives are the industry standard because of their durability and size. A common configuration consists of two half-height floppy drives: a 5 1/4-inch (360 kilobytes or 1.2 megabytes) and a 3 1/2-inch (1.44 megabytes). (See Figure 0.5.)

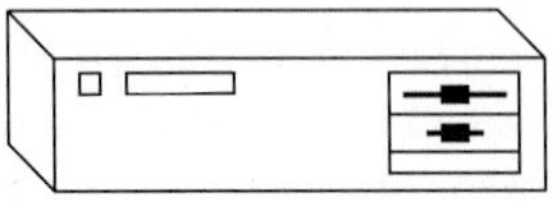

Figure 0.5

A computer with both 5 1/4-inch and 3 1/2-inch disk drives.

Backup Storage

Although disks are reliable, there is always the chance that something might happen to a disk that contains valuable information. In later chapters, you will learn how to use DOS to make backup copies of disks. Then if a disk you need is ruined, you have another containing the same data. Another medium that is also used for this purpose is magnetic tape. Magnetic tape provides a less expensive, more convenient backup for disks. Backing up disks is a time-consuming, but necessary, procedure. Making floppy disk backups usually can take from one to two minutes, while a hard disk backup can take as long as an hour or more, depending on the capacity of the hard disk and on the amount of data on the disk.

As time goes by, optical drives will replace magnetic tape drives as a backup medium because any magnetic medium can be erased by magnetic fields or extreme temperatures, while optical drives are less susceptible to damage.

Input/Output Devices

Although the heart of the computer system is the CPU and temporary storage (RAM), you cannot communicate with these computer parts without input and output (I/O) devices. The number of different devices for input and output to personal computers has increased since the PC was first developed. The most common input device is still the keyboard, but other devices are also becoming popular. The two most common output devices are (1) monitors—screens that look like television screens but are actually windows that allow you to see what is being keyed into RAM, and (2) printers—which are like typewriters used to obtain a hard (paper) copy of the contents of RAM. To use DOS effectively, you need to know something about monitors, keyboards, and printers.

Monitors.   A monitor is simply a screen, similar to a television screen, used to display the communications that occur between you and the computer. Monitors are either monochrome (single color) or color (RGB). Monochrome means single color. Monochrome monitors come in either Amber, Green, or Black and White (also known as paper color). They also come in low, medium, and high resolution. RGB stands for red, green, and blue. When these three "primary" colors are mixed together, any combination of colors can be produced. RGB color monitors are available in four basic types: Color Graphics Adaptor (CGA), Enhanced Graphic Adaptor (EGA), Video Graphics Array (VGA), and Super Video Graphics Array (SVGA).

When color monitors were first introduced, they were called the Color Graphics Adaptor (CGA) monitors because they required an extra computer card called a color graphics adaptor card to be installed in the computer. CGA monitors can display 4 colors in the graphics mode or 16 colors, from a palette of 64, in the text mode. (See Figure 0.6.) CGA monitors use 200 horizontal lines, with 320 pixels per line, for a total of 64,000 pixels per screen. The CGA monitor provides the lowest level of resolution in color monitors.

EGA monitors use the same basic technology found in CGA monitors. They use an additional computer graphics card called the Enhanced Graphics Adaptor card. They allow 16 colors, from a palette of 64, during all uses, but instead of (320 x 200) resolution, the EGA monitor uses (640 x 360) resolution. In other words, the EGA monitor uses 360 lines with 640 pixels per line for a total of 230,400 pixels per screen.

Figure 0.6
Monitors with greater
resolution have a
greater number of
pixels per square inch
and higher scan rates.

Monochrome (Original IBM)

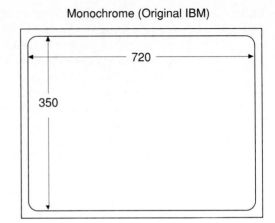

CGA (Color Graphics Adapter)

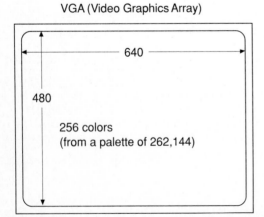

4 colors in graphics mode
16 colors in text mode
(from a palette of 64)

EGA (Enhanced Graphics Adapter)

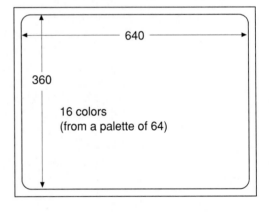

16 colors
(from a palette of 64)

VGA (Video Graphics Array)

256 colors
(from a palette of 262,144)

SVGA (Super Video Graphics Array)

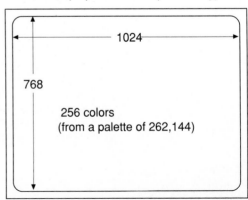

256 colors
(from a palette of 262,144)

VGA monitors use a technology completely different from that used by either CGA or EGA monitors. This new technology allows the VGA monitor to provide 256 colors, from a palette of 262,144 colors, on the screen at any one time. It uses 480 lines with 640 pixels per line for a total of 480,000 pixels per screen.

SVGA monitors are the next generation of VGA monitors. They use (1024 x 768) resolution, or 786,432 pixels. SVGA monitors provide the highest level of resolution. SVGA pictures are almost as sharp as a photograph.

VGA and SVGA monitors are used wherever high resolution computer graphics are required. New 80386 and 80486 computer systems come standard with VGA or SVGA graphics built into the main computer board.

Keyboards.   The keyboards used on PCs and their compatibles consist of three sections:

1. *Function keys* (keys labeled F1 through F12), which use a special storage area of memory called a template. The template stores the last DOS command typed. The function keys can repeat the entire DOS command or part of the command in the template and eliminate the need to retype commands. These keys are either located to the extreme left of the keyboard or appear in a row above the standard alphanumeric (typewriter) keyboard. (See Figure 0.7) You will learn how to use these function keys in later chapters.

2. The standard *alphanumeric keyboard* with the addition of a few special keys. Note the location of these special keys because they will be used with DOS.

3. The *numeric keypad* located at the extreme right-hand side of the keyboard. The numeric keypad can be used to input numbers when the Num Lock key located above the keyboard is depressed. The numeric keypad can also function as cursor movement keys when the Num Lock key is turned off (depressed a second time). The cursor (usually a flashing hyphen or small rectangle) on a screen is the point or place in memory where action is occurring. Two important keys to note on this side of the keyboard are the Ins and Del keys which you will learn to use in later chapters. (See Figure 0.8.)

Tips: When using personal computer keyboards, keep the following tips in mind:

1. Depress the keys lightly, and do not hold down too long. Computer keys are "typematic," meaning they will repeat if held down. The result of depressing the a key too long is aaaaaaaaaaaaaaaaaaaaaa.

2. Be careful not to spill anything onto the keyboards as they are electronic devices. Liquids can irreparably damage a keyboard.

3. Do not despair if you are a fast typist. Sometimes the characters that you type will take a while to echo (display) on the screen.

4. Note that when the Caps Lock key is turned on, you will display a lowercase character if you use a Shift key and a character.

Figure 0.7

Note the position of the keys that are highlighted.

Standard

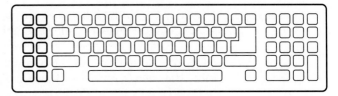

Enhanced

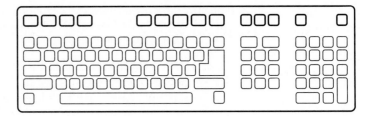

Figure 0.8
Function keys.

Key		Reason Used
⏎	(Return key or Enter key)	Transmits (sends) commands displayed on the screen to computer's memory. After you type a command, you must press the Enter key to tell DOS to execute the command. This key is also called the *transmit key* or *carriage return key*. In this text, we will use Enter to represent the Enter key.
Ctrl	(Control key)	Used simultaneously with other keys for a number of purposes.
Alt	(Alternate key)	Used simultaneously with other keys for a number of purposes.
←	(Backspace key)	Erases a character or space that was just typed. The backspace key deletes the character or space to the immediate left of the cursor.
Caps Lock	(Caps Lock key)	Places alphabetic characters in all uppercase when turned on. This key is a toggle key; it is turned on and off by depressing it. It does not affect symbol keys such as the $, #, and so on.
Shift	(Shift key)	Used like the shift key on a typewriter to capitalize alphabetic letters or to obtain the symbols on the topmost portion of some keys. (Notice that a shift key is positioned at each side of the keyboard.)
PrtSc	(Print screen)	Used with the shift key, it can give you a printout of the material displayed on a screen if your computer has a printer attached and turned on.
Esc	(Escape)	Cancels a line you have typed with DOS and moves the cursor down one line. A backslash (\) indicates a canceled line.
Ins	(Insert)	Inserts a character(s) when used with DOS. Press the INS key once to begin the insert mode and press this key again to end the insert mode.
Del	(Delete)	Deletes a character when used with DOS.
Num Lock		Determines whether the keypad on the right side of the computer will function as cursor movement keys or a numeric keypad.

Other Input Devices.   Because of the cumbersome nature of a keyboard, other input devices have been developed. One of the most widely accepted alternatives to the keyboard is the mouse. A mouse is a pointing device designed originally for art design. It allows the user to point to a specific area on a monitor and either draw a line from one point to another, move a graphic from one place to another on the screen, highlight a section of text for deletion or modification, or perform another activity. A mouse usually has one, two (left and right), or three buttons. On a two-button mouse the left button responds the same way as the Return or Enter key. The right button represents the Esc key. *Clicking* obtained its name from the sound made when a button is pushed; clicking means pressing the left button once on a two-button mouse. Double clicking means pressing the left button twice in rapid succession. When creating art, if you click and hold down the left mouse button and then *drag* the mouse in any direction, and then release, you can draw a line. Some people prefer using a mouse while others prefer using a keyboard for executing commands. A mouse can enhance but cannot totally replace a keyboard.

A scanner is a device that is similar to a copying machine, but instead of producing a hard copy of what it copies, it converts what it reads to a form that can then be used or manipulated in a computer. Scanners come in different sizes and can scan in color or in shades of gray (called gray-scale scanning). They can scan either text or graphics, depending upon the type of scanner.

A digitizer pad is a device used primarily by artists and designers, but is now entering the business world. A digitizer pad uses a pencil-like device that when placed on a digital pad allows the user to draw graphics directly into the computer system. This device usually replaces a mouse.

Printers.   A number of different types of printers have been developed for use with microcomputers. The two categories that they are generally divided into are letter-quality and nonletter-quality printers. Letter-quality printers use various types of printing devices that allow a character to be fully formed. The most common of these devices are print wheels and thimbles. A laser printer is also a letter-quality printer. It uses a photocopying process similar to a copying machine instead of an impact device and produces the fastest, highest quality of print next to phototypeset copy. A disadvantage is that many types of paper cannot be used with laser printers and the printers themselves may be expensive to purchase.

Nonletter-quality printers are generally dot-matrix printers that print characters formed by tiny dots produced by a hairbrushlike device that comes in contact with the paper. Dot-matrix printers are often used for draft purposes because they are less expensive than letter-quality printers and print faster than most printers that use print wheels or thimbles. An advantage is that they can be used to create graphics. Another type of dot-matrix printer that produces a higher-quality print is an ink-jet printer. It produces images by spraying the dots that form the characters onto the page. It is not used as extensively as the other dot-matrix printers because it is more expensive. Higher-resolution color graphics require ink-jet or laser printers, or plotters that print using color.

Modems.   Modems are communication devices used when computers communicate with each other over phone lines. They are used to convert the information you want sent to another computer into signals that can be transmitted over phone lines. Modems can be found either inside the computer (internal) or as separate pieces of hardware (external). (See Figure 0.9.)

Figure 0.9
An external modem.

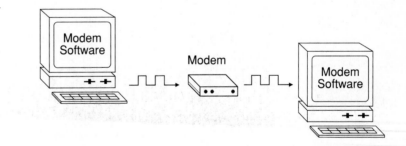

Software

As previously mentioned, computer hardware cannot function without instructions that direct it to perform certain activities. When these instructions are put on disks, they are called *software*.

Software consists of groups of instructions to the computer, called *programs*. The programs are loaded into the memory of the computer from disks. The two general categories of software most commonly used are applications software and systems software.

*Applications
Software*

Applications software is used to perform specific activities such as writing a letter or preparing a budget. Six of the most common general-purpose software packages developed in response to the needs of people whose work involves such common tasks as writing, calculating and planning, recordkeeping, and communicating are the following:

1. Word processing applications software such as WordStar, WordPerfect, Microsoft Word, DisplayWrite, Multimate, and PC Write is used for preparing documents such as letters and reports.

2. Spreadsheet applications software such as Lotus, Math-Plan, Microsoft Excel, and Quatro Pro is used for preparing budgets and forecasting.

3. Database management applications software such as DBase, RBase, Reflex, and FoxPro is used for maintaining client and customer lists.

4. Communications applications software such as SmartCom, PC Talk, and CrossTalk is used for communicating with other computer users located at a distance.

5. Desktop publishing applications software such as Ventura Publisher and PageMaker is used for creating newsletters, brochures, and so on.

6. Graphics applications software such as Harvard Graphics and Corel Draw is used for creating presentations and graphics.

How Software
Programs and
Data Are Stored
on Disks

Software programs and data are stored on disks as files. A file is a grouping of text, numbers, symbols, and so on that you might want to store together. Software programs (both applications software and operating system software) usually consist of a number of files. Each file performs specific tasks related to the software program as a whole. Each of these files have names given to them by the programmer who created them. These names are called *filenames*.

When you use applications software programs, you create your own files and you need to give them filenames. A filename can consist of up to eight characters. When creating filenames, a three-character extension can be added after a period (a separator) if desired. When using word processing applications software, a file might be a letter or other document consisting of one or more pages. A typical filename might be LETTER1.DOC. When using spreadsheet software, it might be a spreadsheet consisting of one or more pages. A typical filename might be SPREAD1.WKS. With database management software, it might be a list of names that takes up a number of pages. A typical filename might be LIST1.DTA. In programming, it might just be the listing of a file or the data that are used in the file. A typical filename might be PROGRAM1.PAS. In Chapter 3, you will learn more about creating files and naming them. (See Figure 0.10.)

A file can be thought of as a chapter in a book. Most chapters that you find in a book consist of similar thoughts or groupings of data. A file on a disk is similar.

If you were writing a book using word processing software, you might create a file for Chapter 1, a file for Chapter 2, and so on.

Figure 0.10(a)

Files can be documents produced by (a) word processing software, …

BMR
Business Media Resources

150 Shoreline Hwy. Bldg. B. Suite 27
Mill Valley, CA 94941   415/331-6021

January 14, 198–

Dear Ms. Ryan:

Thank you for allowing us to submit a proposal for your desktop publishing needs. As our associate, Ms. Gray, indicated to you on the phone, we would make every effort to have your project completed two weeks prior to your requested deadline.

We have enclosed a number of samples of our work to help you make your decision. The third sample is the layout we recommend for your project. You may call Mr. Phillip Heines to further discuss this recommendation.

In any event, may we hear from you by January 28 so we can plan our work schedule for next month.

Sincerely,

Elizabeth Mason
Marketing Representative

Figure 0.10(b)

... (b) spreadsheets, (c) programs created by programmers, or (d) database management software.

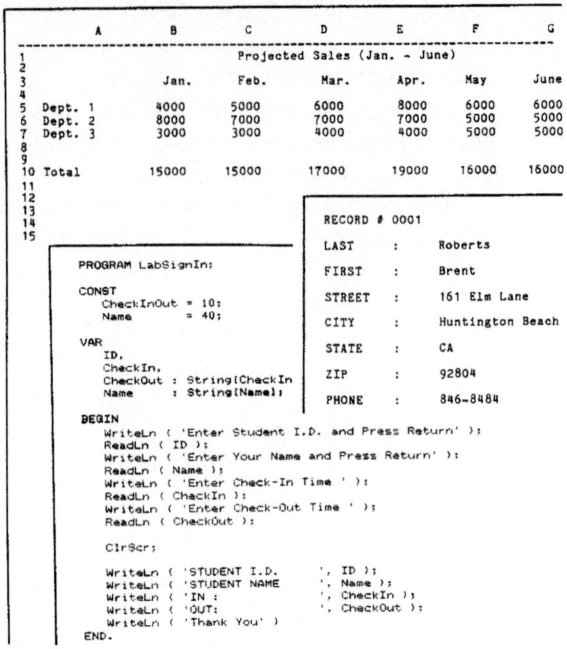

```
        A       B       C       D       E       F       G
-----------------------------------------------------------------
1                       Projected Sales (Jan. - June)
2
3              Jan.    Feb.    Mar.    Apr.    May     June
4
5  Dept. 1    4000    5000    6000    8000    6000    6000
6  Dept. 2    8000    7000    7000    7000    5000    5000
7  Dept. 3    3000    3000    4000    4000    5000    5000
8
9
10 Total     15000   15000   17000   19000   16000   16000
11
12
13
14
15
```

```
                                    RECORD # 0001

                                    LAST     :    Roberts

    PROGRAM LabSignIn:               FIRST    :    Brent

    CONST                            STREET   :    161 Elm Lane
        CheckInOut = 10;
        Name       = 40;             CITY     :    Huntington Beach

    VAR                              STATE    :    CA
        ID,
        CheckIn,                     ZIP      :    92804
        CheckOut : String[CheckIn
        Name     : String[Name];     PHONE    :    846-8484

    BEGIN
        WriteLn ( 'Enter Student I.D. and Press Return' );
        ReadLn ( ID );
        WriteLn ( 'Enter Your Name and Press Return' );
        ReadLn ( Name );
        WriteLn ( 'Enter Check-In Time ' );
        ReadLn ( CheckIn );
        WriteLn ( 'Enter Check-Out Time ' );
        ReadLn ( CheckOut );

        ClrScr;

        WriteLn ( 'STUDENT I.D.     ', ID );
        WriteLn ( 'STUDENT NAME     ', Name );
        WriteLn ( 'IN :             ', CheckIn );
        WriteLn ( 'OUT:             ', CheckOut );
        WriteLn ( 'Thank You' )
    END.
```

(b) Spreadsheet   (c) Program   (d) Database

SPREAD1.WKS   PROGRAM1.PAS   LIST1.DTA

Systems Software

Systems software is the software that controls the operation of your computer system—the input, processing, and output hardware components. Each family of computers has its own system software or operating system. The operating system for IBM and IBM-compatible computers is DOS, an acronym for *disk operating system*.

PC-DOS and MS-DOS

When computers are referred to as "IBM compatible," it means that they can use either the operating system developed by Microsoft Corporation, called MS-DOS, or the IBM equivalent, PC-DOS. International Business Machines (IBM) packages its computers with PC-DOS. Other manufacturers package their IBM-compatible computers with MS-DOS. MS-DOS is actually the product of Microsoft Corporation. IBM made an agreement with Microsoft to allow IBM to use this system for its personal computers and was given the right to make slight alterations and change the name to PC-DOS. In this book, the screens will be displayed in MS-DOS unless noted. Some screens may vary slightly, depending on the type of DOS used. For example, the opening screens for IBM PC-DOS 4.0 and MS-DOS 3.30 differ, as shown in Figure 0.11.

Figure 0.11

PC-DOS and MS-DOS opening screens.

PC-DOS Opening Screen Version 4.0

```
Current time is 7:43:47.67p
Enter new time:
Current date is Fri 03-15-1991
Enter new date (mm-dd-yy):


IBM DOS Version 4.00

C:\>
```

**MS-DOS Opening Screen and
MS-DOS Version 3.30**

```
Current date is Fri 5-3-1991
Enter new date (mm-dd-yy):
Current time is  6:48:22.81
Enter new time:

Microsoft(R) MS-DOS(R) Version 3.30
           (C) Copyright Microsoft Corp 1981-1987


A>
```

Versions of DOS

Another factor that may affect the screen output is what version of DOS you are using. Throughout the years, DOS has repeatedly been upgraded. More and more commands have been added, and other improvements have been made. Each time an improvement is made, a new version results. Figure 0.12 shows the versions and the capabilities that have been added over time. The versions can differ either slightly or can reflect major updates. When major updates occur, the version number increases by one whole number. For example, a major update occurred between 2.0 and 3.0. When minor updates are made, the decimal portion increases by 1. For example, a minor update occurred between versions 2.0 and 2.1.

This book presents the features of DOS that are common to most versions above 3.0, unless otherwise noted. You should consult the DOS operations manual if you have any questions about the version of DOS you are using.

Some of the newer computers such as the IBM PS/2 series require at least a 3.3 version of DOS because of the advances in technology used in these computers. You will later learn how to determine the version you have by using a DOS command.

Figure 0.12

Versions of DOS and why they were introduced.

PC-DOS Version Introduced	Reasons for Change
1.0	IBM PC was developed.
2.0	Fixed disk drive was added to the IBM XT.
2.1	Half-height disk drives for the portable PC were developed.
3.0	1.2-megabyte floppy disks for the AT were developed.
3.1	IBM networking required a DOS up-date.
3.2	3 1/2-inch disk drive required a DOS update.
3.3	Introduced new commands such as APPEND.
4.0	Capacity for running multiple programs simultaneously required a DOS update. This version breaks the 32 megabyte hard-drive size barrier.

Note: All references to DOS commands will refer to MS-DOS version 3.30.

What DOS Does

DOS provides a way for you the user to communicate with the hardware of the computer system. The basic functions of DOS are as follows:

1. DOS acts as a controller of input and output operations (I/O operations) such as moving data from a disk drive to RAM or from RAM to a printer. Without DOS, each applications program would have to contain instructions to tell the computer to perform the various operations involved in input and output in addition to the instructions to perform the activity of the applications program.

2. DOS interprets and executes the DOS commands that you will learn to enter at the keyboard. Without DOS, you would not be able to send the commands to control the system hardware.

3. DOS allows you to manage the information that is stored on disks. A way of visualizing how DOS manages information stored on disks is to think of your computer as an electronic library. Inside the library are large work tables or work spaces, which are equivalent to the RAM memory of the computer. In this library, disks are used instead of books. The information in the books is arranged in files instead of chapters. When you wish to read a chapter (file) from the book, it must be placed on the large work table, that is, in the RAM memory of the computer. In this library, DOS acts as the librarian, performing functions similar to those that you normally perform in a library. You command DOS (the librarian) to retrieve the file you want and place it on the work space in RAM.

4. DOS allows you to configure your system so that your applications software programs can operate at their optimum level.

Many of the specific actions of controlling the computer hardware are performed automatically without your needing to have any knowledge of them. Now, if this is true, you must be thinking, "Why do I have to learn about a computer's operating system?" Let's see why.

Why Learn About DOS?

DOS is not only an operating system, but it is also a very powerful tool for users of applications software programs and computer programmers. DOS allows you to

1. Customize the operation of your computer to meet your personal needs.

2. Make the operation and use of applications programs more efficient and user-friendly.

3. Control the flow of information to and from your hardware components.

4. Work efficiently to manage your disks and files.

Knowing how to use DOS puts you in control of your computer.

Summary Points

1. A computer system consists of both hardware and software.

2. The most common pieces of hardware in a computer system are a keyboard, a system unit containing memory and a CPU, a monitor, and a printer. Many computers also are connected to modems, which allow communication with other computers.

3. Computers perform three functions: input, processing, and output.

4. Processing is the ability to change or manipulate data to produce information.

5. In order to process data into information, data must be entered into the computer by means of a keyboard or other input device.

6. Supplying the computer with data is called *input*.

7. Displaying, storing, or printing the final product is called *output*.

8. The computer's power is based upon its processing and storage capabilities.

9. The processing unit contains a microprocessor chip, also known as the *central processing unit* (CPU), and a number of temporary storage or internal storage chips.

10. The type of microprocessor chip used determines how fast the computer will process instructions and data.

11. A *word* is the unit of data that is processed at one time. It does not correspond to a word in English. A larger word size means that more data can be processed at a time.

12. *Megahertz* is the unit for measuring how fast the clock runs that processes data and instructions. A megahertz is one million cycles per second.

13. In microcomputers, the hardware used to provide a temporary save area in the computer is called a *memory chip*.

14. A memory chip provides short-term memory. Short-term memory is called RAM, *random access memory*.

15. RAM memory has a limited storage capacity. The amount of storage depends on the number of memory chips present in your computer.

16. RAM stores data as long as the computer is running. When the computer is turned off, the data are lost.

17. Data are stored permanently on magnetic disks, magnetic tapes, or optical disks.

18. Magnetic disks are the most common type of permanent storage.

19. Disks may be floppy disks (also called *diskettes*) or hard disks.

20. Floppy disks (or diskettes) are thin, light-weight, and flexible. They are sealed in plastic jackets to protect their recording surfaces.

21. Floppy diskettes are available in two sizes: 3 1/2 inches, 5 1/4 inches. The 3 1/2-inch and 5 1/4-inch sizes are the most frequently used sizes for personal computers.

22. Hard disks for most computers are Winchester disks. Winchester disks consist of one or more rigid disks called *platters*.

23. Data are transferred to and from floppy or hard disks by way of a disk drive. The disk drive is composed of a motor that spins the disk(s) and one or more read/write heads, which copy data to the disk from RAM or read data from the disk surface into RAM.

24. Disk drives are identified by a letter followed by a colon, for example, A:, B:, C:, D:.

25. Floppy disk drives can be categorized as full-height or half-height. They can also be either horizontal or vertical.

26. The contents of a disk can be copied to another disk for backup purposes. Magnetic tape provides a less expensive and more convenient backup for disks.

27. The most common input device used is the keyboard, but other devices are becoming popular.

28. The two most common output devices are monitors and printers. Monitors display the contents of RAM to the screen. Printers display the contents of RAM to paper (hard copy).

29. The four basic types of monitors are monochrome, CGA, EGA, and VGA.

30. CGA, EGA, and VGA monitors display in the three primary colors (red, green, and blue), which the eye interprets as a variety of colors. For this reason, CGA, EGA and VGA monitors are also called *RGB monitors*.

31. Monitors are evaluated according to the resolution—sharpness or clarity—of images.

32. Keyboards for PCs and compatibles consist of three sections: function keys, alphanumeric keyboard, and numeric keypad.

33. The two categories of printers used with microcomputers are letter-quality and nonletter-quality printers.

34. Modems are communications devices used when computers communicate with each other over phone lines.

35. The majority of people who use computers today use applications software packages designed to increase their personal productivity. Applications software cannot be used without an operating system such as DOS.

36. Applications software is used to perform specific activities such as writing a letter or preparing a budget.

37. Systems software is the software that controls the operation of your computer.

38. DOS is an acronym for *disk operating system*.

39. When computers are said to be IBM PC compatible, it means that they can use either the operating system developed by Microsoft Corporation (MS-DOS) or the IBM equivalent (PC-DOS).

40. Several different versions of DOS have been developed. Versions are distinguished by numbers (1.0, 2.0, 2.1, 3.1, and so on). The versions can differ slightly or can reflect major updates. When a major update occurs, the version number increases by one whole number (2.0 and 3.0). When a minor update occurs, the decimal portion increases by 1.

41. DOS provides a way for you the user to communicate with the computer. It puts you in control of your computer.

Comprehension Questions

Supply the answers to the following questions.

1. List the parts of a computer.

2. Explain the difference between temporary and permanent storage.

3. Explain how disk drives are named.

4. Distinguish between floppy disks and hard disks.

5. Draw a diagram depicting the various types of disk drives.

Completion Exercises

Complete the following sentences by supplying the proper answer(s).

1. _____ is the physical equipment of a computer system.

2. The functions a computer performs are _____, _____, and _____.

3. The _____ _____ is the temporary storage area within the computer.

4. Two categories of disks used for permanent storage of information are _____ disks and _____ disks.

5. The input device you will use most when working with DOS is a _____.

Matching Exercises

Choose the correct letter from the right-hand column

1. Num Lock

2. Esc

3. Shift key

4. Enter key

5. Ins

a. Used simultaneously with other keys for a number of purposes.

b. A single-color monitor.

c. Cancels a line you have typed in DOS.

d. Determines whether the keys on the far right of a keyboard will be cursor movement keys or a numeric keypad.

e. A multicolor (16-color) monitor that requires a color graphics card.

6. Del

f. Places characters all in uppercase when depressed along with the character.

7. Ctrl key

g. Transmits (sends) commands displayed on the screen to the computer's memory.

8. Monochrome

h. Inserts a character at a time when used with DOS.

9. CGA

i. Deletes a character at a time when used with DOS.

10. VGA

j. A multicolor (256-color) monitor that produces high-resolution graphics.

1

Getting Started in a Floppy Disk/ Hard Disk/LAN Environment

When you have completed this chapter, you will be able to

Learning Objectives:

1. Explain what "booting the system" means.

2. Explain what a system prompt is.

3. Explain what a DOS command is.

4. Describe how to handle disks properly.

Performance Objectives:

1. Insert a disk properly.

2. Perform a cold boot.

3. Find the version of DOS you are using.

4. Perform a warm boot.

5. Enter the time and date.

6. Change the time and date.

Chapter Overview

The majority of people who work with computers today use applications software packages to increase personal productivity. Applications software packages cannot function without an operating system such as DOS.

To use any of the applications software packages available for your personal computer, you need to become acquainted with at least a few of the DOS operating system commands. The more you learn about DOS, the more control you will have over your software packages and your computer.

In this chapter, you will learn how to start your computer using DOS. While starting DOS, you will also learn to

1. Enter the time and date. When the current time and date are entered, the clock inside the computer will be correct. When you store the documents you create, the proper date and time they were created will be recorded.

2. Find the version of DOS you are using. When you use certain applications programs, you will be required to use a certain DOS version.

3. Clear all information in memory and restart the computer. When you exit one applications software package and go to the next, you may want to clear the computer's memory without turning the computer off and starting all over.

Without understanding these basics, you might be able to start your computer, but you might not be as efficient as you could be.

Booting the System

The first step in using your computer is to load DOS into your computer system. Your computer system is unable to operate without an operating system like DOS. Loading DOS into the computer is called "booting the system." The two ways that you can boot a system are (1) by turning the computer power switch on (cold boot) or (2) by restarting the system by clearing the computer's memory and reloading DOS (warm boot). To perform a warm boot, hold the Ctrl key down while pressing the Alt followed by the Del key. After all three have been depressed together, release them simultaneously.

The only difference between a cold boot and a warm boot is that during a cold boot the computer runs a full start-up diagnostic routine while a warm boot bypasses the diagnostic routine; it just clears the computer memory and reloads DOS. A cold boot takes a few more seconds than a warm boot. A computer should be turned off for at least 15 seconds before attempting a cold boot; otherwise, the computer perceives the off-and-on power flow as a surge and, to protect itself, may not restart. Many computers also have a reset button that, when pressed, performs a warm boot.

When using a floppy-disk system, you must have a DOS disk in Drive A: while performing a cold or warm boot. When using a hard-disk system, DOS must be installed on the hard disk. During a hard-disk system boot (cold or warm), the computer first checks to see if a DOS disk is in Drive A:; if not, it will look for DOS on the hard disk. If there is a hard disk failure, this check allows you to boot the system from the A: drive. When you turn on a hard-drive system, the computer may bypass the system prompt and load a menu system that has been installed for ease of loading applications programs; if so, locate the exit-to-DOS choice to return to DOS.

When a computer is installed on a local area network (LAN), it is usually set up to bypass the normal DOS prompt during a system boot and enter the LAN menu system. If you are using a computer on a LAN system and wish to return to DOS, it is necessary to exit the menu system rather than reboot the computer. A reboot would just reload the LAN system menu. On many LAN menus, you will find an option labeled "exit to DOS." If you do not have this option, you may try exiting the LAN to return to DOS by using a LOGOFF command. Check your LAN documentation for appropriate exit procedures.

How Do You Know That You Have Loaded DOS?

Whenever DOS is loaded, you will be given a system prompt. The system prompt is an A> if a DOS disk is placed in Drive A: and a warm or cold boot performed. If you have a hard disk system, the system prompt is normally a C>. The prompt itself may look slightly different as will be discussed in a later chapter. The system prompt indicates that DOS has been loaded into the computer and is awaiting a command. Before looking further into these DOS commands, let's look at what they really are.

What is a DOS COMMAND?

A DOS command can be either a name of a file that contains instructions (software) that tell the computer system to perform a certain action or a command that you can give DOS at any system prompt.

There are two types of DOS commands: Internal (RAM-resident) and External (disk-resident). This book covers almost all of the Internal commands and about half of the External commands. Refer to your DOS manual for more information about the commands not covered.

Internal commands are loaded into RAM during the system boot and are available at any system prompt. For this reason they are called RAM resident. You will not find them listed on the Directory of a disk because they are not independent files. They are part of the DOS file COMMAND.COM that is loaded into the computer's memory during the system boot. The Internal commands available to you depend on the version of DOS you are using. Internal commands are used to set the computer's date and time, display the version of DOS you are using, copy files, rename files, delete and erase files, clear the screen, and much more.

In addition to the standard Internal commands, there are several Internal commands used within special files called Batch files. These Internal commands as well as Batch files will be covered in Chapter 7.

External DOS commands are files found on a DOS disk. For this reason they are called disk-resident commands. These commands will be listed on the directory of a DOS disk, or on a hard disk. DOS External commands are used to format disks, check the status of disks, backup and restore files to and from hard drives, sort files, find specified strings of text, and much more. Most versions of DOS contain two diskettes: a Startup disk and an Operating disk. If your DOS files are contained on two disks, make sure that you are using the disk with the correct file(s) on it.

Hands-On Activities

In the following section, you will learn how to handle diskettes, start up a computer, enter the appropriate time and date, change the time and date, find out what version of DOS you are using, and restart a computer by clearing the computer's memory.

How to Handle Diskettes

Since you will be using a DOS diskette to start your computer, you need to know the correct procedure for inserting diskettes. Your disk drive is either a horizontal or vertical disk drive. If your disk drive is horizontal, follow the procedure shown in Figure 1.1(a) or (c). If your disk drive is vertical, follow the procedure shown in Figure 1.1(b) or (d).

Figure 1.1

How to insert disks into drive. The procedure for inserting disks into (a) a horizontal 5 1/4-inch disk drive, (b) a vertical 5 1/4-inch disk drive, (c) a horizontal 3 1/2-inch disk drive, and (d) a vertical 3 1/2-inch disk drive.

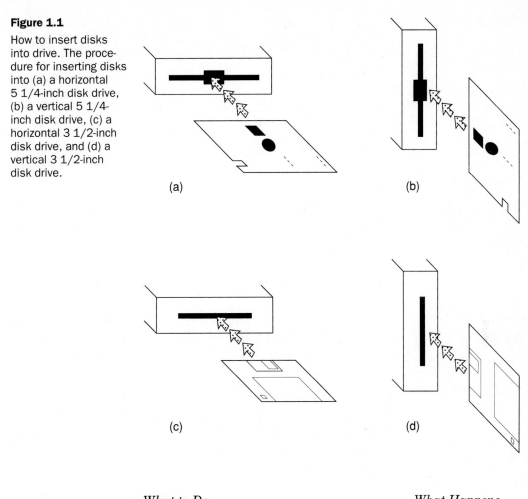

(a)   (b)

(c)   (d)

	What to Do	*What Happens*
Step 1	Hold the DOS diskette in your hand with your thumb on the label as shown in Figure 1.1.	Nothing.
Step 2	Open the door to Disk Drive A:.	
Step 3	Insert the disk carefully into Drive A:.	Nothing.
Step 4	Close the disk drive door.	

Note: Be careful not to force a disk into a drive or to force a door to close. Either of these actions can destroy a disk.

In addition, keep in mind the tips listed in Figure 1.2 when handling diskettes.

Figure 1.2

Disks must be handled with care. The vinyl jacket (protective cover) is the only surface that should be touched.

Do's

1. Keep floppies dust-free by storing them in their protective envelopes.
2. Store floppies in an up-right position.
3. Label diskettes with appropriate names for the contents of the disks.
4. Use a felt-tip pen to write on diskette labels.

Don'ts

1. Never touch the recording surface—the part not protected by the protective covering.
2. Do not bend, fold, or staple.
3. Do not expose disks to magnetic surfaces.
4. Do not use disk immediately after exposure to extreme heat or cold.
5. Do not remove a diskette from a drive while the drive light is on.

How to Perform a Cold Boot on a Floppy-Disk System

Before performing a cold boot on a floppy-disk system, you need to locate the on/off switch of the computer (CPU) and monitor that you are using. The switches are normally located as follows:

Computer (CPU).   The switch appears either on the left or right side of the unit, toward the back. Otherwise, look at the right or left side of the back panel. Power switches for the IBM PS/2 models are located on the front of the system unit. The switch has two positions—"O" and "–": "O" means off and "–" means on.

Monitor.   The switch normally appears on the right-hand side of the monitor next to the screen, but may be located at the top of the monitor or on the lower right or left corner. Usually two knobs are found next to one another—one for power and one to adjust screen brightness. Sometimes these knobs are hidden behind a panel.

When you are booting the system, DOS must be in Drive A:. In a one- or two-floppy-disk drive system, you must put the disk containing DOS into Drive A:. The system must then be turned on—both the screen (monitor) and the computer (CPU) must be turned on.

The following steps are used to perform a cold boot on a one- or two-floppy-disk drive system.

Perform the following steps. If the steps lead you to an unsuccessful attempt, you have skipped a step or performed a step incorrectly, and you should start over with the first step in the section. You may skip this section if you are using a hard-drive or a computer in a LAN.

	What to Do	*What Happens*
Step 1	With the DOS diskette in Drive A:, check that the disk drive door is closed.	Nothing.
Step 2	Turn the power on for the computer and screen.	Sometimes numbers will be displayed on the screen, while the computer checks its memory and tests to ensure that other hardware components are working. A cursor begins to flash on the screen. The red drive light will go on. A beeper sounds.

A prompt (a request for a user response) similar to the following one appears, depending on the version of DOS you are using:

```
Current date is Sun 3-17-1991
Enter new date (mm-dd-yy):
```

Note: *You cannot enter a date earlier than 1/1/80.*

Step 3   Type the current date using the format   See screen that
              MM-DD-YY and press Enter. For example,   follows.
              type 04-28-91 and press Enter.
              Note: Do not type the name of the day;
              DOS will fill this in for you.

The following message appears

```
Current date is Sun 3-17-1991
Enter new date (mm-dd-yy): 4-28-91          ▶The date you type.
Current time is 8:00:16.00
Enter new time:
```

Note: If the current time and date are correct, you do not have to reenter
           them. Just tap the Enter key twice. The date and time should be
           correct if your computer has a built-in clock.

Step 4   Type the current time based on the 24-hour   See the screen that
              clock. For example, if the time is 4:05 P.M.,   follows.
              type 16:05 and press Enter. You may be
              more precise and add seconds.

Note: DOS assumes a 24-hour clock. Thus, 1 A.M. to noon is 01 to 12
           respectively, 1 P.M. becomes 13, 2 P.M. is 14, and so on.

The following message appears

```
Microsoft(R) MS-DOS(R)    Version 3.30
         (C) Copyright Microsoft Corp. 1981-1987

A>_                                              ▶Flashing cursor.
```

Note: This message will vary depending on the version of DOS you are using.

Variations in
Entering the
Time and Date

The following variations can be used when you enter time and date:

1. Enter hours using military time from 0 to 23.

2. Enter hours in the form of hours/minutes/seconds/hundredths of seconds, or leave off the seconds and hundredths of seconds.

3. Use a / or – (or . in DOS version 3.1) to separate date entries.

4. Use a : (or . in DOS version 3.1) to separate time entries.

5. Enter or omit leading zeros when entering the date.

6. Enter or omit the century part of a date.

Tips:

1. Wait at least 15 seconds to turn a computer back on after it has been turned off.

2. Do not remove a disk when the disk drive light is on.

*How to Change
the Date
and Time*

You need to use the DOS DATE and TIME commands

1. If you entered either date or time or both incorrectly during the system boot.

2. If you were not asked for the time and date at all.

3. If your computer's internal clock has malfunctioned and is no longer keeping the correct time.

When using these two commands, DOS not only displays the date and time found in its memory, but also prompts you for a new date and time.

What to Do	*What Happens*
Step 1 At the A > type DATE and press Enter. (Uppercase, lowercase, or a combination of upper- and lowercase can be used.)	See screen that follows.

```
A>DATE
Current date is Sun 4-28-1991
Enter new date (mm-dd-yy):
```

▶*DATE is what you
type in.*

Note: *You cannot enter a date earlier than 1/01/80.
The "current date" may vary.*

Step 2	Enter a new date and press Enter.	An A > appears.
Step 3	At the A > type TIME and press Enter.	See screen that follows.

```
A>TIME
Current time is 13:31:13.43
Enter new time:
```

▶ *TIME is what you type in.*

The "current time" will vary.

Step 4	Enter a new time and press Enter.	An A > appears.

Note: If the current time and date are correct, just tap the Enter key twice. The date and time should be correct if your computer has a built-in clock.

Review Exercises

1. Use the DOS internal command DATE to enter the date of your next birthday.

2. Use the DATE command again to find out the day of the week your birthday will fall on.

How to Find the Version of DOS You Are Using

At times you may need to check the version of DOS that you are using, to see if it is appropriate for your intended use. For example, some applications program packages require certain versions of DOS. A program might require DOS 3.3 and will not work with other versions.

To find the version of DOS that you are using, at the A > type VER.

	What to Do	*What Happens*
Step 1	At the A > type VER and press Enter.	See screen that follows.

If you are using MS-DOS version 3.30, the following message is displayed:

```
A>VER

MS-DOS Version 3.30

A>_
```
▶*Flashing cursor.*

How to Reboot the System (Warm Boot)

If you are working with one applications program and you wish to use a different applications program, you will want to clear the computer's memory and obtain the system prompt again. You perform a warm boot by depressing three keys (Ctrl, Alt, Del) simultaneously while the machine is running. You do not have to be at the A > to use this procedure. You can use this procedure any time you wish to obtain an A > after DOS has been booted.

	What to Do	*What Happens*
Step 1	Depress the Ctrl key, the Alt key, and the Del key simultaneously.	You have rebooted the system. Therefore, you must enter the date and time again.

Tip: If pressing Ctrl, Alt, and Del simultaneously does not reboot the system, perform a cold boot.

How to Perform a Cold Boot on a Hard-Disk System

Before performing a cold boot on a hard disk system, you need to locate the on/off switch of the computer (CPU) and monitor that you are using. The switches are normally located as follows:

Computer (CPU).   The switch appears either on the left or right side of the unit, toward the back; look at the right or left side of the back panel. Newer systems might locate the switch on the front panel adjacent to a reset switch. Power switches for the IBM PS/2 models are located on the front of the system unit. The switch has two positions—"O" (off) and "–" (on).

Monitor.   The switch normally appears on the right-hand side of the monitor next to the screen, but may be located at the top of the monitor or on the lower-right or -left corner. Usually two knobs are found next to one another—one for power and one to adjust screen brightness. Sometimes these knobs are hidden behind a panel. Both the screen (monitor) and the computer (CPU) must be turned on.

The following steps are used to perform a cold boot on a hard disk system.

Perform the following steps. If the steps lead you to an unsuccessful attempt, you have skipped a step or performed a step incorrectly, and you should start over with the first step in the section.

	What to Do	*What Happens*
Step 1	Make sure that Drive A: does not contain a diskette.	
Step 2	Turn the power on for the computer and screen.	A cursor may begin to flash on the screen. Sometimes numbers will also be displayed on the screen, while the computer checks its memory and tests to ensure that other hardware components are working. One or more drive lights will go on. A beep sounds.

Note: Other information may also appear on the screen during this process.

A prompt (a request for a user response) similar to the following one normally appears, depending on the version of DOS you are using:

```
Current date is Sun 3-17-1991
Enter new date (mm-dd-yy):
```

Note: *You cannot enter a date earlier than 1/1/80.*

Note: Steps 2 and 3 may be reversed.

| Step 3 | Type the current date using the format MM-DD-YY and press Enter. For example, type 04-28-91 and press Enter. *Note:* Do not type the name of the day; DOS will fill this in for you. | See screen that follows. |

The following message appears:

```
Current date is Sun 3-17-1991
Enter new date (mm-dd-yy): 4-28-91
Current time is 8:00:35.11
Enter new time:
```
▶*The date you type.*

Note: If the current time and date are correct, just tap the Enter key twice. The date and time should be correct if your computer has a built-in clock.

| Step 4 | Type the current time based on the 24-hour clock. For example, if the time is 4:05 p.m., type 16:05 and press Enter. You may be more precise and add seconds. | See the screen that follows. |

Note: DOS assumes a 24-hour clock. Thus, 1 A.M. to noon is 01 to 12 respectively, 1 P.M. becomes 13, 2 P.M. is 14, and so on.

The following message may appear

```
Microsoft(R) MS-DOS(R)    Version 3.30
          (C) Copyright Microsoft Corp. 1981-1987
C>_
```

▶*Flashing cursor.*

Note: What appears next on the screen of your computer depends on what it has been programmed to do following a system boot. Many computers bypass the DOS system prompt C:\> and immediately load a list of choices (a menu) from which users can select the application they wish to use. The file that tells the computer what to do is called the AUTOEXEC.BAT batch file. You will learn how to create and edit the AUTOEXEC.BAT file in a later chapter.

Variations in Entering the Time and Date

The following variations can be used when you enter time and date:

1. Enter hours using military time from 0 to 23.

2. Enter hours in the form of hours/minutes/seconds/hundredths of seconds, or leave off the seconds and hundredths of seconds.

3. Use a / or – (or . in DOS version 3.1) to separate date entries.

4. Use a : (or . in DOS version 3.1) to separate time entries.

5. Enter or omit leading zeros when entering the date.

6. Enter or omit the century part of a date.

Tips: 1. Wait at least 15 seconds to turn a computer back on after it has been turned off.

2. Do not remove a disk when the disk drive light is on.

How to Change the Date and Time

You need to use the DOS DATE and TIME commands

1. If you entered either date or time or both incorrectly during the system boot.

2. If you were not asked for the time and date at all.

3. If your computer's internal clock has malfunctioned and is no longer keeping the correct time.

Most 80286, 80386, and 80486 computers have built-in clocks that keep accurate track of the date and time. These clocks are powered by their own independent batteries. If the battery fails or the clock experiences a power surge, it might lose track of either or both the date and time. If this occurs, use the DATE and TIME DOS commands to reset the clock. If resetting the clock by this means does not work, your computer may have a set-up program that will help you reset the clock. If so, check your computer manual for the appropriate steps.

When using these two commands, DOS not only displays the date and time found in its memory, but also prompts you for a new date and time.

	What to Do	*What Happens*
Step 1	At the C:\> type DATE and press Enter. (Uppercase, lowercase, or a combination of upper- and lowercase can be used.)	See screen that follows.

```
C:\>DATE
Current date is Fri 04-28-1991
Enter new date (mm-dd-yy):
```

▶*DATE is what you type in.*

Note: *You cannot enter a date earlier than 1/01/80. The "current date" may vary.*

Step 2	Enter a new date and press Enter.	A C:\> appears.
Step 3	At the C:\> type TIME and press Enter.	See screen that follows.

```
C:\>TIME
Current time is 16:07:43:47.67
Enter new time:
```

▶*TIME is what you type in.*

The "current time" will vary.

Step 4	Enter a new time and press Enter	A C:\> appears.

Note: If the current time and date are correct, just tap the Enter key twice. The date and time should be correct if your computer has a built-in clock.

| *Review Exercises* | 1. Use the DOS internal command DATE to enter the date of your next birthday. |
| | 2. Use the DATE command again to find out the day of the week your birthday will fall on. |

| *How to Find the Version of DOS You Are Using* | At times you may need to check the version of DOS that you are using, to see if it is appropriate for your intended use. For example, some applications program packages require certain versions of DOS. A program might require DOS 3.3 and will not work with other versions. |

To find the version of DOS that you are using, at the C:\> type VER.

	What to Do	*What Happens*
Step 1	At the C:\> type VER and press Enter.	See screen that follows.

If you are using MS-DOS version 3.30, the following message is displayed:

```
C>VER

MS-DOS Version 3.30

C>_
```

►*Flashing cursor.*

| *How to Reboot the System (Warm Boot)* | If you are working with one applications program and you wish to use a different applications program, you will want to clear the computer's memory and obtain the system prompt again. You perform a warm boot by depressing three keys (Ctrl, Alt, Del) simultaneously while the machine is running. You do not have to be at the C:\> to use this procedure. You can use this procedure any time you wish to obtain a C:\> after DOS has been booted. |

	What to Do	*What Happens*
Step 1	Depress the Ctrl key, the Alt key, and the Del key simultaneously.	You have rebooted the system. Therefore, you must enter the date and time again.

Tip: If pressing Ctrl, Alt, and Del simultaneously does not reboot the system, perform a cold boot.

Note: Although you have learned to boot your system, the exercises in this book require that you reboot your computer with a floppy DOS disk in Drive A:.

How to Perform a Cold Boot on a Computer in a LAN

The computer that you are using in a LAN may be either a "dumb terminal" or a computer that has its own hard drive. A dumb terminal is a computer without a CPU; it is just a keyboard and a monitor. The main item that you must remember when using a LAN is that the LAN simply gives you access to greater processing power and storage than a single computer; otherwise, using a LAN is similar to using a single computer. You still must load DOS into the computer system when you start. This process is called "booting the system." The two ways that you can boot the system are (1) by using a cold boot (turning the computer power switch on) or (2) by performing a warm boot (restarting the system by clearing the computer's memory).

Before performing a cold boot, you need to locate the on/off switch of the computer (CPU) and monitor that you are using. The switches are normally located as follows:

Computer (CPU). The switch usually appears on either the left or right side of the unit, toward the back. Look at the right or left side of the back panel.

Power switches for the IBM PS/2 models are located on the front of the system unit. The switch has two positions—"O" (off) and "–" (on).

Monitor. The switch normally appears on the right-hand side of the monitor next to the screen, but may be located at the top of the monitor or on the lower-right or -left corner. Usually two knobs are found next to one another—one for power and one to adjust screen brightness. Sometimes these knobs are hidden behind a panel.

Note: For many LANs to operate, all the computers in the LAN must be turned on.

The following steps are used to perform a cold boot on a computer in a LAN environment. Do not attempt to do these steps if you are not using a computer in a LAN environment.

Perform the following steps. If the steps lead you to an unsuccessful attempt, you have skipped a step or performed a step incorrectly, and you should start over with the first step in the section.

	What to Do	*What Happens*
Step 1	Make sure that Drive A: is empty unless your system requires a floppy disk for the system boot.	Nothing.
Step 2	Turn the power on for the computer and screen.	A cursor begins to flash on the screen. The red drive light will go on. A beep sounds. Sometimes numbers will also be displayed on the screen, while the computer checks its memory and tests to ensure that other hardware components are working.

As the LAN program installs itself, other items of information will appear on the screen. The LAN program will then ask you to sign on to the system. This is called the LOGON or sometimes, LOGIN.

As the LOGON procedures differ for various LANs, you will need to identify the exact LOGON procedures for your particular LAN.

Use the following section to enter your LOGON procedures for your LAN.

What to Do	*What Happens*
Step 1	
Step 2	
Step 3	
Step 4	
Step 5	

After logging on the LAN, a list of choices (a menu) should appear. One of the choices on the menu should be "Exit to DOS." Often you exit to DOS by pressing the F10 function key. This process is called "backing out of the LAN." You back out of the LAN in order to arrive at a DOS prompt. The DOS prompt that you are returned to will normally be other than a C:\> prompt. It will probably be an F:\>, G:\>, H:\>, or other drive. This means that you can now access DOS, but only from within the LAN. DOS is not active in your hard drive but in a hard drive located somewhere else on the LAN.

Exit to DOS

Since your instruction for backing out of the LAN may differ from the previous example, use the following section to enter your procedures to back out of the LAN.

What to Do	*What Happens*
Step 1	
Step 2	

If you do not have a menu item labeled "Exit to DOS," use the following to enter your LOGOFF procedures.

LOGOFF

LOGOFF procedures also return you to the LAN system prompt; for example, F:\>, G:\>, H:\>.

Use the following section to enter your LOGOFF procedures.

What to Do	*What Happens*
Step 1	
Step 2	

Even if you log off, you still need to return to your own computer's hard disk to utilize DOS in your computer.

Use the following section to enter the procedures you need to follow to return to your computer's hard-drive DOS system prompt.

What to Do	*What Happens*
Step 1	
Step 2	

If you have a floppy-disk system, use the steps for a cold boot in a floppy-disk environment.

Now that you are at your own computer's DOS prompt, check the date and time.

Variations in Entering the Time and Date

The DOS DATE and TIME internal commands can be answered with many different variations.

The following variations can be used when you enter time and date.

1. Enter hours using military time from 0 to 23.

2. Enter hours in the form of hours/minutes/seconds/hundredths of a second, or leave off the seconds and hundredths of a second.

3. Use a /, –, or . (in DOS version 3.1) to separate date entries.

4. Use a . or : (in DOS version 3.1) to separate time entries.

5. Enter or omit leading zeros when entering the date.

6. Enter or omit the century part of a date.

Tips:

1. Wait at least 15 seconds to turn a computer back on after it has been turned off.

2. Do not remove a disk when the disk drive light is on.

How to Change the Date and Time

You need to use the DOS DATE and TIME commands

1. If you entered either the date or time or both incorrectly during the system boot.

2. If you were not asked for the time and date at all.

3. If your computer's internal clock has malfunctioned and is no longer keeping the correct time.

Most 80286, 80386, and 80486 computers have built-in clocks that keep accurate track of the date and time. These clocks are powered by their own independent battery. If the battery fails or the clock experiences a power surge, it might lose track of either or both the date and time. If this occurs, use the DATE and TIME DOS commands to reset the clock. If resetting the clock by this means does not work, your computer may have a set-up program that will help you reset the clock.

When using these two commands, DOS not only displays the date and time found in its memory, but also prompts you for a new date and time.

	What to Do	*What Happens*
Step 1	At the C:\> type DATE and press Enter. (Uppercase, lowercase, or combination of upper- and lowercase can be used.)	See screen that follows.

```
C:\> DATE
Current date is Tue 1-01-1980
Enter new date:
```
▶ *Date is what you type in.*

Note: *You cannot enter a date earlier than 1/01/80. The "current date" may vary.*

Step 2	Enter a new date and press Enter.	A C:\> appears.
Step 3	At the C:\> type TIME and press Enter.	See screen that follows.

```
C:\> TIME
Current time is 0:04:12.27
Enter new time:
```
▶ *TIME is what you type in.*

The "current time" will vary.

Step 4	Enter a new time and press Enter.	A C:\> appears.

Review Exercises

1. Use the DOS internal command DATE to enter the date of your next birthday.

2. Use the DATE command again to find out the day of the week your birthday will fall on.

How to Find the Version of DOS You Are Using

At times you may need to check the version of DOS that you are using, to see if it is appropriate for your intended use. For example, some applications program packages require certain versions of DOS. A program might require DOS 3.3 and will not work with other versions.

To find the version of DOS that you are using, at the C:\> type VER.

What to Do	*What Happens*
Step 1	At the C:\> type VER and press Enter.	See screen that follows.

If you are using MS-DOS version 3.30, the following message is displayed:

```
C>VER

MS-DOS Version 3.30

C>_
```

How to Reboot the System (Warm Boot)

Rebooting the system usually only reloads the LAN software. You will still need to back out of the LAN to use DOS on your computer. A warm boot will merely take you back into the LAN. However, some hard-disk-based computers in LANs may allow you to select using DOS or the LAN during a system boot. If you are presented with this choice or are given a DOS prompt to begin with, you do not have to worry about backing out of the LAN. You may wish to try a warm boot after you have exited the menu on your LAN to see what happens.

What to Do	*What Happens*
Step 1	Depress the Ctrl key, the Alt key, and the Del key simultaneously.	You have rebooted the system.

Tip: If pressing Ctrl, Alt, and Del simultaneously does not reboot the system, perform a cold boot.

Summary Points

1. Certain procedures must be followed when handling diskettes to prevent damage from occurring.

2. Loading DOS is called "booting the system."

3. A prompt is a request from the system for a user response.

4. When the computer system is booted, the computer prompts the user for the date and time.

5. Time is entered in military time—the 24-hour clock.

6. The A > (or C > if you are using a hard disk drive) is called the *system prompt*.

7. TIME and DATE allow you to change the time and date.

8. VER allows you to find the version of DOS you are using.

The disks that you will be using and their contents.

DOS Disk   Practice Disk

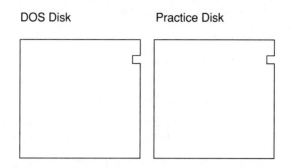

Application Exercises

At your computer, perform the following application exercises:

1. Attach a label to a blank disk—newly purchased disk that does not contain DOS. With a felt-tip pen, label the disk "Practice."

2. Insert a DOS disk into the computer and obtain an A>.

3. Reboot the system and enter the date April 26, 1991, using this exact format. Explain what happens.

4. Convert the time 8:30 P.M. to the 24-hour clock.

5. Perform a "warm boot" and reenter the current time and date.

6. At an A> type VER. Explain what happens.

Comprehension Questions

Write the answers to the following questions:

1. Suppose you inserted a disk into Drive A:, turned on the computer, and received the following message:

```
Non-System Disk or disk error
Replace and strike any key when ready
```

What would you say happened?

2. Suppose you accidently put DOS disk into Drive B: instead of Drive A: when you started up the computer. What would happen?

3. Suppose you entered the time 86:00. What would happen?

4. Explain why June 1, 1987, could not be entered as the date when starting your computer.

5. Explain how to change the date after the current date is entered.

6. Explain how to change the time after the current time is entered.

7. Explain how to determine what version of DOS you are using.

Completion Exercises

Complete the following sentences by supplying the proper answer(s):

1. Loading DOS is called _____ the system.

2. Many computers have a _____ button used to perform a warm boot.

3. The DOS command used to find the version of DOS you are using is _____.

4. When DOS is loaded a _____ appears.

5. On a hard drive, the system prompt is normally _____.

Matching Exercises

Choose the correct letter from the right-hand column.

1. Prompt	a. System prompt
2. A>	b. Turning the computer on with DOS and obtaining an A>
3. Warm boot	c. Request for a user response
4. Cold boot	d. 0–23 hours
5. Military time	e. Ctrl, Alt, and Del depressed simultaneously obtaining an A>
6. DATE, TIME, VER	f. DOS commands

2

Preparing Disks for Use

When you have completed this chapter, you will be able to

Learning Objectives:

1. Differentiate between internal and external DOS commands.
2. Explain how to find out what files are on the disk.
3. Explain why it is necessary to format a disk.
4. Explain what formatting a disk means.
5. Explain the purpose of CHKDSK.

Performance Objectives:

1. Display the contents of a disk using DIR with various options.
2. Format a disk.
3. Copy the operating system onto the disk you are formatting.
4. Use CHKDSK to check a formatted disk.
5. View the directory of another drive.
6. Change default drives.
7. Format a disk with a volume label.
8. Find the name of a volume label.
9. Change a volume label.
10. Use Esc to delete a line before the Enter key is depressed.
11. Use Ctrl-C to cancel a DOS command.

Chapter Overview

As a user of application software programs, you will work with disks that contain the instructions to perform tasks such as word processing or database management. With these programs, you will create letters, memos, reports, lists, or other documents. The documents that you create must also be stored on disks, if you wish to keep them for future use.

Although the applications software diskettes will most likely be ready for you to use, the diskettes on which your data will be stored must first be prepared so that they can operate on your equipment. In this chapter, you will learn how to prepare disks for use and check the status of a disk before using it. To prepare for these activities, let's take a closer look at DOS files.

DOS Files

A listing of the DOS diskette includes the following files: (1) COMMAND.COM, the file that places the internal DOS commands into memory when the system is booted and that produces the system prompt A > (or C > on a hard disk drive), and (2) filenames of the external DOS command files.

External commands are *disk-resident commands*, meaning that they reside on a disk. These commands can only be given to DOS when the DOS disk is placed in a disk drive or when DOS has been loaded onto your computer's hard disk.

Internal commands are *RAM-resident or memory-resident commands*, meaning that they reside in RAM memory after DOS is loaded. These commands can be given to DOS without a DOS disk being placed in a disk drive.

The Internal DOS Commands

The commands that you have learned—DATE, TIME, VER—do not appear on the DOS diskette directory list. They do not appear on the DOS diskette listing because they are internal commands that have been placed in memory for use when the computer was booted. Unlike the external commands that require a DOS diskette to be present in a disk drive, the internal commands can be performed anytime after DOS has been booted. All they require is the presence of a DOS prompt. The DOS prompt A > (or C > on a hard disk drive) represents the default drive, the drive where DOS looks when a command is given unless otherwise directed. The complete list of the internal commands for MS-DOS version 3.3 are:

3.3 Dos Internal Commands

BREAK	MD
CALL	MKDIR
CD	NOT
CHDIR	PATH
CLS	PAUSE
COPY	PROMPT
CTTY	RD
DATE	REM
DEL	REN
DIR	RENAME
ECHO	RMDIR
ERASE	SET
ERRORLEVEL	SHIFT
EXIST	TIME
EXIT	TYPE
FOR	VER
GOTO	VERIFY
IF	VOL

The External DOS Commands

All DOS external files have filenames and extensions. When you wish to use a DOS external command, type only the filename at any DOS prompt and press Enter. The extension does not have to be typed.

A list of the external commands for MS-DOS version 3.3 follows.

3.3 Dos External Commands

APPEND	EXE	GWBASIC	EXE
ASSIGN	COM	JOIN	EXE
ATTRIB	EXE	KEYB	COM
BACKUP	COM	LABEL	COM
CHKDSK	COM	LINK	EXE
COMMAND	COM	MODE	COM
COMP	COM	MORE	COM
DEBUG	COM	NLSFUNC	EXE
DISKCOMP	COM	PRINT	COM
DISKCOPY	COM	RECOVER	COM
EDLIN	COM	REPLACE	EXE
EXE2BIN	EXE	RESTORE	COM
FASTOPEN	EXE	SELECT	COM
FC	EXE	SHARE	EXE
FDISK	COM	SORT	EXE
FIND	EXE	SUBST	EXE
FORMAT	COM	SYS	COM
GRAFTABL	COM	TREE	COM
GRAPHICS	COM	XCOPY	EXE

Finding Out What Files Are on a Disk

To find out what files are on a disk, you can display a directory of the disk. You may need to look at the directory for several reasons:

1. If you have an applications program, you may need to display the directory to see what filename calls up the program you want to use.

2. If you have a data disk, you may need to locate the filename of a file you have created and wish to retrieve.

3. If you are using DOS, you can check to see what external DOS commands are available on a particular DOS disk. Different versions of DOS contain different DOS files.

DIR

The DOS internal command DIR allows you to see the contents of the disk directory. The directory command DIR can be used by itself or with several different options.

The DIR command lists the filename and extension, the size of the files (in bytes), and the date and time each file on the disk was created. A listing of the DOS version 3.3 disk displays the files:

```
A>DIR

 Volume in drive A is MS330APP01
 Directory of A:\

4201       CPI    17089   2-02-88  12:00a
5202       CPI      459   2-02-88  12:00a
ANSI       SYS     1647   2-02-88  12:00a
APPEND     EXE     5794   2-02-88  12:00a
ASSIGN     COM     1530   2-02-88  12:00a
ATTRIB     EXE    10656   2-02-88  12:00a
BACKUP     COM    30280   2-09-88  12:00a
CHKDSK     COM     9819   2-02-88  12:00a
COMMAND    COM    25308   2-02-88  12:00a
COMP       COM     4183   2-02-88  12:00a
COUNTRY    SYS    11254   2-02-88  12:00a
DEBUG      COM    15866   2-09-88  12:00a
DISKCOMP   COM     5848   2-02-88  12:00a
DISKCOPY   COM     6264   2-02-88  12:00a
DISPLAY    SYS    11259   2-02-88  12:00a
DRIVER     SYS     1165   3-01-89   3:00p
EDLIN      COM     7495   2-02-88  12:00a
EGA        CPI    49065   2-09-88  12:00a
EXE2BIN    EXE     3050   2-02-88  12:00a
FASTOPEN   EXE     3888   2-02-88  12:00a
FC         EXE    15974   2-09-88  12:00a
```

```
FDISK      COM   48983   2-02-88  12:00a
FIND       EXE    6403   2-02-88  12:00a
FORMAT     COM   11671   2-02-88  12:00a
GRAFTABL   COM    6136   2-02-88  12:00a
GRAPHICS   COM   13943   2-02-88  12:00a
GWBASIC    EXE   80592   2-09-88  12:00a
JOIN       EXE    9612   2-02-88  12:00a
KEYB       COM    9041   2-02-88  12:00a
KEYBOARD   SYS   19735   2-09-88  12:00a
LABEL      COM    2346   2-02-88  12:00a
LCD        CPI   10752   2-09-88  12:00a
LINK       EXE   43988   2-09-88  12:00a
MODE       COM   15440   2-02-88  12:00a
MORE       COM     282   2-02-88  12:00a
NLSFUNC    EXE    3029   2-02-88  12:00a
PRINT      COM    9011   2-02-88  12:00a
PRINTER    SYS   13559   2-09-88  12:00a
RAMDRIVE   SYS    8225   2-09-88  12:00a
RECOVER    COM    4268   2-02-88  12:00a
REPLACE    EXE   13234   2-09-88  12:00a
RESTORE    COM   35650   2-09-88  12:00a
SELECT     COM    4132   2-02-88  12:00a
SHARE      EXE    8608   2-09-88  12:00a
SORT       EXE    1946   2-02-88  12:00a
SUBST      EXE   10552   2-02-88  12:00a
SYS        COM    4725   2-02-88  12:00a
TREE       COM    3540   2-02-88  12:00a
XCOPY      EXE   11216   2-09-88  12:00a
     49 File(s)      745984 bytes free

A>
```

▶ *The information above this line may scroll off the screen as the files are listed.*

Filename	Ext	Size	Date File Created	Time File Created

The filename is also the name of the DOS command that you type to perform a particular DOS activity.

At the bottom of a directory listing, you will find two other important items: (1) the number of files on the disk and (2) the amount of space available for use on the disk (in bytes).

Notice that the period does not show up between the filename and the extension on a disk directory listing. The filenames in the DOS disk are the names used to identify the DOS files for the external DOS commands.

DIR /P (Pause)

When there are more files than fit on a screen at one time, using the DIR will cause the first files to scroll off the screen faster than they can be read. A way of pausing the screen after a screenful of files appears is to type DIR /P at the >. When DIR /P is used, 23 files display. Then DOS waits for you to instruct it to continue. Depressing any key will cause the next screenful of the files to appear on the screen.

```
A>DIR /P

 Volume in drive A is MS330APP01
 Directory of A:\                              ──────────▶  Everything above
                                                            this line scrolls off
 4201      CPI   17089   2-02-88 12:00a                     the screen.
 5202      CPI     459   2-02-88 12:00a
 ANSI      SYS    1647   2-02-88 12:00a
 APPEND    EXE    5794   2-02-88 12:00a
 ASSIGN    COM    1530   2-02-88 12:00a
 ATTRIB    EXE   10656   2-02-88 12:00a
 BACKUP    COM   30280   2-09-88 12:00a
 CHKDSK    COM    9819   2-02-88 12:00a
 COMMAND   COM   25308   2-02-88 12:00a
 COMP      COM    4183   2-02-88 12:00a
 COUNTRY   SYS   11254   2-02-88 12:00a
 DEBUG     COM   15866   2-09-88 12:00a
 DISKCOMP  COM    5848   2-02-88 12:00a
 DISKCOPY  COM    6264   2-02-88 12:00a
 DISPLAY   SYS   11259   2-02-88 12:00a
 DRIVER    SYS    1165   3-01-89  3:00p
 EDLIN     COM    7495   2-02-88 12:00a
 EGA       CPI   49065   2-09-88 12:00a
 EXE2BIN   EXE    3050   2-02-88 12:00a
 FASTOPEN  EXE    3888   2-02-88 12:00a
 FC        EXE   15974   2-09-88 12:00a     ──▶ When you strike
 FDISK     COM   48983   2-02-88 12:00a         any key, any
 FIND      EXE    6403   2-02-88 12:00a         remaining files on
 Strike a key when ready . . .                  the directory
                                                list will appear.
```

DIR /W (Wide)   If you only want to obtain a list of the filenames and are not concerned with the other information found in a directory, you can use the option / W to use the full width of the screen.

```
A>DIR /W

 Volume in drive A is MS330APP01
 Directory of A:\

4201     CPI   5202     CPI   ANSI     SYS   APPEND   EXE   ASSIGN   COM
ATTRIB   EXE   BACKUP   COM   CHKDSK   COM   COMMAND  COM   COMP     COM
COUNTRY  SYS   DEBUG    COM   DISKCOMP COM   DISKCOPY COM   DISPLAY  SYS
DRIVER   SYS   EDLIN    COM   EGA      CPI   EXE2BIN  EXE   FASTOPEN EXE
FC       EXE   FDISK    COM   FIND     EXE   FORMAT   COM   GRAFTABL COM
GRAPHICS COM   GWBASIC  EXE   JOIN     EXE   KEYB     COM   KEYBOARD SYS
LABEL    COM   LCD      CPI   LINK     EXE   MODE     COM   MORE     COM
NLSFUNC  EXE   PRINT    COM   PRINTER  SYS   RAMDRIVE SYS   RECOVER  COM
REPLACE  EXE   RESTORE  COM   SELECT   COM   SHARE    EXE   SORT     EXE
SUBST    EXE   SYS      COM   TREE     COM   XCOPY    EXE
    49 File(s)         745984 bytes free

A>
```

DIR /W /P   For longer directories, such as might be found on a hard disk, both the "wide" and the "pause" options can be included with the DIR command. The order in which the /W and /P appear does not matter.

Why Format?

If you performed a DIR on a brand new disk, you would most likely (unless you had purchased preformatted empty disks) obtain an error message because the disk first must be prepared or formatted for use on your particular system. The way that information is stored on disks varies for different families of computers. To cope with this problem, disk manufacturers have standardized disk production. When you purchase a disk, the disk can be used by a variety of microcomputers, using a number of different operating systems. What you are buying is essentially a blank disk that must be customized for use with your particular operating system.

If you recall, we said that files can be compared to chapters of a book. Before you can store the information on a page, the pages of the book must be created. The pages on a disk are the tracks and sectors that are created, providing addressable areas of the disk where information can be safely stored and located. Creating this structure is called *formatting the disk.*

What is Formatting?

When you format a disk, invisible concentric rings or tracks are laid down on the surface of the disk and are sectioned into pie-shaped sectors. These tracks are where data are stored. A 5 1/4-inch disk has 40 tracks; a 3 1/2-inch disk has 80 tracks. Each track is divided up usually into nine pie-shaped sectors. (See Figure 2.1.)

Once the disk is formatted, the read/write head of a disk drive can store or locate data that have been stored. To visualize the process, think of a phonograph record as being a disk and a needle as being a read/write head.

The general command for formatting a disk is FORMAT. During the formatting process, other activities are taking place:

1. The disk is being checked for damage. Formatting the disk allows you to determine if there are any recording areas (tracks or sectors) on the disk that are not acceptable for storing data.

2. A space is allocated for the directory of the disk. The directory is like a card catalogue drawer in a library.

3. If the option /V follows the FORMAT command, a volume label is added to the directory of the disk.

4. If the option /S follows the FORMAT command, the DOS file COMMAND.COM and two hidden files are placed on the disk allowing the disk to boot the system. Transferring the DOS system files onto another disk with the /S option is in violation of copyright laws, unless you purchased a DOS disk from a licensed distributor.

5. If you want to format a 5 1/4-inch low-capacity disk in a 5 1/4-inch high-capacity drive, use the /4 option.

6. If you want to format a 3 1/2-inch low-capacity disk in a 3 1/2-inch high-capacity drive, use the options /t:80 and /n:9, where t = the number of tracks and n = the number of sectors (FORMAT A: /t:80 /n:9).

Figure 2.1

A disk with the tracks (rings) and sectors (pie-shaped wedges) shown.

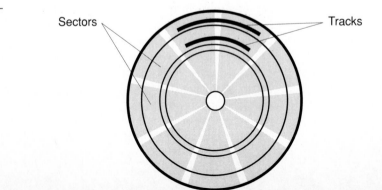

Sectors

Tracks

Other options can be used with the FORMAT command. These other options and how they affect the formatted disk are listed in the DOS manual. You should consult the DOS manual whenever you have any questions regarding the capabilities of the DOS version that you are using.

Where Should Disks Be Formatted?

Whenever you format a disk(s), you should format the disk(s) on your own computer, or on one that has the same hardware as yours, because computers format disks differently. If you format a disk on a computer that does not match your computer's hardware, you might not be able to use it. Even computers in the same family do not always have compatible disk formats. For example, if you format a disk on an IBM PS/2 or Compaq 386, the disk might not work on a earlier-model family computer such as the PC, XT, or AT. The IBM PS/2 or Compaq 386 both use high-capacity floppy drives that allow more information to be stored on a disk. Therefore, the tracks are too close together (and narrower) for the earlier family computer to read. Technologically advanced computers can store more files on the same type of disk. If you try to access these files using computers that have lower-capacity disk drives, you will obtain a disk error when trying to read the file(s).

The incompatibility in this respect will continue as newer computers make older computers obsolete. However, the positive side is that if you format a disk on a computer that is not as advanced (such as an IBM PC, IBM XT, or IBM AT), the more advanced one (such as the PS/2) can usually use the disk formatted by the PC, XT, or AT. When the disk is formatted for PC, XT, or AT use, the tracks or sectors are laid out in accordance with the individual computer's capabilities. After the tracks are created, almost any computer from the same level or above may be able to read or write onto the disk.

What Version of DOS Should You Use?

The types of hardware each DOS version supports varies. As mentioned in the introduction, DOS evolved because it had to keep up with the advances in hardware technology. Before booting a computer with DOS, make sure that the DOS version can support your computer's hardware. A list of computer-disk types and versions of DOS needed to support them is as follows:

Hardware	DOS Version
5 1/4-inch 360k Low-Capacity Disk	2.0 and above
5 1/4-inch 1.2M High-Capacity Disk	3.0 and above
3 1/2-inch 720k Low-Capacity Disk	3.0 and above
3 1/2-inch 1.44M High-Capacity Disk	3.3 and above

In the introduction, you learned that floppy disks, both 5 1/4- and 3 1/2-inch, can store different amounts of information, depending on disk and drive type.

A 5 1/4-inch double-density (low-density) disk can store 360,000 bytes of information. A 5 1/4-inch high-density disk can store 1.2 million bytes of information.

The 3 1/2-inch disk also comes in two types: double-density (low-density) and high-density. Low-density disks can store 720,000 bytes of information; high-density disks, 1.44 million bytes.

Floppy-disk drives come in the same four categories. A 5 1/4-inch 360k drive can format 5 1/4-inch double-density disks to store 360k bytes. A 5 1/4-inch high-capacity drive can format both double-density and high-density floppy disks. To format a high-density disk on a high-capacity drive, just use the DOS FORMAT command. To format a 360k double-density disk on a high-capacity drive, use the DOS FORMAT command with the /4 option as follows:

```
C:\>FORMAT A: /4
```

Note: You can format a 360k double-density disk as a 1.2 megabyte high-density disk, but the disk will be unreliable.

The 3 1/2-inch drive performs like the 5 1/4-inch drive. A 720k drive primarily uses and formats a double-density 3 1/2-inch disk, whereas a 1.44 megabyte drive can format both 720k and 1.44 megabyte disks. To format a 1.44 megabyte disk on a 1.44 megabyte drive, use the FORMAT command alone. To format a 720k disk on a 1.44 megabyte drive, use the FORMAT command with the options as follows:

```
C:\>FORMAT A: /t:80 /n:9      80 = number of tracks,
                               9 = number of sectors
```

Both types of high-capacity drives (5 1/4- and 3 1/2-inch) can store and retrieve information from low-density disks. Low-density drives cannot access high-density formatted disks.

Note: Some disks (usually bulk purchased disks) do not list whether they are double-density or high-density. Make sure you purchase the right type.

Floppy disks can also be referred to as follows:

Disk Type	Alternate Names
5 1/4-inch Double-density	Double Sided, Double Density (DS, DD)
5 1/4-inch High-density	Double Sided, High Density (DS, HD) (MD2-HD) (HD)
3 1/2-inch Double-density	Micro Floppy, Two Sides, Double Density (MF2-DD)
3 1/2-inch High-density	Micro Floppy, Two Sides, High Density (MF2-HD)

DOS Disks, Program Disks, and Data Disks

The three categories of disks that you will use are DOS diskettes, applications program diskettes, and data diskettes.

DOS Disks

When applications programs are used, a disk containing DOS files must first be used to boot the system. Use the following procedure:

1. Boot the system with the DOS disk in the default drive or with Drive A: empty if you have a hard disk with DOS loaded on it.

2. Remove the DOS disk, if using a floppy disk system.

3. Load the applications program by inserting the application program disk into the drive and typing the filename that calls up the program or by just typing in the application name if the application program is loaded on your hard disk.

Applications Program Disks

Applications program disks purchased from the manufacturer cannot be used to boot the computer because they do not contain the necessary DOS system files. Because of software copyright laws, application program manufacturers are not allowed to place the DOS system files on their disks.

Disks that are intended to hold applications software programs should be formatted with the system added. In Chapter 4, you will learn to use disks formatted with the DOS system files to make self-booting applications software diskettes. To transfer the DOS system files to a disk while formatting, the DOS command FORMAT is used with the option / S. (See Figure 2.2.) The command looks like this:

A>FORMAT /S   formats a disk with DOS system files added.

A>FORMAT /S/V   adds a volume label to a disk formatted with the DOS system files added.

The DOS system files can also be transferred to applications software program disks by using the DOS SYS command. The SYS command transfers the system files to a disk (hard or floppy) only if there is available space. The first step in making a self-booting applications program disk is to format a disk with the system. The other steps will be shown in Chapter 4.

Data Disks

A data disk is used for file storage only. The DOS system files do not need to be placed on data disks because data disks are not normally used to boot the computer. One reason why you might not want to place the system files on a data disk is that the system files occupy valuable storage space. PC-DOS Version 2.1 system files occupies 40,960 bytes of disk space. Version 3.1 occupies 62,464 bytes for regular drives and 61,440 bytes for high-capacity drives.

Figure 2.2

A DOS system disk, an applications software system disk (program disk), and a data disk. The DOS system files can be transferred to the applications software disk.*

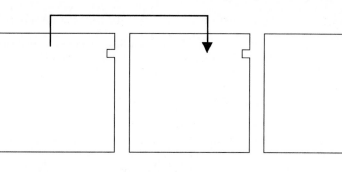

DOS system disk   Applications software system disk (program disk)   Data disk

Applications software is used to perform specific activities such as writing a letter or preparing a budget. Five of the most common general-purpose software packages developed in response to the needs of people whose work involves such common tasks as writing, calculating and planning, record-keeping, and communicating are the following: word processing applications software such as WordStar, Word Perfect, MS Word, DisplayWrite, Multimate, and PC Write is used for preparing documents such as letters and reports; spreadsheet applications software such as Lotus 1-2-3, Microsoft Excel, and Borland's Quatro Pro is used for preparing budgets and forecasting; database management applications software such as DBase, RBase, and Reflex is used for maintaining client and customer lists; communications applications software such as SmartCom, PC Talk, and CrossTalk is used for communicating with other computer users located at a distance; desktop publishing applications software such as Ventura Publisher and PageMaker is used for creating newsletters, presentations, brochures, and so on.

The commands to format a data disk are

A>FORMAT	to format a disk using one drive.
A>FORMAT B:	to format a disk in Drive B: without having to remove the DOS disk from Drive A:.
A>FORMAT /V	adds a volume label to a data disk.
A>FORMAT B: /V	adds a volume label to a data disk formatted in Drive B:.

For people using high-capacity drives, several options can be used with this command. One option (/4) allows you to format a 5 1/4-inch disk for use in a 360k drive. Check your DOS manual for other formatting options.

Note: If you do not specify additional options when formatting a disk, your computer will attempt to format the disk according to your computer's hardware.

CHKDSK

At the end of the format process, DOS lists the following:

1. If the /S was used, a message stating that the system was transferred.

2. The total disk space in bytes.

3. Bytes used by the system (number of bytes that the DOS system files occupy).

4. Bytes in bad sectors (number of bytes unavailable for storage because tracks or sectors have been damaged).

5. Bytes available on a disk (number of bytes available for storage).

Although this information is displayed during the formatting process, there may be other times when you will need to know this information and formatting your disk would erase all your files. The DOS external command CHKDSK allows you to view this information without destroying files. In addition to the information provided during the format process, CHKDSK provides you with a few more details:

1. Although it does not display the number of bytes used by each of the DOS system files, CHKDSK does list the number of hidden files and number of bytes occupied by them (such as the two DOS hidden files IBMBIO.COM and IBMDOS.COM). IBMBIO.COM and IBMDOS.COM are two of the three DOS system files. COMMAND.COM is the third system file and is found on the directory listing of a disk because it is considered a user-file. A user-file is any file that you can access without the assistance of a special program.

2. It lists the number of bytes used by user-files.

3. It lists the total amount of RAM memory your system has and the amount of RAM memory that is available (free). From this information, you can determine how many bytes are currently being used.

Hands-On Activities

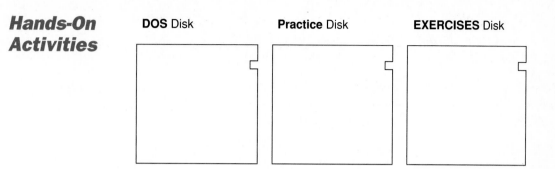

DOS Disk   **Practice** Disk   **EXERCISES** Disk

In this section you will:

1. Display the contents of a disk using DIR with various options.

2. Format a disk using one drive.

3. Format a disk using two drives.

4. Copy the operating system onto the diskette you are formatting.

5. Use CHKDSK to check a formatted diskette.

6. Change default drives.

7. Label a disk with a volume label.

8. Find the name of the volume label.

9. Use ESC to delete aline before the Enter key is depressed.

10. Use Ctrl-C to cancel a DOS command.

How to Obtain a Directory Listing Using DIR

With the DOS diskette in Drive A:

	What to Do	*What Happens*
Step 1	At the A> type DIR and press Enter.	See screen that follows.

```
A>DIR

Volume in drive A is MS330APP01
Directory of A:\

4201       CPI    17089   2-02-88  12:00a
5202       CPI      459   2-02-88  12:00a
ANSI       SYS     1647   2-02-88  12:00a
APPEND     EXE     5794   2-02-88  12:00a
ASSIGN     COM     1530   2-02-88  12:00a
ATTRIB     EXE    10656   2-02-88  12:00a
BACKUP     COM    30280   2-09-88  12:00a
CHKDSK     COM     9819   2-02-88  12:00a
COMMAND    COM    25308   2-02-88  12:00a
COMP       COM     4183   2-02-88  12:00a
COUNTRY    SYS    11254   2-02-88  12:00a
DEBUG      COM    15866   2-09-88  12:00a
DISKCOMP   COM     5848   2-02-88  12:00a
DISKCOPY   COM     6264   2-02-88  12:00a
DISPLAY    SYS    11259   2-02-88  12:00a
DRIVER     SYS     1165   3-01-89   3:00p
EDLIN      COM     7495   2-02-88  12:00a
EGA        CPI    49065   2-09-88  12:00a
EXE2BIN    EXE     3050   2-02-88  12:00a
FASTOPEN   EXE     3888   2-02-88  12:00a
FC         EXE    15974   2-09-88  12:00a
FDISK      COM    48983   2-02-88  12:00a
FIND       EXE     6403   2-02-88  12:00a
FORMAT     COM    11671   2-02-88  12:00a
GRAFTABL   COM     6136   2-02-88  12:00a
GRAPHICS   COM    13943   2-02-88  12:00a
GWBASIC    EXE    80592   2-09-88  12:00a
JOIN       EXE     9612   2-02-88  12:00a
```

▶ *Scrolls off the screen.*

```
KEYB       COM    9041   2-02-88 12:00a
KEYBOARD   SYS   19735   2-09-88 12:00a
LABEL      COM    2346   2-02-88 12:00a
LCD        CPI   10752   2-09-88 12:00a
LINK       EXE   43988   2-09-88 12:00a
MODE       COM   15440   2-02-88 12:00a
MORE       COM     282   2-02-88 12:00a
NLSFUNC    EXE    3029   2-02-88 12:00a
PRINT      COM    9011   2-02-88 12:00a
PRINTER    SYS   13559   2-09-88 12:00a
RAMDRIVE   SYS    8225   2-09-88 12:00a
RECOVER    COM    4268   2-02-88 12:00a
REPLACE    EXE   13234   2-09-88 12:00a
RESTORE    COM   35650   2-02-88 12:00a
SELECT     COM    4132   2-02-88 12:00a
SHARE      EXE    8608   2-09-88 12:00a
SORT       EXE    1946   2-02-88 12:00a
SUBST      EXE   10552   2-02-88 12:00a
SYS        COM    4725   2-02-88 12:00a
TREE       COM    3540   2-02-88 12:00a
XCOPY      EXE   11216   2-09-88 12:00a
     49 File(s)     745984 bytes free

A>
```

Screens may vary according to DOS version and disk type.

How to Use	Since there are more files than fit on a screen, a way of reading a

How to Use
DIR /P (Pause)

Since there are more files than fit on a screen, a way of reading a screen of files is to type DIR /P at the A>. Depressing any key will cause the rest of the file to appear on the screen.

With the DOS diskette in Drive A:

What to Do	*What Happens*
Step 1	At the A> type DIR /P and press Enter.	See screen that follows.

```
A>DIR /P

 Volume in drive A is MS330APP01
 Directory of A:\

4201      CPI    17089   2-02-88  12:00a
5202      CPI      459   2-02-88  12:00a
ANSI      SYS     1647   2-02-88  12:00a
APPEND    EXE     5794   2-02-88  12:00a
ASSIGN    COM     1530   2-02-88  12:00a
ATTRIB    EXE    10656   2-02-88  12:00a
BACKUP    COM    30280   2-09-88  12:00a
CHKDSK    COM     9819   2-02-88  12:00a
COMMAND   COM    25308   2-02-88  12:00a
COMP      COM     4183   2-02-88  12:00a
COUNTRY   SYS    11254   2-02-88  12:00a
DEBUG     COM    15866   2-09-88  12:00a
DISKCOMP  COM     5848   2-02-88  12:00a
DISKCOPY  COM     6264   2-02-88  12:00a
DISPLAY   SYS    11259   2-02-88  12:00a
DRIVER    SYS     1165   3-01-89   3:00p
EDLIN     COM     7495   2-02-88  12:00a
EGA       CP1    49065   2-09-88  12:00a
EXE2BIN   EXE     3050   2-02-88  12:00a
FASTOPEN  EXE     3888   2-02-88  12:00a
FC        EXE    15974   2-09-88  12:00a
FDISK     COM    48983   2-02-88  12:00a
FIND      EXE     6403   2-02-88  12:00a
Strike a key when ready . . .
```

▶ *Scrolls off the screen.*

Screens may vary according to DOS version and disk type.

When DOS asks you to strike a key when ready, it means that the information (directory list) was more than could fit on one screen. When you are finished reading the first screen, just depress any key and DOS will list the next screen.

| Step 2 | Strike a key when ready. | See screen that follows. |

```
FORMAT     COM    11671    2-02-88  12:00a
GRAFTABL   COM     6136    2-02-88  12:00a
GRAPHICS   COM    13943    2-02-88  12:00a
GWBASIC    EXE    80592    2-09-88  12:00a
JOIN       EXE     9612    2-02-88  12:00a
KEYB       COM     9041    2-02-88  12:00a
KEYBOARD   SYS    19735    2-09-88  12:00a
LABEL      COM     2346    2-02-88  12:00a
LCD        CPI    10752    2-09-88  12:00a
LINK       EXE    43988    2-09-88  12:00a
MODE       COM    15440    2-02-88  12:00a
MORE       COM      282    2-02-88  12:00a
NLSFUNC    EXE     3029    2-02-88  12:00a
PRINT      COM     9011    2-02-88  12:00a
PRINTER    SYS    13559    2-09-88  12:00a
RAMDRIVE   SYS     8225    2-09-88  12:00a
RECOVER    COM     4268    2-02-88  12:00a
REPLACE    EXE    13234    2-09-88  12:00a
RESTORE    COM    35650    2-02-88  12:00a
SELECT     COM     4132    2-02-88  12:00a
SHARE      EXE     8608    2-09-88  12:00a
SORT       EXE     1946    2-02-88  12:00a
SUBST      EXE    10552    2-02-88  12:00a
Stike a key when ready . . .
SYS        COM     4725    2-02-88  12:00a
TREE       COM     3540    2-02-88  12:00a
XCOPY      EXE    11216    2-09-88  12:00a
     49 File(s)      745984 bytes free

A>
```

Screens may vary according to DOS version and disk type.

How to Use *DIR /W (Wide)*	The DIR / W is used to enable the entire directory to be displayed in a horizontal format. Only the filenames and extensions are displayed when the DIR /W command is used.	
	DOS should be in Drive A:.	
	What to Do	*What Happens*
Step 1	At the A> type DIR /W and press Enter.	See the screen that follows.

```
A>DIR /W
 Volume in drive A is MS330APP01
 Directory of A:\

4201      CPI   5202      CPI   ANSI      SYS   APPEND    EXE   ASSIGN    COM
ATTRIB    EXE   BACKUP    COM   CHKDSK    COM   COMMAND   COM   COMP      COM
COUNTRY   SYS   DEBUG     COM   DISKCOMP  COM   DISKCOPY  COM   DISPLAY   SYS
DRIVER    SYS   EDLIN     COM   EGA       CPI   EXE2BIN   EXE   FASTOPEN  EXE
FC        EXE   FDISK     COM   FIND      EXE   FORMAT    COM   GRAFTABL  COM
GRAPHICS  COM   GWBASIC   EXE   JOIN      EXE   KEYB      COM   KEYBOARD  SYS
LABEL     COM   LCD       CPI   LINK      EXE   MODE      COM   MORE      COM
NLSFUNC   EXE   PRINT     COM   PRINTER   SYS   RAMDRIVE  SYS   RECOVER   COM
REPLACE   EXE   RESTORE   COM   SELECT    COM   SHARE     EXE   SORT      EXE
SUBST     EXE   SYS       COM   TREE      COM   XCOPY     EXE
        49 File(s)      745984 bytes free

A>
```

Screens may vary according to the DOS version.

Note: You can also use DIR /W /P if you have a large number of files on your disk. If you use DIR /W /P with the DOS 2.1 disk, the /P option would not be of any value because there are not enough files on the list.

Directory Attempt on an Unformatted Disk

When you attempt to perform a directory on an unformatted disk in Drive A:, you will receive the message

```
Disk error reading drive A.
Abort, Retry, Ignore?
```

The error message may vary according to the DOS version.

To return to the A>, type A.

Note: Obtain a new unformatted disk and label it "PRACTICE."

Place the unformatted **Practice** disk in Drive A:.

What to Do	*What Happens*
Step 1 At an A>, type DIR and press Enter.	The disk drive lights up. See screen that follows.

```
A>DIR

General failure error reading drive A
Abort, Retry, Ignore?
```

Screens may vary according to the DOS version.

Step 2	Type A.	The A> returns.

Note: You were instructed to type A for Abort during this exercise because both of the other choices would have only caused DOS to attempt another DIR of the same disk, thus obtaining the same disk error message.

Anytime you receive this message, you can select A to return to the A>, R to retry the command if you think you have received the error incorrectly, or I to ignore the error message. It is not a good practice to ignore error messages. You could destroy a file or files.

How to Format a Data Disk Using One Drive

Use the unformatted disk labeled **Practice** disk in Drive A:.

	What to Do	*What Happens*
Step 1	At an A>, insert **Practice** disk in Drive A: and close the drive door.	Nothing.
Step 2	Type in the command DIR and then press Enter. (This ensures that you are not going to format over valuable files.)	See DOS reply as follows.

WARNING! When you format a disk, be sure that you check the directory of the disk first. If you format over important files, they are lost forever!

```
Disk error reading drive A
Abort, Retry, Ignore?
```

Screens may vary according to the DOS version.

If you obtain this message, you have an unformatted disk.

Write-Protect Your Disks!

If DOS responds with a directory listing of the disk, make sure that you are not going to format a disk that contains important files. To protect a 5 1/4-inch disk that you do not wish to have formatted, cover the write-protect tab with one of the foil tabs supplied with the disks that you purchased, as shown in Figure 2.3. If you ever wish to write to a disk that has protective tabs, you need to remove the tabs. To protect a 3 1/2-inch disk, slide the write-protect tab over the opening. (See Figure 2.3.)

WARNING! Write-protect your DOS disk. If you accidentally format it, you will be sorry!

If the disk you are using contains files and you wish to save them, obtain an unformatted disk and attach a label to it. With a felt-tip pen, label the disk **Practice** and start over with Step 1.

Tip:	*Do not* use the following FORMAT commands:
	
	`C>FORMAT`
	`A>FORMAT C:`
	
	Both of these commands will wipe out the contents of a hard disk.	

Step 3	Remove the **Practice** disk and insert the DOS disk into Drive A: and close the drive door.	Nothing.
Step 4	Type A and press Enter (to return to the system prompt).	An A> appears.
Step 5	Type in the command FORMAT A: and press Enter.	See screen that follows.

```
A>FORMAT A:
Insert new diskette for drive A:
and strike ENTER when ready
```

Step 6	Remove the DOS disk and insert the **Practice** disk in Drive A: and press Enter.	See screen that follows.

```
Formatting...

Head: 1  Cylinder: 37
```

When the red disk drive light is on, do not remove the disk.

Note: You will either see a message that says "Formatting" or see DOS counting the actual heads and cylinders being formatted. If you receive an error message, see note on page 83.

When the formatting is completed, the message is

```
Format complete
    1457664 bytes total disk space
    1457664 bytes available on disk

Format another (Y/N)?
```

▶ *Size of a 3 1/2-inch disk (high density)*

Note: Formatting messages may vary according to the version of DOS you are using.

You will then be asked whether you wish to format another. If you do not, type an N.

```
Format another (Y/N)?
```

Step 7   Type N and press Enter.   An A> appears.

Note: If a disk has been formatted and contains bad tracks or sectors, DOS will inform you of this condition following the total disk space message above. In this event, you should try to reformat. If reformatting does not cure the problem, use another disk.

Tips: 1. You can return a disk with bad tracks or sectors to most suppliers and receive a replacement.

2. When you buy a box of disks, you should always format them as data disks at one sitting. You will then not have to stop and format a disk whenever you need a new one. If you decide you need to have a disk formatted as a system disk, the system can be added later.

Figure 2.3

Protect your files from being erased: use your write-protect tab covers.

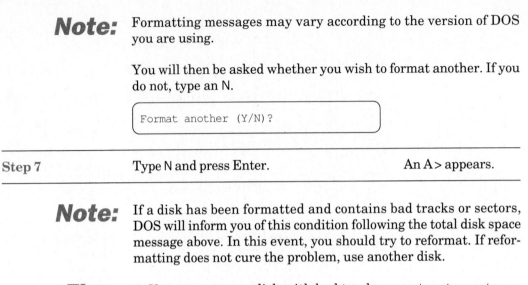

Review Exercise   Use the DIR command to check the contents of the **Practice** disk.

How to Format a Data Disk Using Two Drives

If you have a two-floppy drive system, you can use drive designators within a DOS command to direct DOS to perform the action on the disk located in the drive you specify.

An external DOS command such as FORMAT can be typed in at any system prompt—A>, B>, or so on. The prompt specifies the drive that DOS is going to look to for the file (command) that you request. If the DOS disk resides in a disk other than the default drive, you must label that drive after the system prompt, but prior to the command. The drive designator after the system prompt tells DOS where the DOS file "FORMAT" is located. The final drive letter tells DOS where to perform the action.

```
A>B:FORMAT A:
```

A>   means that DOS normally would look to the A drive for the DOS file (FORMAT).

B: tells DOS to look to Drive B: for the DOS file (source drive).

FORMAT   tells DOS what command to perform (in this case, to FORMAT).

A: tells DOS to perform the format procedure on the disk located in Drive A: (target drive).

The drive where DOS will look for the DOS file is called the source drive. The drive where DOS will execute the command is called the target drive. If the source and/or target drives are not specified, DOS will use the default drive for both the source and target drives. The default drive is the drive designated in front of the >. If the DOS diskette is in the default drive, you need to specify only the target drive when using the DOS command FORMAT.

In summary, when using DOS external commands such as FORMAT, the system prompt and the drive designators can vary depending on the default drive, on where the DOS disk is located, and on where the disk is located that you wish to format.

An advantage of using disk drive designators is that you will not have to manually switch disks between drives to perform certain commands.

Before you begin the next exercise, you will need to format another disk. Obtain another floppy disk that is compatible with your computer's B: drive and label it "BACKUP."

	What to Do	*What Happens*
Step 1	Place the DOS disk in Drive A:.	Nothing.
Step 2	Obtain an A>.	Nothing.
Step 3	Type FORMAT B:	DOS asks you to place a disk in Drive B:.
Step 4	Place the **BACKUP** disk in Drive B: and press the Enter key.	DOS begins to FORMAT the disk. See the screen that follows.

```
A>FORMAT B:
Insert new diskette for drive B:
and strike ENTER when ready
```

Note: To stop the formatting procedure, you can use Ctrl-C. If you receive an error message, see note on page 83.

	What to Do	*What Happens*
Step 5	After DOS is finished formatting the **BACKUP** disk, you will be asked if you want to format another disk.	Nothing.
Step 6	Press N and then Enter.	An A> appears.

```
Format complete

    362496 bytes total disk space
    362496 bytes available on disk

Format another (Y/N)?n
A>
```

Numbers will vary according to disk and drive types.

Notes: If a disk has been formatted and contains bad tracks or sectors, DOS will inform you of this condition after the preceding total disk space message.

If you receive an error message when you try to format a disk, make sure that the disk you are using is compatible with the disk drive. To format a disk in Drive B: with a DOS disk in Drive A:, refer to the following:

5 1/4-inch 360k low-density disk in a 360k low-capacity drive	`A:>FORMAT B:`
5 1/4-inch 360k low-density disk in a 1.2m high-capacity drive	`A:>FORMAT B: /4`
5 1/4-inch 1.2m high-density disk in a 1.2m high capacity drive	`A:>FORMAT B:`
3 1/2-inch 720k low-density disk in a 720k low-capacity drive	`A: >FORMAT B:`
3 1/2-inch 720k low-density disk in a 1.44m high-capacity drive	`A:>FORMAT B: /t:80 /n:9`
3 1/2-inch 1.44m high-density disk in a 1.44m high capacity drive	`A:>FORMAT B:`

Tips:

1. If you type any letters in a command incorrectly and have not yet depressed the Enter key, you can remove the incorrect character(s) by depressing the Backspace key. The Backspace key removes the character to the left of the cursor. The Backspace key appears at the upper right-hand portion of the keyboard.

2. If you wish to cancel the entire command or a line before the Enter key is depressed, depress the Esc key and then press the Enter key to return to the system prompt.

3. To cancel a DOS command prior or after you have depressed the Enter key, depress the C while holding down the Ctrl key.

Review
Exercise

Use the DIR command to check the contents of the **BACKUP** disk.

How to Add the
System While
Formatting

To add the system while formatting, use the /S option. Use this option when you wish to prepare a disk that later will store an applications program. This disk will then be able to boot the system. The rules governing the use of drive designators also apply to using the options. When using options, use them after the command and drive designators:

```
A>FORMAT B: /S
```

Use the **BACKUP** disk in Drive B.

Note:

If you have a one-floppy-disk drive system, you can use this command, but you will have to switch the DOS disk and the disk you wish to format in and out of the drive as you are prompted. DOS believes that the one-floppy drive is actually two drives, A: and B:. In the following chapters, many exercises will be based on a two-floppy-disk drive system. Use the commands as listed, but be prepared to switch disks on being prompted by DOS.

	What to Do	*What Happens*
Step 1	Insert DOS disk in Drive A: and close the drive door.	Nothing.
Step 2	Type the command FORMAT B: /S and press Enter. (You may omit the space after the colon.)	See screen that follows.

```
A>FORMAT B: /S
Insert new diskette for drive B:
and strike ENTER when ready
```

Note: If you receive an error message when you try to format a disk, make sure that the disk you are using is compatible with the disk drive. To format a disk in Drive B: with a DOS disk in Drive A:, refer to the following:

5 1/4-inch 360k low-density disk
in a 360k low-capacity drive   `A:>FORMAT B: /s`

5 1/4-inch 360k low-density disk
in a 1.2m high-capacity drive   `A:>FORMAT B: /s /4`

5 1/4-inch 1.2m high-density disk
in a 1.2m high capacity drive   `A:>FORMAT B: /s`

3 1/2-inch 720k low-density disk
in a 720k low-capacity drive   `A:>FORMAT B: /s`

3 1/2-inch 720k low-density disk
in a 1.44m high-capacity drive   `A:>FORMAT B: /s /t:80 /n:9`

3 1/2-inch 1.44m high-density disk
in a 1.44m high capacity drive   `A:>FORMAT B: /s`

Step 3	Insert **BACKUP** disk in Drive B:.	Nothing.
Step 4	Press Enter to begin the FORMAT process.	See screen that follows.

```
Format complete
System transferred

    362496 bytes total disk space
     78848 bytes used by system
    283648 bytes available on disk

Format another (Y/N)?
```

▶ *The number of bytes depends on the version of DOS and the type of disk being used.*

Screens may vary according to the DOS version.

Step 5	Type N and press Enter when DOS asks you if you wish to format another disk.	DOS returns you to the A>.

How to Use CHKDSK

CHKDSK is an external DOS command that requires the presence of DOS in a disk drive. It is used to check the number of useful bytes available on a disk (check disk). In this exercise, you will use CHKDSK to determine whether the DOS system files were transferred during the FORMAT / S command. If the files were transferred, you will find one user file and two hidden files.

	What to Do	*What Happens*
Step 1	Obtain an A >.	Nothing.
Step 2	Check that the DOS Disk is in Drive A: and **BACKUP** is in Drive B:.	Nothing.
Step 3	Type CHKDSK B: and press Enter.	See screen that follows.

```
A>CHKDSK B:

362496 bytes total disk space
 53248 bytes in 2 hidden files
 25600 bytes in 1 user files
283648 bytes available on disk
654336 bytes total memory
598896 bytes free

A>
```

▶ *IBMBIO and IBMDOS*
▶ *COMMAND.COM*

▶ *RAM memory size*
▶ *Available RAM memory*

Note: 1. The number of bytes you see on your screen may vary. RAM memory size will vary depending on your computer's memory. Available RAM memory will also vary.

2. Because of the different types of drives and floppy disks, the screen display shown after the CHKDSK command will vary.

How to Look at a Directory of Another Drive

To view the contents of any drive other than the default drive, simply designate the desired drive after the command DIR. For example, if you are at an A> (default drive) and want to see the contents of the disk in Drive B:, use the internal command DIR with the drive designator B:.

```
A>DIR B:
```

Notice that no DOS disk is required.

Use **BACKUP** disk in Drive B:.

What to Do	*What Happens*
Step 1 At an A>, type DIR B: and press Enter.	See screen that follows.

```
A>DIR B:

 Volume in drive B has no label
 Directory of B:\

COMMAND   COM   25308   2-02-88 12:00a
     1 File(s)      283648 bytes free

A>
```

In Chapter 3, you will learn more about using the directory command. You can also obtain a directory of the contents of Drive B: by first moving to the drive and then requesting a directory with the DIR commands. To move to another drive is called "changing the default drive."

How to Change Default Drives

During a system boot, DOS is always inserted into the default disk drive. As mentioned before, the default drive is the drive that is designated for you to use, unless you decide to change it. The default drive on a two-disk drive system is A:. When it appears on the screen, you see A>. On a hard-disk system, the default disk drive is C:. When it appears on the screen, you see C>.

To change from one drive to another, you simply enter the drive letter followed by a colon and press Enter at any DOS > (prompt). For example, when in Drive A :, at the A>, type B: and then press Enter.

Now let's look at the difference between asking for a directory of B: while in Drive A: versus moving to Drive B: and asking for a directory.

When in Drive A: When in Drive B:

A>DIR B: B>DIR

The results are the same. Note that attempting to change to a drive that contains an unformatted disk will not work.

Make sure the **BACKUP** disk is in Drive B:.

To change from Drive A: to Drive B:

	What to Do	*What Happens*
Step 1	At the A> type B: and press Enter.	The B> appears.
Step 2	At the B> type DIR and press Enter.	See screen that follows.

```
B>DIR

 Volume in drive B has no label
 Directory of B:\

COMMAND    COM    25308    2-02-88 12:00a
    1 File(s)        283648 bytes free

B>
```

Since the **BACKUP** disk has been formatted with the system on it, it contains the two hidden files and the COMMAND.COM file. As shown above, the only listing within the directory is the COMMAND.COM file, because hidden files are not displayed within a directory. The COMMAND.COM file information will vary depending on the DOS version.

To change back to Drive A:

Step 3	At the B> type A: and press Enter.	The A> appears.

Tips:

1. Before you can use any disk drive, a disk must be placed in the drive.

2. If you wish to compare the directories of two disks on one screen, use the DIR command on the first disk and then change drives and use the DIR command again.

How to Format a Data Disk with a Volume Label

In a short period of time, you will be amazed to find the number of disks that you can accumulate. For that reason you should label all your disks. In addition to the label on the outside of the disk, you can label the disk within the disk directory. This label is called a volume label, similar to an encyclopedia volume. It should not be confused with volume in reference to a specific size. (See Figure 2.4.)

A volume label is placed on a disk during the format process or by using the DOS external command LABEL found in Version 3.0 and later versions. You can add or change the label at any time. Some commercial programs are also available that allow you to add or change a label (for example, Norton Utilities).

Figure 2.4

Disks can be labeled just as books are labeled. The volume labels should be meaningful.

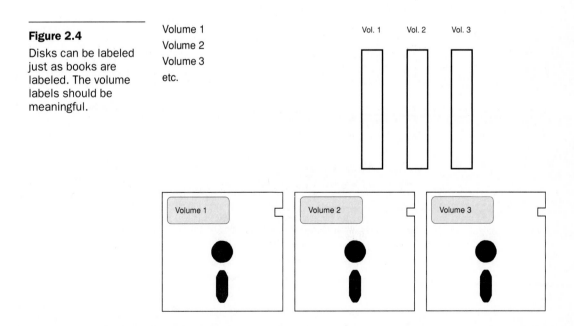

Use **Practice** disk.

	What to Do	*What Happens*
Step 1	At the A> insert DOS disk into Drive A: and close the drive door.	Nothing.
Step 2	Type in the command FORMAT A:/V and press Enter. (V stands for VOLUME.)	See screen that follows.

```
A>FORMAT A: /V
Insert new diskette for drive A:
and strike ENTER when ready
```

Note: If you receive an error message when you try to format a disk, make sure that the disk you are using is compatible with the disk drive. To format a disk in Drive B: with a DOS disk in Drive A:, refer to the following:

5 1/4-inch 360k low-density disk
in a 360k low-capacity drive   A:>FORMAT B: /v

5 1/4-inch 360k low-density disk
in a 1.2m high-capacity drive   A:>FORMAT B: /v /4

5 1/4-inch 1.2m high-density disk
in a 1.2m high capacity drive   A:>FORMAT B: /v

3 1/2-inch 720k low-density disk
in a 720k low-capacity drive   A:>FORMAT B: /v

3 1/2-inch 720k low-density disk
in a 1.44m high-capacity drive   A:>FORMAT B: /v /t:80 /n:9

3 1/2-inch 1.44m high-density disk
in a 1.44m high capacity drive   A:>FORMAT B: /v

| Step 3 | Remove DOS and insert **Practice** disk in Drive A: and press Enter. | See screen that follows. |

DOS will then say that it has finished formatting your disk and ask you for a VOLUME (11 characters).

```
Format complete
Volume label (11 characters, ENTER for none)?
```

| Step 4 | Type PRACTICE and press Enter. Up to 11 characters can be used to create a volume label. | See screen that follows. |

```
Volume label (11 characters, ENTER for none)? PRACTICE

    1457664 bytes total disk space
    1457664 bytes available on disk

Format another (Y/N)?
```

| Step 5 | Type N and press Enter. | DOS returns you to the A>. |

Note: A volume label can also be placed onto a system disk during FORMAT /S. The command is FORMAT /S /V (or FORMAT B: /S /V if two drives are used). The options /V /S are interchangeable, meaning that it does not matter which comes first, the /V or the /S, when they are used together.

How to Find the Name of the Volume Label	Whenever you need to know the label of a volume, type the DOS internal command VOL.	
	Use **Practice** disk in Drive A:.	
	What to Do	*What Happens*
Step 1	At an A>, type VOL and press Enter.	See screen that follows.

```
A>VOL

Volume in drive A is PRACTICE

A>
```

Review Exercise	Use the VOL command to check the volume label of the **BACKUP** disk.

Note:	You can also find the volume label of a disk in a drive other than the default drive by typing in the drive designator following the VOL command (for example, A>VOL B:). The volume label can also be displayed using the DIR command.

How to Change a Disk's Volume Label	To change the Label of a disk, use the DOS command LABEL.	
	What to Do	*What Happens*
Step 1	Make sure the DOS disk is in Drive A: and the **BACKUP** disk is in Drive B:.	Nothing.
Step 2	Obtain an A>.	Nothing.

Step 3	Type LABEL B:.	DOS displays the disk's current label and asks you to type in the new label.
Step 4	Type in your name and press Enter.	

Review Exercise

Using the VOL command, check to see that the volume label was changed. Change the volume label of the **BACKUP** disk from your name to BACKUP.

Summary Points

1. Before formatting a disk, you should make certain that the disk does not contain any files that you may later need.

2. The command used to format a disk is FORMAT. It can be used with other options such as /S and /V.

3. Disks should be formatted on the equipment where they are going to be used.

4. CHKDSK allows you to obtain information found using the FORMAT disk without destroying files. It also lists some additional information.

DOS	EXERCISES	PRACTICE	BACKUP
	Formatted Contains files (already prepared for you)	Formatted Data Disk PRACTICE	Formatted Data Disk BACKUP

Application Exercises

At your computer, perform the following application exercises.

1. Find out the volume label of the disk labeled **EXERCISES**. Does it match the external label (EXERCISES)? Yes ____ No ____

2. Use the disk labeled **EXERCISES** with the DOS internal command DIR and any options if necessary to find out the following information. Fill in the blanks with this information.

   Number of files _____

   Number of bytes free _____

   The number of files with COM extensions _____

   When the COM files were created _____

3. At the A>, type the following:

   My name is _____.

   Use the Esc key to cancel the line and press Enter.

4. Use DIR to obtain a directory listing of the disk labeled **EXERCISES**; while the files are listing, type Ctrl-C.

Comprehension Questions

Supply the answers to the following questions.

1. Explain what formatting a disk does.

2. Can you add a volume to a disk after you have formatted the disk? How?

3. If you have formatted an old disk and DOS tells you that certain tracks and/or sectors are bad, what does that mean? Can you store files there?

4. How do you determine what the volume label of a disk is?

5. What happens if you try to use DIR on an unformatted disk?

6. How do you return to the A> if you try to attempt to use DIR on an unformatted disk?

Completion Exercises

Complete the following sentences by supplying the proper answer(s).

1. Placing tracks and sectors on a disk is called _____ the disk.

2. Before you use a data disk, you must _____ it.

3. To return to the A> after the following message

```
Disk error reading drive B
Abort, Retry, Ignore?
```

you would type a/an ____ .

4. A disk that does not contain any DOS files nor any applications programs can be a _____ disk.

5. Explain what each of the following commands do. Be sure to tell what is done and where each disk is located.

   a. `A>DIR B:/P`

   b. `A>DIR B: /W`

   c. `B>A:`

   d. `A>FORMAT`

   e. `A>FORMAT B:`

   f. `A>FORMAT /S/V`

   g. `A>FORMAT /V`

   h. `A>FORMAT B:/V`

   i. `A>VOL B:`

   j. `A>B:`

   k. `A>CHKDSK B:`

Matching Exercises

Choose the correct letter from the right-hand column.

1. DIR

a. Copies the DOS system files to a disk while formatting.

2. FORMAT /S

b. An option added to allow you to view a directory listing by pausing until a key is struck.

3. /P

c. An option added to allow you to view a directory in a wide or horizontal format.

4. DIR B:

d. Allows you to change from Drive A: to Drive B:.

5. /W

e. The same as A>DIR B:

6. A>B:

f. Allows you to see a directory of Drive B.

7. B>DIR

g. Allows you to see what files are on a disk in a vertical format.

8. Esc

h. Removes the character to the left of the cursor.

9. Backspace

i. Used before the Enter key is depressed to cancel a line.

10. Ctrl-C

j. Cancels an entire command.

3

Creating and Displaying Files

When you have completed this chapter, you will be able to

Learning Objectives:

1. Explain how files are created and displayed.

2. Explain how to display the contents of a file using the DOS internal command TYPE.

3. Explain how output can be redirected to a printer or other devices.

4. Explain how to stop a directory list or a file from scrolling off the screen.

Performance Objectives:

1. Create a file from the keyboard using the DOS internal command COPY and the keyboard device name CON.

2. Use the DOS internal command TYPE to display the contents of a file.

3. Display the contents of a file to the printer.

4. Find out if a file is on a disk without listing the entire directory.

5. Display from the directory of a disk selected files using the DOS (? and *) wildcards.

6. Use Ctrl-S to stop a directory list from scrolling off the screen too fast.

7. Obtain a directory of selected files using wildcards and send the list to the printer.

Chapter Overview

Although applications software program files will be created for you, you can create your own files using DOS that will help you use your applications programs more efficiently. In this chapter, you will learn to

1. Create a file using DOS.

2. Display the contents of a file to a screen.

3. Send the contents of a file to a printer.

4. Find out if a file is on a disk without having to list the whole directory.

5. Obtain a partial directory of selected files.

6. Send the directory listing to a printer.

You will also learn some DOS editing commands that will help you key in your commands more efficiently.

Creating Filenames

When you name files, the computer does not allow you to give the same name to two different files. However, it does not stop you from giving names that are totally meaningless—a practice you should avoid. Otherwise, you could spend a great deal of time reading endlessly through files to determine which file contains the data you are looking for.

You should give files meaningful names, in order to quickly locate the files and data you need. You can name your files anything you wish, with some minor restrictions: in general,

1. The filename length cannot be longer than eight characters. Either upper- or lowercase characters or both can be used.

2. A three-character extension can be used to further identify files.

3. Although certain symbols can be used such as / ! @ # $ % & ( ) – _ { } ` ', you should avoid using punctuation or symbols in naming files because certain symbols are unacceptable. Some symbols, such as * and ?, have specific meanings in DOS.

4. A period (separator) is used to separate the filename from the extension.

5. Spaces cannot be used in either the filename or extension.

Any filename longer than eight characters or any extension longer than three characters will not be recognized by DOS. DOS will shorten filenames to the first eight characters and extensions to three characters to conform with the proper filename length.

The Filename

The filename should also reflect what is in a file. For example, if you are writing the first draft of an essay on President Jimmy Carter, you might name your file CARTER1. The numeral 1 is used to label it as your first draft. The key is to make the filename simple and at the same time make it reflect what the file contains.

File Extensions

In addition to the name of the file, you might want to add an extension or file type designator. Extensions follow the filename and are used to classify the type of file it is. For example, let's say that while writing your essay on Carter you decided to create a mailing list of professors whom you might wish to ask for information using database management software. To distinguish the file containing the essay prepared using word processing software from the mailing list prepared (using database management software), you might label your text file CARTER1.TXT and your mailing list or data file CARTER1.DBF. In this example, TXT stands for *text* and DBF stands for *data*. The period (.) is used as a separator only and is found between the filename and extension.

Certain types of software provide their own filename extensions that allow you to distinguish their text files from other types of software. For example, Multimate word processing software provides the extension DOC, and Turbo Pascal provides the extension PAS. Some software also automatically creates backup files that contain the version of the file before it was revised. These filenames have the extension BAK (BACKUP).

File Types

You should be aware of the file type extensions shown in Figure 3.1.

Figure 3.1

Types of filename extensions.

COM or EXE	Command files	An extension of .COM or .EXE means that the contents of the file is an executable file or a program. It is a file created by using a programming language such as "C" or Pascal. By typing the filename (with or without this extension), the computer will assume you want a command executed.
		You will find .COM and .EXE files on applications program and operating system program disks.
SYS	System files	SYS files are files that command your computer to perform such actions as reroute its outputs, and so on. An example is CONFIG.SYS.

BAT	Batch files	BAT files are files that carry out a series of commands. An example is AUTOEXEC.BAT, which you will learn about in later chapters.
BAK	Backup files	BAK files provide copies of files created by DOS or applications software when the original file was altered so that your original is saved. A user can also use BAK as an extension to indicate a backup copy.
DOC or TXT	Document or text files	DOC or TXT files are created by using word processing applications software.
WKS	Worksheet files	WKS files are created by using Lotus and other spreadsheet applications software.
DBF or DTA	Database files	DBF or DTA files are created by using database applications software.
OVR	Overlay files	OVR are files found in applications software.
BAS	BASIC files	BAS are files created when using the BASIC programming language.
PAS	Pascal files	PAS files are created when using the Pascal programming language.

Other extensions can also be used, as long as they follow the rules for creating filenames. See Figure 3.2 for invalid and Figure 3.3 for valid ways of naming files.

Figure 3.2

Invalid ways of constructing filenames.

Invalid	Why Invalid
MY STORY.TXT	Contains a space
.TXT	Does not have a filename
MY,STORY.TXT	Contains a comma
MY:STORY.TXT	Contains a mark of punctuation (colon)
MYSTORY.TXTE	Extension contains more than three characters
PRN.TXT	Contains a device name (PRN)
COPY.TXT	Contains a DOS command (COPY)
WP.COM	Contains an applications software filename (WP.COM)
MY*STORY.TXT	Contains a wildcard (*)

Figure 3.3	**Valid Filename**	**What It Represents**
Valid ways of	LETTER.TXT	A text file
constructing	REVENUE.DBF	A database file
filenames.	AUTOEXEC.BAT	A DOS "batch" file
	1234ABCD.333	A filename and an extension
	5551212.XXX	A filename and an extension
	%$#%@812	No extension designator
	HELLO	No extension designator

Note: Filenames can be all caps (uppercase), all lowercase, or upper- and lowercase. When displayed in a directory, the letters will all be displayed in uppercase.

Creating a File

The files created for various types of applications are created by programmers using a variety of different programming languages. The user creates data files when using these applications programs. The files that call up an applications program that have the extension COM are called COMMAND files. You can retrieve a COM file by typing in the filename.

Within DOS, files can be created by using the DOS editor EDLIN or by copying from the console to a file, using the DOS internal command COPY and the keyboard device name CON (console). The DOS editor is more versatile in that it allows you to make corrections once a file has been created. COPY CON provides an easy method of creating a small file without requiring an external DOS command. That is, you do not need to have the DOS disk present in a drive. All COPY CON requires is a DOS prompt, and a usable disk in the default drive.

The disadvantage of using COPY CON is that you cannot edit a file once it has been created. The only way to edit your mistakes while creating a file is to make sure that each line of text is correct before you depress Enter. After a line of text has been entered using COPY CON, the only way to correct the error without resorting to EDLIN is to rewrite over the same file, using COPY CON.

In this chapter, you will learn how to create a file using COPY CON, but you will not see the real advantage of creating a file with DOS until Chapter 7.

Tip: Words of caution—when you create a file, you must name the file using a filename that has not already been used, or you will erase the file (with the same name) that was present before.

Displaying the Contents of a File

The DOS internal command TYPE is used to list the contents of a file onto the screen. Certain files such as Command (COM) and Executable (EXE) files will appear as symbols when displayed in this way. These files have been created using a programming language and converted into machine-readable code that is unreadable to the average person. Files that you create with DOS are called *text files*. When you use the command TYPE, they display as text characters as you have written them, not as symbols. If a file is displayed to the screen in symbols, you should not attempt to alter the symbols in any way or you might ruin the file.

Redirecting Output

If you wish to send a copy of the contents of your file to the printer instead of to the screen, DOS allows you to do so. When you use a command to send output to a device other than the screen (default device), it is called *output redirection*. The command to redirect information/data away from the screen to the printer is

```
>PRN
```

PRN is the DOS device name for *printer*.

Directory Listing of a Single File

To find out if a file exists without listing an entire directory, you can use DIR with the filename. When you use this command, DOS searches the directory of the disk for the filename listed and, if found, displays the same information about that file that would appear in a complete directory listing. The command appears as

```
A>DIR FILENAME.EXT
```

If found, DOS will list the file. If not found, DOS responds that the file was not found.

Note:

DOS will respond with a "not found" message if you mistype any part of the filename or extension.

Obtaining Partial Directories with Wildcards

When you work with long lists of files, you may find it difficult to locate certain files that are on the directory. By using wildcards, you can obtain partial directories of certain types of files. Wildcards are symbols that can be used in place of known or unknown characters in filenames or extensions. The DOS manual refers to them as *global filename characters*. The two wildcards are ? and * (question mark and asterisk). The ? can take the place of one unknown character. The * can take the place of more than one unknown characters.

To obtain a directory listing of all the files with the COM extension, the command would be

```
A>DIR *.COM
```

The other uses of the wildcards will be explained in the Hands-On Activities.

Hands-On Activities

DOS	EXERCISES	PRACTICE	BACKUP
	Formatted Data Disk VOL=EXERCISES	Formatted Data Disk VOL=PRACTICE	Formatted Data Disk VOL=BACKUP

In the following exercises, you will learn how to (1) create a file using COPY CON, (2) look at a directory to see that the file was created, (3) display the contents of a file onto the screen, (4) redirect the output to display to the printer, (5) display a directory of a single file, and (6) display a directory of selected files using the wildcards. In addition, you will learn to use Ctrl-S to stop the scrolling of a directory.

How to Use COPY CON to Name and Create a File

COPY CON is usually used to create a small file to help you use your applications software. The following files that you create are not practical files that you would normally create. They are intended just to give you practice in creating files with COPY CON.

Use **Practice** disk in Drive A:.

	What to Do	*What Happens*
Step 1	At A> type in COPY CON MYNAME.TXT and press Enter.	You name a file MYNAME.TXT.
Step 2	Type your name and press Enter.	

Step 3	Depress Ctrl and Z simultaneously, release, and then press Enter.	See screen that follows.

```
A>COPY CON MYNAME.TXT
MARK D. ALLEN
^Z
         1 File(s) copied

A>
```

▶ *You insert your name.*

Notes:

1. In the future, when two keys are used together separated by a hyphen, you are to press the two keys simultaneously. Ctrl and Z will be written Ctrl-Z.

2. Ctrl-Z or the key F6 can be used to produce ^Z.

3. The Ctrl-Z is used to signify the end of input. If followed by Enter, the file is copied.

Now you should check the disk in your default drive to make sure the file was created. If the disk contained a write-protection covering, the file would not have been copied. DOS would have given you a message to that effect when you tried to save the file with Ctrl-Z and Enter. If this happens, you need to remove the write-protection before copying.

Step 4	Type DIR and press Enter for disk directory.	See screen that follows.

```
A>DIR
 Volume in drive A is PRACTICE
 Directory of A:\
MYNAME    TXT      15   5-13-91 12:08p
    1 File(s)    1457152 bytes free
A>
```

▶ *These numbers will vary.*

Notice that your file may not contain the same number of bytes. The letters and spaces used to create your name and any Enter or Ctrl characters are all added to arrive at the number of bytes used. The more characters in your name, the greater the number of bytes that are used. If your name differs in size from the name shown and you add extra spaces or returns, the number of bytes will vary from those on the screen.

**Review
Exercises**

1. Create a file using COPY CON and name the file DAYDATE.TXT. In the file, place the following contents: Current day of the week, and the month, day, and year separated by / 's.

2. Create a file using COPY CON and name it SCHEDULE.TXT. In the file, place the following contents:

MONDAY	Go to the bank.
TUESDAY	Call tax consultant.
WEDNESDAY	Call for a doctor's appointment.
THURSDAY	Pay phone bill.
FRIDAY	Visit the dentist.

Note: If you make a typing mistake, use COPY CON again to recreate the file. By saving the file again, you erase the old file.

*How to Display
the Contents
of a File*

If you wish to display the contents of a file, first list the files on a disk using the DIR command. If you see the file you want on the directory list, you can then look into the file to see the contents of the file. To do this, you need to use the TYPE command.

Use the **Practice** disk.

What to Do	*What Happens*
Step 1 — The **Practice** disk should be in Drive A:. Type TYPE MYNAME.TXT and press Enter.	See screen that follows.

```
A>TYPE MYNAME.TXT
MARK D. ALLEN


A>
```

▶*Your name should
appear here.*

1. a. Display the contents of DAYDATE.TXT to the screen.

   b. Using DIR, find the number of bytes in the file.

      Record your answer: __290 304__

   c. Will everyone's file be the same size?   NO

2. a. Display the contents of SCHEDULE.TXT to the screen.

   b. Using DIR, find the number of bytes in the file.

      Record your answer: __290 304__

   c. Will everyone's file be the same size?   NO

Answers

1. b. Answers will vary.

   c. No.

2. b. Answers will vary.

   c. No.

*How to
Redirect Output
to a Printer*

The TYPE command can also be used to display the contents of a file to a printer. *Be sure that the printer is attached and turned on before using the TYPE command to display to a printer.* The command as it appears on the screen to display a file in Drive A: is as follows:

```
A>TYPE DAYDATE.TXT>PRN
```

Use **Practice** disk in Drive A:.

What to Do	*What Happens*
Step 1 At the A> type TYPE DAYDATE.TXT > PRN and press Enter.	See printout that is created by the printer (Figure 3.4).

If you want to print out the contents of a file that is located in Drive B:, use the following command:

```
A>TYPE B:DAYDATE.TXT>PRN
```

Note: If you are using a laser printer, you will need to turn the On Line button off and press the form feed. Remember to turn the On Line button back on.

Tip: Do not use > PRN unless you have a printer attached and the on-line light on, or the computer will lock up until the printer is on line. The message "Not ready error writing device PRN" appears.

Figure 3.4

Printout for redirected output (example).

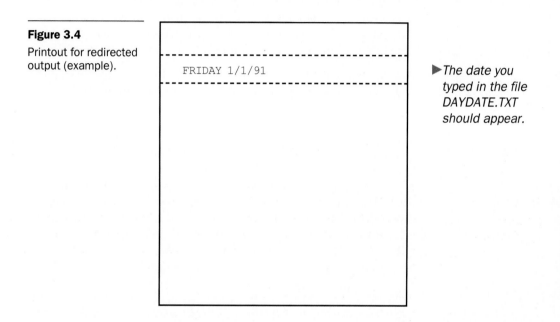

```
FRIDAY 1/1/91
```

▶The date you typed in the file DAYDATE.TXT should appear.

Use **Practice** disk in Drive A: and **BACKUP** disk in Drive B:.

	What to Do	*What Happens*
Step 1	Type B: and press Enter.	A B > appears.
Step 2	At the B > type TYPE A:DAYDATE.TXT > PRN and press Enter.	The contents of that file displays to the printer.

*Review
Exercises*

Use the disk labeled **EXERCISES**.

1. Display the contents of the file README.DOC (using the DOS command TYPE) located on the disk labeled **EXERCISES**. (Notice that the file displays so quickly that you cannot read what is on the screen.)

2. At the A> type README and press Enter. Answer the questions. This file illustrates the power that you will have over your computer by learning DOS. In Chapter 7, you will learn to create this type of file, called a *batch file*. If it is easier for you to work from hard copy, display the contents of the README.DOC file to the printer, using the TYPE command, and answer the questions.

3. Display the contents of README.ANS to the printer using the TYPE command to check your answers to Exercise 2. You can also check your answers to Exercise 2 by typing ANSWER.BAT.

You can practice creating files using COPY CON until you feel comfortable with creating them. You need to learn to use COPY CON because it is a very useful tool when creating batch files—a number of commands that execute consecutively one after another. README is an example of a batch file. Users of hard (fixed) disks especially need to know how to use batch files to simplify movement within the vast storage area of the hard disk. In later chapters, batch files will be discussed. How to delete the files you just created and/or rename them will be discussed in Chapter 4.

*How to Locate
a Specific File
on a Disk*

Anytime you wish to see if a specific file is on a directory list without listing the entire directory, DOS allows you to do so. For example, if you want to find out if a file called README.DOC exists on a disk without listing the whole DIR, you would do the following:

Use the disk labeled **EXERCISES** in Drive A.

	What to Do	*What Happens*
Step 1	Obtain an A>.	Nothing.
Step 2	Type DIR README.DOC and press Enter.	See screen that follows.

```
A>DIR README.DOC

 Volume in drive A is EXERCISES
 Directory of A:\

README     DOC     2340  1-04-80 12:09a
     1 File(s)       626688 bytes free
```

►*Numbers may vary.*

If DOS responds with a directory listing of the file you requested, the file is on the disk.

How to Display Selected Files in a Directory

Files that have similar characters within their filenames or extensions can be displayed by using either the * or ? wildcards. Using these wildcards, you could perform operations that list only all the command files (files with the extension COM) or all the text files (files with the extension TXT).

The * Wildcard

Suppose that you have two files named CARTER, one that is a database file and one that is a word processing text file. Although they have the same filename CARTER, they might have different extensions (DBF) and (TXT). To locate these files on a directory, you could use an asterisk in place of the extension, as shown:

A>DIR CARTER.*   tells DOS to search for any file with the filename CARTER and any extension.

Another reason for using the * wildcard is for listing all the files with the same extension. For instance, if you wanted to list only the files that had the extension TXT, you would use the command as follows:

A>DIR *.TXT   tells DOS to list the directory of any file with the extension TXT.

Using the * wildcard in place of both the filename and the extension would produce the same result as using the DIR command alone.

A>DIR *.* would produce the same affect as A>DIR. The first asterisk stands for any filename. The second asterisk stands for any extension.

The asterisk can be used in the following ways:

A>DIR CARTER.*   lists all files named CARTER regardless of their extensions (DBF) or (TXT) in Drive A:.

A>DIR *.DOC   lists all files with the extension (DOC) in Drive A:.

A>DIR *.*   lists all files located in Drive A: regardless of filename or extension.

The ? Wildcard

The ? wildcard can be thought of as replacing any one character. For example, if you want to list a number of files that begin with CARTER but are followed by the numbers of the draft CARTER1.TXT, CARTER2.TXT, CARTER3.TXT, CARTER4.TXT, CARTER5.TXT, you cannot use the DIR command and say DIR Carter.*. DOS would search the disk for any filename with only six letters CARTER. The numerals are the seventh character in the filename. Since the last character of each filename differs from file to file, a wildcard can be used in place of that character within the filename that is different in each file:

A>DIR CARTER?.TXT   Lists all the files containing the first part of the root CARTER and any one character following the word CARTER.

When using a ? for a character within a filename while using the DIR command, DOS will look for a filename with the characters that surround the question mark and list any files that fit into the parameters. (See Figure 3.5.)

However, if you have several files such as CARTER1.TXT and CARTER12.TXT, DOS will only list the file CARTER1.TXT using the previous command because you only used one ? following filename CARTER, and CARTER12 has two characters after the common characters CARTER. In this example, to list both files, you would need to list two ?'s following the common characters CARTER.

A>DIR CARTER??.TXT   Uses two question marks because the maximum number of characters following CARTER was two. If three characters follow a similar root, then three question marks must be used.

As you can see, using several ?'s could get confusing at times. You might find it easier to use the * in place of two or more ?'s. For example, A > DIR CARTER??.??? is the same as A > DIR CARTER*.* and A > DIR ??CARTER.??? is the same as A > DIR *CARTER.*.

Figure 3.5

Using a wildcard to search the files (example).

The Files on a Disk	Using	Results
CHAP1.TXT	DIR CHAP?.TXT	CHAP1.TXT
CHAP2.TXT		CHAP2.TXT
CHAP3.TXT		CHAP3.TXT
CHAP4.TXT		CHAP4.TXT
CHAP1A.TXT		
CHAP2A.TXT	DIR CHAP?A.TXT	CHAP1A.TXT
CHAP3A.TXT		CHAP2A.TXT
CHAP4A.TXT		CHAP3A.TXT
CHAP1B.TXT		CHAP4A.TXT
CHAP2B.TXT		
CHAP3B.TXT	DIR CHAP1?.TXT	CHAP1.TXT
CHAP4B.TXT		CHAP1A.TXT
CHAP1.DOC		CHAP1B.TXT
CHAP2.DBF		
CHAP3.WKS	DIR CHAP1.*	CHAP1.TXT
CHAP1.WKS		CHAP1.DOC
CHAP2.WKS		CHAP1.WKS
CHAP3.DBF		

Wildcards accelerate the process of locating specific files when several files have similar characters.

The * Wildcard Replacing an Extension

In this exercise, you will learn how to obtain a list of all the files with the same filename, but an unknown extension. You will obtain a list of all the files with the filename README, but different extensions.

Use the disk labeled **EXERCISES** in Drive A:.

	What to Do	*What Happens*
Step 1	Obtain an A>.	Nothing.
Step 2	Type DIR README.* and press Enter.	See screen that follows.

```
A>DIR README.*

 Volume of drive A is EXERCISES
 Directory of A:\

 README    ANS    2082   1-04-80  12:24a
 README    DOC    2340   1-04-80  12:09a
 README    SC3     553   1-04-80  12:12a
 README    BAT      94   1-01-80  11:46p
 README    AN2    1033   1-04-80  12:30a
 README    SC1    1015   1-03-80  12:24a
 README    SC2     774   1-04-80  12:11a
 README    AN3     475   1-04-80  12:26a
 README    AN1     626   1-04-80  12:27a
      9 File(s)      626688 bytes free

 A>
```

▶*Numbers may vary.*

The * Wildcard Replacing a Filename

In this exercise, you will learn how to obtain a list of all the files with the same extension, but unknown filenames. You will obtain a list of all the files with the extension COM, but different filenames.

Use the disk labeled **EXERCISES** in Drive A:.

	What to Do	*What Happens*
Step 1	Obtain an A>.	Nothing.
Step 2	Type DIR *.COM and press Enter.	See screen that follows.

```
A>DIR *.COM

 Volume of drive A is EXERCISES
 Directory of A:\

 WP        COM   16707   1-01-80 12:19a
 DB        COM   24432   8-26-87  3:58p
 SS        COM   21330   8-26-87  3:59p
 REPLY     COM      14   9-17-87 12:34p
      4 File(s)       626688 bytes free

 A>
```

▶*Numbers may vary.*

This command lists a directory of all the files with the COM extension.

In the next exercise, you will learn how to obtain a list of all the files with the same filename and one unknown character in the extension. You will obtain a list of all the README files with the extension that begins with AN.

Use the disk labeled **EXERCISES** in Drive A:.

	What to Do	What Happens
Step 1	Obtain an A>.	Nothing.
Step 2	Type DIR README.AN? and press Enter.	See screen that follows.

```
A>DIR README.AN?

 Volume of drive A is EXERCISES
 Directory of A:\
 README    ANS    2082   1-04-80 12:24a
 README    AN2    1033   1-04-80 12:30a
 README    AN3     475   1-04-80 12:26a
 README    AN1     626   1-04-80 12:27a
      4 File(s)       626688 bytes free

 A>
```

▶*Numbers may vary.*

Both the ? and the * can be used together to obtain the desired directory.

The > PRN can be used with the preceding commands to send the contents of a directory to the printer; for example,

```
A>DIR *.COM>PRN
```

As you can see, wildcards help you obtain the directory listing you want.

Review Exercises

1. Using the **EXERCISES** disk, send the directory of the files that contain the filename README to the printer. What command did you use?

2. Using the **EXERCISES** disk, send the directory of all the COM files to the printer. What command did you use?

3. Using the **EXERCISES** disk, send the directory of all the files that contain the filename README and the first two characters of the extension AN. What command did you use?

4. Using the **EXERCISES** disk, send the directory of all the files that contain the letters CHAP in the filename. (The directory should list four files.) What command did you use?

Answers

1. `A>DIR README.*>PRN`

2. `A>DIR *.COM>PRN`

3. `A>DIR README.AN?>PRN`

4. `A>DIR CHAP*.*>PRN`

How to Use Ctrl-S

Sometimes a disk contains so many files that the DIR scrolls all the filenames faster than you can read them. By using the Ctrl-S keys together, you can stop a directory from scrolling off the screen. Ctrl-S is similar to DIR /P, except that with Ctrl-S you can control the portion of the directory displayed on the screen at a time. After typing in your DIR command, but before pressing the Enter key, place one finger over the Ctrl key and one finger over the S key. Once you have pressed the Enter key to begin listing the directory, press the Ctrl-S keys simultaneously to stop the scrolling. If the file you are looking for is on the screen and you have obtained the information that you desire, press any key to continue the scrolling of the directory. If the file you are looking for is not on the screen when you first stop the directory, be ready to press the Ctrl-S keys again to stop the list after you have pressed a key to begin the scrolling.

Tip: It is easy to leave the Ctrl key pressed and only worry about pressing the S key to start and stop the scrolling.

Use the disk labeled **EXERCISES** in Drive A:.

	What to Do	*What Happens*
Step 1	At an A > type TYPE README.DOC and press Enter.	The contents of README.DOC display on the screen.
Step 2	Depress Ctrl-S.	Scrolling stops.
Step 3	Depress any key to continue.	Scrolling continues.

Two-key combinations that are useful now that you are listing file directories using DIR and the contents of individual files using the TYPE command are Ctrl-C and Ctrl-S. When you type DIR and the contents of the screen begin to scroll, you can stop the scrolling by depressing Ctrl-S. Any key depressed will resume the scrolling. On the other hand, if you wish to abort the command, you can type Ctrl-C (or Ctrl Break), and you will be returned to the >. You can do the same after the TYPE command is issued.

Summary Points

1. The computer does not allow you to give the same name to two different files.

2. It does allow you to give meaningless names—a practice you should avoid.

3. A filename cannot be longer than eight characters. Upper- or lowercase characters or both can be used.

4. A three-character extension can be used with a filename.

5. You should avoid using punctuation or symbols in naming files because certain symbols are unacceptable. Spaces cannot be used.

6. A period (separator) is used to separate the filename from the extension.

7. Any filename longer than eight characters or extension longer than three characters will not be recognized by DOS.

8. Some extensions are commonly used by applications software and system software developers; for example, COM or EXE, SYS, BAT, BAK, DOC or TXT, WKS, DBF or DTA, OVR, BAS, PAS.

9. The files created for various types of applications are created by programmers using a variety of different programming languages.

10. The user creates data files when using applications programs.

11. You can retrieve a COMMAND (COM) or an Executable (EXE) file to call up an applications program by typing in the filename.

12. Within DOS, files can be created by using the DOS editor EDLIN or by copying from the console to a file using the DOS internal command COPY and the keyboard device name CON (console).

13. An advantage of using COPY CON is that it provides an easy method of creating a small file without requiring an external DOS command. That is, you do not need to have DOS present in a drive. All COPY CON requires is an A>.

14. When you create a file, you must name the file using a file name that has not already been used, or you will erase your existing file.

15. The DOS internal command TYPE is used to list the contents of a file onto the screen.

16. Certain files such as COMMAND (COM) and Executable (EXE) files will appear as symbols when displayed using the TYPE command. These files have been created using a programming language and converted into machine-readable code.

17. Files that you create with DOS are considered text files. They can be displayed as text when you use the DOS internal command TYPE.

18. The DOS command to redirect the printer away from the screen to a printer device is TYPE filename.EXT > PRN. PRN is the DOS name for printer.

19. You can use the directory command with a filename to search the directory of the disk for a file and display the information as found on a directory listing.

20. Wildcards make it possible to list selected files from a directory.

21. Wildcards are symbols that can be used in place of known or unknown characters. The DOS manual refers to them as *global filenames*.

Application Exercises

Do the following exercises at your computer.

1. On **Practice** disk, create a file called LETTER1.DOC using the DOS COPY CON command. The contents of the file should be:

```
September 1, 199-

Professor Alvin Tomas
P.O. Box
Santa Clara, CA 92734
```

2. On **Practice** disk,

   a. Create three files with the contents as shown:

Filename	Contents
CHAP1.TXT	Chapter 1
CHAP2.TXT	Chapter 2
CHAP3.TXT	Chapter 3
	Text
	Application Exercises

   b. Display the contents of the previous three files on the screen using the TYPE command.

   c. Send the contents of the files to the printer.

3. On **Practice** disk,

   a. Create three files and the contents as shown:

Filename	Contents
DATA1.DBF	Your own name
	Your own address
DATA2.DBF	Your own phone number
DATA3.DBF	Your own birthdate
	Your own Social Security number

   b. Display the contents of the previous three files on the screen.

   c. Send the contents of the three files to the printer.

4. Try to create a file named ??123.TXT with the word "Hi" in it on **Practice** disk.

   a. Did DOS accept the filename?

   b. Why would you want to avoid using the ? wildcard in this way? Check the directory using DIR *.TXT.

5. Using **Practice** disk, enter a filename that has a space in it using COPY CON. Explain what happens. *You get a Bad command or file name*

6. List the directory of **Practice** disk in Drive A: and use Ctrl-S. Explain what happens.

7. Display the directory of **EXERCISES** disk in Drive A: and use Ctrl-C (Ctrl Break). Explain what happens.

8. Display the contents of WP.COM on the **EXERCISES** disk using the TYPE command. Explain what you see.

9. Send the directory of **Practice** disk to the printer. What command did you use?

Comprehension Questions

Answer the following questions.

1. If you are in Drive A: and wanted to create a file in Drive B: using COPY CON, how would you do it?

2. When is the COPY CON method of creating a file most useful?

3. Explain the difference between Ctrl-S and Ctrl-C.

4. What would happen if you tried to enter a filename or extension that has more characters than is allowed?

5. Why is the TYPE command used?

6. Explain the difference between the command to display to the screen and the command to display to the printer.

7. What does "output redirection" mean?

Completion Exercises

Complete the following sentences.

1. A _filename_ is any group of text, numbers, or symbols stored under one name.

2. The main portion of a filename is called the _extension_.

3. _extension_ follow the filename and are used to classify the type of file it is.

4. Write valid or invalid after each filename.

a. PRN.TXT _____valid_____

b. CHAP 1.TXT _____invalid_____

c. CHAP1.TEXT _____invalid_____

d. 1CHAP.TXT _____invalid_____

e. CHAPTER12.TXT _____invalid_____

f. TO:JOE.LET _____invalid_____

g. JONES,J.LET _____invalid_____

Matching Exercises

Choose the correct letter from the right-hand column.

B 1. BAK

A 2. CON

C 3. COPY CON

E 4. Esc

F 5. Ctrl-S

H 6. TYPE FILENAME.EXT>PRN

D 7. Ctrl-C

G 8. PRN

a. DOS name for console

b. A file extension used for backup files

c. A key used to cancel anything written after an >

d. A means of copying a file created at the keyboard

e. A means of aborting a command and returning to the >

f. A means of stopping the scrolling of text when the directory command DIR or TYPE is used

g. Sends the contents of a file to a printer

h. DOS name for printer

4

Copying and Deleting Files

When you have completed this chapter, you will be able to

Learning Objectives:

1. Explain the purpose of copying.

2. Distinguish between COPY and DISKCOPY.

3. Explain the restrictions that apply to copying.

4. Explain how to copy one file at a time using the COPY command.

5. Explain how to copy several files at a time using the COPY command.

6. Explain the use of RENAME.

7. Explain the purpose of DEL and ERASE.

8. Explain the purpose of the function keys.

Performance Objectives:

1. Use DISKCOPY to copy a disk.

2. Copy a single file to the same disk.

3. Copy a single file to another disk.

4. Copy multiple files to the same disk.

5. Copy multiple files to another disk.

6. Rename a file.

7. Use function keys to edit a command.

8. Use CLS.

Chapter Overview

When working with applications programs, you should always be sure to make backup copies of your DOS disk, your applications program disk, and your data disks. Whenever you purchase an applications program disk, you should immediately make a copy of it and put the original (master copy) away. As soon as you are finished creating important data files, backups should be made and stored in a safe place.

Making backups is an important function of copying, but just as important is the flexibility that copying gives you to move files around. Files are copied either to produce a duplicate of a file or disk or to transfer a file or files from one disk to another. In this chapter, in addition to learning how to back up disks, you will learn how to

1. Move files around within a disk and to other disks

2. Delete unnecessary files

3. Combine the contents of several files under one filename

4. Rename files

Why Make Backups?

Although disks are sturdy, a number of different problems may occur, making backups a necessity: You may accidentally erase a file by (1) using the DOS command that deletes a file, (2) depressing the wrong key(s) in an applications program by mistake, (3) exposing the disk to magnetic fields, or (4) experiencing a computer malfunction. If you are using floppy disks, it is also easy to misplace them or accidently bend or mutilate them.

When you ruin or lose an application program disk, you will have to contact the manufacturer for another copy. Losing or ruining a disk with data files is often a disaster. It often means that hours of your hard work will have to be repeated.

Why Use DISKCOPY?

One DOS command used for making backups is DISKCOPY. The DOS external command DISKCOPY makes an electronic duplicate of a disk in its entirety, including both hidden and visible files. It is convenient for making backups because you do not have to format the backup disk. DISKCOPY makes a duplicate copy of the source disk and formats the target disk at the same time. (See Figure 4.1.)

Figure 4.1

DISKCOPY copies all the files on the source diskette to the target diskette and reformats the target diskette.

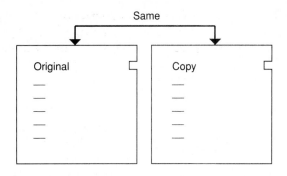

If the target disk already contains files, the files are erased and the disk is reformatted. For this reason, you should be careful when copying a disk using DISKCOPY.

DISKCOPY can be used with either a single-disk drive or with a dual-disk (two-disk) drive system. When using DISKCOPY with a single-disk system, you will have to manually switch your source and target disks. After typing DISKCOPY and pressing ENTER, DOS will prompt you when to switch between the source and target disks. For example, the command for copying a disk in drive A: is

```
A>DISKCOPY A:
```

If you have a dual-diskette system, with two identical disk drives, you can use the DISKCOPY command with the disk drive designators to indicate that the source is in Drive A: and the target disk in Drive B:, as follows:

```
A>DISKCOPY A: B:
```

After this command is executed, you must follow the prompts on the screen. You can copy another disk by typing Y when DOS asks you if you want to copy another (Y / N).

Since DISKCOPY is an external command, the DOS disk must be placed in a drive to initiate the command. DISKCOPY cannot be used for copying to or from a hard disk because of the size of the disk. You can use the DOS file DISKCOPY if it is on a hard disk to copy floppy diskettes. DISKCOPY.COM must be available on Drive C:. The commands are

```
C>DISKCOPY A: B:
```

or

```
C>DISKCOPY B: A:
```

Figure 4.2

DISKCOPY destroys existing files because the disk is formatted at the same time. COPY adds the files to be copied to already existing files.

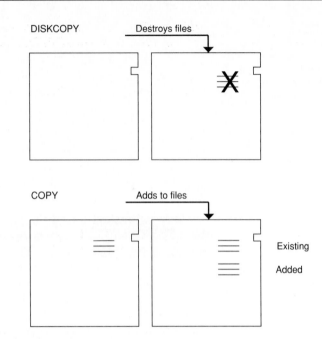

Why Use DISKCOMP?

After you copy a disk using DISKCOPY, you should check to see that the two disks contain the same files. DISKCOMP is an external DOS command that allows you to check to see if the two disks are the same.

Why Use the COPY Command?

You may not want to copy the entire disk, but you may wish to copy one or more files. The COPY command allows you to copy a single file, a selected group of files, or the contents of an entire disk (with the exception of hidden files) to another disk(s). It does not destroy the existing contents of a target disk. It merely adds the new files.

Tips:

Before issuing the COPY command, you should look at the directories of both the source disk (the disk that contains the file or files that you are going to copy) and the target diskette (the disk to which the file or files will be copied).

1. Check the directory of the source disk to determine the size of the file to be copied. Then check the directory of the target diskette to determine if there is enough room to hold the file or files (number of bytes free).

2. Check the target disk to determine if the name(s) of the file(s) that you wish to copy already appear on the target diskette. If they do, the files on the target drive with the same name as those being copied will be written over with the contents of the file or files from the source diskette.

Summary of the Difference Between DISKCOPY and COPY

DISKCOPY is an external DOS command that allows you to copy the contents of an entire disk, making an exact duplicate of it. If the disk is not formatted, it will also format at the same time.

The DISKCOPY command destroys any files that exist on the disk to which the files are being copied. COPY allows you to add files to an already formatted disk. (See Figure 4.2.)

Restrictions on Copying Files

When copying files, you must pay attention to the copyright laws of the software manufacturers. Most software manufacturers allow you to make copies of your disks for backup purposes. If you make a copy of a DOS disk or an applications program disk that you do not own, you are in violation of the copyright laws pertaining to software and can be prosecuted. Some applications programs have built-in write-protection prohibiting you from making usable copies.

Why Copy an Individual File?

When using applications programs, you may find that you have placed a number of data files on a disk. To organize your files, you need to move some to other disks. The COPY command makes this possible. You may also wish to copy a file and rename it with another name so that you have a backup of the file.

In order to use the COPY command, you need to supply DOS with additional information (parameters). The COPY command requires the name of the drive in which the source file(s) resides (unless the source is in the default drive), the filename of the source, and the destination of the copy.

A general format for the COPY command is shown in Figure 4.3.

Figure 4.3
Format for the COPY command.

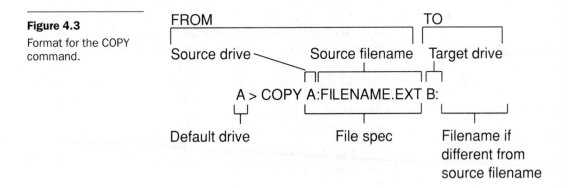

The COPY command allows you to copy a single file in the following manner:

```
A>COPY B:CHAP1.DOC A:
```
copies from the disk in Drive B: the file CHAP1.DOC to the disk in Drive A:.

```
A>COPY CHAP1.DOC B:
```
copies from the disk in Drive A: the file CHAP1.DOC to the disk in Drive B: (DOS assumes that CHAP1.DOC is located in Drive A: because A is the default drive).

In the first example, the source file is identified as being on the disk in Drive B: and the target drive—the drive that contains the disk being copied to—as Drive A:. In the second example, the source file is assumed to be the drive indicated by the DOS prompt A>.

You need to specify your source and target disk drives, unless your source disk is located in the default drive, the drive indicated by the DOS prompt. DOS always looks to the default drive for the file to copy if a drive is not specified in the file spec before the filename. (The file spec consists of the source drive, filename, and extension, if any.)

The following is not an acceptable method of copying a single file:

```
A>COPY CHAP1.DOC
```
does not copy.

If you used this command, you would be trying to copy CHAP1.DOC onto itself and would receive a message telling you that you cannot do this. You have not specified a new location for the copy.

When you ask for a file to be copied, DOS looks for the file. If you have not given a source drive label, DOS will look in the default drive for the file. If you have given a source drive label, DOS will go to that drive and look for the file. It will load the file into RAM and read the drive name to which the file is to be copied. At this point, DOS will scan the directory of the diskette in that drive and see if enough space exists there to copy the file.

If there is not enough space, DOS will not copy the file. Instead it will give you a "Disk full" message. When the COPY command is issued and there is not enough disk space, the following message appears:

```
Insufficient disk space, 0 file(s) copied.
```

When the COPY command is issued and there is enough disk space, the drive that contains the source disk lights up as the file is loaded into RAM. Then the drive that contains the target disk lights up as the file is copied to the disk there.

When the process is complete, DOS displays the message

```
One file copied.
```

You will then be returned to the prompt of your default drive.

Why Use COMPARE?

After you have made a copy of a file, it is wise to check to see that the two files are identical. The external DOS command COMPARE allows you to check to see if the two files are the same.

Why Use Wildcards with COPY?

If you do not want to make a disk copy, but want to copy several files, copying files using the wildcards is much faster than copying individual files.

Filenames or extensions that have one or more similar characters in common can be copied by using either the * or ? wildcards. Using these wildcards, you could perform such operations as copy all the command files (files with the extension COM), or copy all the text files (files with the extension TXT) from one disk to another. Wildcards accelerate the copying process.

The ? Wildcard

As explained in Chapter 3, the ? wildcard can be thought of as standing for any single character. For example, if you have to copy a number of files that begin with CARTER but are followed by the numbers of the draft, CARTER1.TXT, CARTER2.TXT, CARTER3.TXT, CARTER4.TXT, and CARTER5.TXT, you cannot use the COPY command and say COPY CARTER. The last character of the file differs from file to file. A wildcard, however, can be used in place of the seventh character of the file:

```
A>COPY CARTER?.TXT B:
```
copies all the files containing the first part of the root CARTER and any one character following the word CARTER to Drive B:.

Note: When using a ? for a character within a filename, DOS will look for a filename with the characters that surround the question mark and copy any names that have these common characters.

If you have files such as CARTER1.TXT and CARTER12.TXT, you will only be able to copy CARTER1.TXT using the previous command. To copy CARTER12.TXT, you would need two question marks following CARTER to transfer this file:

`A>COPY CARTER??.TXT B:`   uses two question marks because the maximum number of characters following CARTER was two. If three characters follow a similar root, then three question marks must be used.

The COPY command followed by ????????.??? and a disk drive designation is the same as the COPY command followed by *.* and a disk drive designation. It transfers all the files from one disk to another.

*The * Wildcard*   Another way to copy selected files is through the use of the * wild card. For example, if you have a file named CARTER that was a database file and one that was a word processing text file, they might have different extensions (DBF) and(TXT) but the same filename CARTER. The asterisk can be used in place of the filename or extension or both. It can also substitute for part of the filename.

The asterisk can be used in the following ways:

`A>COPY CAR*.* B:`   copies all files that begin with CAR regardless of their extensions (DBF) or (TXT) from Drive A: to Drive B:.

`A>COPY CARTER.* B:`   copies all files named CARTER regardless of their extensions (DBF) or (TXT) from Drive A: to Drive B:.

`A>COPY *.TXT B:`   copies all files with the extension (TXT) from A: to B:.

`A>COPY *.* B:`   copies all files located on Drive A: to Drive B:.

When the COPY command is used to copy multiple files, the files will copy one by one, and DOS will pack the files as close together as possible without gaps.

The use of the COPY command requires that the target disk be formatted. The COPY command will not destroy existing files on the target diskette, but it will write over a file of the same name.

Why Combine Files?

Sometimes when you are using applications software, you may find that you wish to combine the contents of two files. You may have two or more files containing paragraphs that you think should belong on one file. Rather than retype the paragraphs, you could merge the files. Most of the time this capability is present when you are using applications software. The DOS capability of combining files, however, provides a convenience. The DOS command COPY lets you merge the files without being in the applications program. Files merged together are said to be "concatenated." An example of how DOS allows you to merge the contents of a number of files together and store the results in another file is as follows:

```
A>COPY          CHAP1.DOC+CHAP2.TXT          A:CHAP.OLD
```
copies the contents of CHAP1.DOC and the contents of CHAP2.DOC and stores the result in CHAP.OLD.

You can also use wildcards. However, the former method allows you to choose the order in which the files will be added together.

Why Rename Files?

Since you cannot have two exact filenames of a file on a disk, for backup purposes you may wish to leave the filename the same but change the extension. With the COPY command, you can copy a file and rename it simultaneously.

Copy While Renaming

Either the root or the extension of the filename can be changed by using the COPY command. Here are two cases where you might want to change the names of the files with the COPY command:

1. Suppose you have just finished the third draft of the term paper you are writing on Carter. You have named the file CARTER3.DOC. You want to copy the document from Drive A: to Drive B: as a backup, but you want the extension to be BAK not DOC. The procedure for copying and renaming the extension of the file is

```
A>COPY A:CARTER3.DOC B:CARTER3.BAK
```

```
A>COPY
```

from

```
A:CARTER3.DOC
```

to

```
B:CARTER3.BAK
```

Note: The A: preceding CARTER3 is not necessary.

2. Suppose you have been using NEW as your extension for all your lessons. You wish to rename as OLD all the chapters in Drive A: that are backups and store them on a disk located in Drive B:. You can rename while copying all the files with the extension OLD by the following:

```
A>COPY *.NEW B:*.OLD

A>COPY
```

from

```
*.NEW
```

to

```
B:*.OLD
```

Renaming a File

Sometimes you just need to change the name of a file for organization purposes. The DOS command RENAME allows you to change the name without copying the file.

1. Suppose you have just finished working on the chapter of a book that you named CHAP3.DOC, but you discover that this chapter should actually be Chapter 4. You can rename it by doing the following:

```
A>RENAME A:CHAP3.DOC A:CHAP4.DOC

A>RENAME
```

from

```
A:CHAP3.DOC
```

to

```
A:CHAP4.DOC
```

Note: The A: preceding CHAP3 and CHAP4 is not necessary.

2. Suppose you have been naming the chapters you have been working on as CHAP1, CHAP2, and so on. You decide that instead of chapters, the units should be called lessons. You can rename the file and extension if you wish.

```
A>RENAME A:CHAP3.DOC A:LESSON3.BAK
```

```
A>RENAME
```

from

```
A:CHAP3.DOC
```

to

```
A:LESSON3.BAK
```

Note: The A: preceding CHAP3 and LESSON3 is not necessary.

COPY allows you to copy and rename at the same time. It is useful when backups of files are needed. RENAME allows you to organize files that have names that are no longer relevant. It allows you to rename without creating a new file.

Why Erase or Delete Files?

When using applications programs, you will discover that unless you are careful you can end up with several copies of the same file, even several version of the same file. The DOS commands ERASE and DEL allow you to delete old files to organize your disk or to create room for other files that you wish to keep on a disk.

When you delete a file, you may wonder why it seems that a file that took a long time to create disappears so quickly. The commands ERASE and DEL (delete) do not really erase a file, they simply replace the first character of the file with a Greek character. The Greek character is the ASCII character 229. (Sometimes this character is shown as a ? when utility software is used.) ASCII (American Standard Code for Information Interchange) is a code for representing data and programs to the computer. Letters of the alphabet, numbers, and symbols all have corresponding ASCII symbols. When ERASE or DEL are used, DOS does not recognize the file as existing any longer even though it still does exist on the disk. Therefore, if you accidentally delete a file, you should immediately take your disk out of the disk drive. You can then use any one of a number of different commercial software utility packages that enable you to recover your files. With these packages, you can list out a directory of deleted files and change the ? (or other symbol) to the correct character, making the files readable again.

ERASE or DEL can be used to delete a single file or a selected group of files in the following ways:

```
A>ERASE REPORT1.TXT
```
erases REPORT1.TXT from a disk located in Drive A:.

```
A>ERASE A:REPORT.TXT
```
erases REPORT.TXT from a disk located in Drive A:.

```
A>ERASE B:REPORT1.BAK
```
erases REPORT1.BAK from a disk located in Drive B:.

```
A>ERASE B:*.*
```
erases all the files from the disk in Drive B:.

```
A>ERASE A:*.BAK
```
erases all the files with the extension BAK from the disk in Drive A:.

```
A>ERASE A:LET??.TXT
```
erases all the files starting with LET and any two unknown characters that follow with the extention TXT from the disk in Drive A:.

```
A>ERASE ?LET.TXT
```
erases all the files starting with an unknown character followed by LET and the extension TXT from Drive A:.

Other ways to delete the contents of an entire disk are by reformatting the disk using the FORMAT command, copying over the disk using DISKCOPY, or using a magnetic eraser.

Protecting Files

In addition to the file directory that appears when you use the DIR command, file information is also stored in an area on the disk called the File Allocation Table (FAT). In the FAT, additional items of information on each file are also kept, such as the location(s) of where the file is stored on the disk, whether the file should be hidden from the directory, whether the file should be read-only (protected from deletion), and whether the file has been archived (backed up). The last three items are called file attributes. They are like flags that either appear or do not appear next to the filename. You can use the DOS command ATTRIB to change either the read-only flag or the archive flag. The read-only flag is used to protect files from deletion and to protect files from computer viruses. To protect a file by changing its read-only flag to the "on" position, you use the command:

```
A>ATTRIB filename.ext +r
```

To turn the read-only flag to the "off" position, you use the command:

```
A>ATTRIB filename.ext -r
```

The archive flag is used to mark each file as being archived or backed up. This command enables DOS to quickly reference for backup all files without the archive flag. This attribute is normally associated with hard-disk BACKUP and RESTORE DOS commands that you will learn in a later chapter. To turn the archive flag to the "on" position, you use the command:

```
C>ATTRIB filename.ext +a
```

To turn the read-only flag to the "off" position, you use the command:

```
C>ATTRIB filename.ext -a
```

The hidden file flag is not accessible through DOS. However, there are several file maintenance programs, such as PCTools and Norton Utilities, that allow you to change all three file attributes. One of these file maintenance programs should be installed on all hard disk computers because they also allow you to recover (undelete) a file that has been accidently deleted.

Recovering Files

When a file is deleted, the file information is not erased. What happens is that DOS converts the first character of the filename to a ?. The file will then not appear on the directory listing and its space is marked for reuse. If you inadvertently delete a file, stop what you are doing. Any new files saved to the disk may overwrite the undeleted files space. To recover a deleted file, you can use PCTools, Norton Utilities, or a number of other file maintenance programs. These programs allow you to view all recently deleted files and change the ? back to the original character.

What are Archiving and Repacking Files and Disks?

From time to time, you will need to archive old files—store them away for safekeeping. Another practice you may wish to follow is to repack your files. Repacking files is useful if you have done a lot of copying, adding, and deleting of files. Repacking files frees up disk space.

What is Disk and File Maintenance?

Disk and file maintenance is the process of (1) analyzing the contents of a file or disk to determine whether the file or files are useful or obsolete and (2) updating the current files. The process includes

1. Using the DIR command to find out what files are on the disk and the characteristics of the files, such as file type (COM, EXE, TXT, DOC, WKS, DBF), size in bytes (characters), and creation date and time.

2. Using the external DOS command CHKDSK to determine the amount of usable storage space available on the disk.

3. Repacking useful files onto a new disk.

4. Archiving onto a disk old files you may want to retrieve at a later date.

5. Eliminating obsolete files by using the DOS commands DEL, ERASE, or FORMAT.

Why Maintain Disks and Files?

As you work with disks, you will find that file and disk maintenance becomes important for organizational purposes. Some reasons why disks and files must be maintained are the following:

1. Some application programs and programming language compilers automatically create file backup copies when you edit or change a file. This leaves you with a current version and an old version. In other words, your original version is protected. Sometimes you may wish to save your original version or subsequent versions that would be lost due to this automatic backup process because only the current and last files are kept. If you wish to keep these old files from being written over, you need to rename them.

2. Many manufacturers of applications programs constantly update their software to keep pace with user demands and advances in technology. Some manufacturers have several versions of the same program. They may be named Version 1.0, 1.1, 2.0, 2.1, 3.0. Usually a version with minor changes is incremented by a decimal-point value or a letter character following the version number, such as 1A. Major changes in a program are designated by integer increases: 3.0, 4.0. If you have a registered copy, the manufacturer will allow you to upgrade your software to the new version for a minimal cost. Because most newer versions are more powerful, it is advisable to make the upgrade and eliminate the old program disks.

3. In working on a project over a period of time, you may acquire multiple versions of the same report or chapter that occupy valuable disk space and can create disorganization.

4. In working on several projects, you may overflow to another disk. For example, you may have three small projects labeled Project 1, Project 2, and Project 3 on a single disk. Project1 may increase in size beyond available disk space. At this point, you would want to transfer all of Project1 to a disk with enough space to accommodate the whole project, rather than split it up onto two disks.

5. Over a period of time, some files may become obsolete. These files should be either archived or deleted, depending on future needs.

6. When you have copied to or deleted files from a disk frequently, the disk may have areas or sections of storage space scattered throughout the disk that is wasted. In this instance, you would want to repack these files onto a new disk using the wildcard copy command (*.*) and then reformat the old disk.

7. Due to the physical makeup of disks, disk space may become unusable.

Hands-On Activities

In this section, you will

1. Make a backup of your **EXERCISES** disk.

2. Compare the two disks used in the copy process to see that they are identical.

3. Copy a single file from one disk.

4. Compare two files to see that they are identical.

5. Copy several files at once.

6. Combine several files into one file.

7. Rename a file.

8. Rename a file while copying it.

9. Delete a single file using ERASE and DEL.

10. Delete selected files. After performing these activities, you will have the skills necessary to maintain your files and disks.

In addition, you will learn to use the F1 and F3 function keys to enable you to edit your DOS commands more quickly and the CLS command to clear your screen when it becomes cluttered.

How to Copy a Single File from One Disk to Another	Usually, you will be copying a single file from a floppy disk to a hard disk, but for these exercises you will be copying files from one floppy disk to another. Before you begin this exercise, you will need to reformat the disk labeled **BACKUP**.	
	What to Do	*What Happens*
Step 1	Place the DOS disk in Drive A:.	Nothing.
Step 2	Obtain an A>.	Nothing.
Step 3	Type FORMAT B: /V and press the Enter key.	DOS asks you to place a disk in Drive B:.
Step 4	Place the **BACKUP** disk in Drive B: and press the Enter key.	DOS begins to FORMAT the disk.
Step 5	When DOS asks for a label, type BACKUP and press the Enter key.	See the screen that follows.

```
A>FORMAT B: /V
Insert new diskette for drive B:
and strike ENTER when ready

Format complete

Volume label (11 characters, ENTER for none)? BACKUP
     362496 bytes total disk space
     362496 bytes available on disk

Format another (Y/N)?N
A>
```

Note: For the following exercise you will be copying the CHAP1.TXT file that you created on the **Practice** disk onto the disk labeled **BACKUP**. To copy the CHAP1.TXT file to the disk labeled **BACKUP**, you would do the following:

Use **Practice** disk in Drive A: and **BACKUP** disk in Drive B:.

	What to Do	*What Happens*
Step 1	Obtain an A >.	Nothing.
Step 2	Type COPY CHAP1.TXT B: and press Enter. (*Note:* You must switch disks manually if you have a single floppy disk drive.)	See screen that follows.

```
A>COPY CHAP1.TXT B:
        1 File(s) copied

A>
```

Tip: When using the COPY command, the REN, and the ERASE/DEL comands, you need to specify the source and target drives unless one or both are the default drive. DOS will not allow you to copy a file onto itself, so you must list the source and target drives as being different.

How to Use Function Keys to Edit Commands

Two of the function keys (keys labeled F1–F10) that enable you to recall your DOS command are

Function Key	Function
F1	Recalls the last DOS command character by character, left to right.
F3	Recalls the last DOS command in its entirety. Once recalled, you can depress the Enter key and perform a task again or edit a section of the line without having to retype the whole line.

You can also use the Ins and Del keys to edit a recalled DOS command. Use the left arrow key to place the cursor over the desired character, depress the Insert key, type in the desired additions, and then use the right arrow key to bring back the rest of the line.

Now you will use the F1 and F3 keys to copy the files Chap2.TXT and Chap3.TXT from **Practice** disk to **BACKUP** disk.

Use **Practice** disk in Drive A: and **BACKUP** disk in Drive B:.

	What to Do	*What Happens*
Step 1	At the A>	Nothing.
Step 2	Press the F1 key. The first character of the COPY command from before is listed. Press the F1 key several times, until you see only the CHAP part of the command. If you go past the CHAP part of the command, use the back arrow until only A>COPY CHAP is seen.	See screen that follows.

```
A>COPY CHAP
```

To enter the correct characters for the new COPY command, do the following:

Step 3	Press the number 2, and then press the forward arrow, or the F1 key, until the whole command is shown. (Be sure Num Lock is not on.)	See screen that follows.

```
A>COPY CHAP2.TXT B:
```

Step 4	Press the Enter key to execute the command.	See screen that follows.

```
A>COPY CHAP2.TXT B:
        1 File(s) copied

A>
```

Now you need to copy the last of the three files, CHAP3.TXT. You can use the F3 key to recall the last command A>COPY CHAP2.TXT B: and then change the 2 to a 3 using the arrow keys. See the following steps:

	What to Do	*What Happens*
Step 1	At the A>	Nothing.
Step 2	Press the F3 key. The last DOS command, A>COPY CHAP2.TXT B: is displayed.	See screen that follows.

```
A>COPY CHAP2.TXT B:
```

Now use the back arrow key to move back to the number 2 so you can change it to a 3.

	What to Do	*What Happens*
Step 3	Press the back arrow key eight times.	See screen that follows.

```
A>COPY CHAP
```

To re-enter the correct characters for the new COPY command, do the following:

	What to Do	*What Happens*
Step 4	Press the number 3, and then press the forward arrow, or the F1 key, until the whole command is shown.	See screen that follows.

```
A>COPY CHAP3.TXT B:
```

	What to Do	*What Happens*
Step 5	Press the Enter key to execute the command.	See screen that follows.

```
A>COPY CHAP3.TXT B:
        1 File(s) copied

A>
```

Check the directory of **BACKUP** to make sure that the files were copied.

If you want to copy the same file(s) to several disks, you can use the F3 key to recall the DOS command, so that you do not have to re-enter the command each time. You will only have to switch the target diskettes into and out of the target drive.

Tip: If you enter a DOS command such as COPY and then wish to use the F1 or F3 keys to recall it, you cannot enter another DOS command such as DIR and then recall the COPY command. The F1 and F3 keys can be used to recall only the last DOS command.

How to Compare Two Files

To make sure that the file(s) you copied are identical, you can use the DOS external command COMP.

To check the two files called CHAP3.TXT on the **Practice** disk and **BACKUP** disk, do the following:

	What to Do	*What Happens*
Step 1	At the A>	Nothing.
Step 2	Insert a DOS disk into Drive A:.	
Step 3	Type COMP and press Enter.	See screen that follows.

```
A>COMP

Enter primary file name
```

Step 4	Remove the DOS disk from Drive A: and insert the disk labeled **Practice**. Also insert the disk labeled **BACKUP** into Drive B:	Nothing.
Step 5	Type CHAP3.TXT and press Enter.	See screen that follows.

```
CHAP3.TXT

Enter 2nd file name or drive id
```

| Step 6 | Type B: and press Enter. | See screen that follows. |

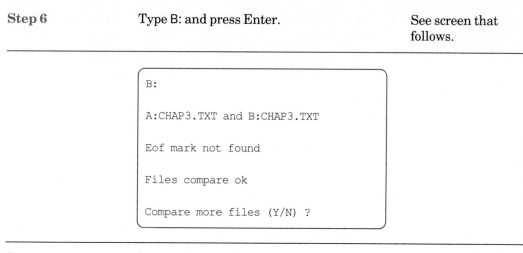

```
B:

A:CHAP3.TXT and B:CHAP3.TXT

Eof mark not found

Files compare ok

Compare more files (Y/N) ?
```

| Step 7 | Press N for No. | An A> appears. |

You may also use the COMP DOS command to compare two files within the same disk. (See the following screen.)

```
A>COMP

Enter primary file name
A:CHAP4.TXT
Enter 2nd file name or drive id
CHAP4.OLD
```

Notes: *Do not* do what is printed on this screen.

If you are using two different disk drives or different disks, your files may not be identical.

Review
Exercises

1. Copy CHAP3.TXT from **EXERCISES** disk in A: to **BACKUP** disk in B:.

2. Use **EXERCISES** disk in Drive A: and **BACKUP** disk in Drive B:; compare the following files and list the files that are the same and the files that are different. *Hint:* You must use a DOS disk in Drive A: to begin.

Files	Same	Different
a. CHAP1.TXT		
b. CHAP2.TXT		
c. CHAP3.TXT		

3. Reformat the **BACKUP** disk with the VOL label before continuing.

Answers

2. a. Different.

   b. Different.

   c. Same.

How to Copy Several Files at Once Using the COPY Command and Wildcards

You can use the COPY command with wildcards to copy several or all the files, except the hidden files, from one disk to another. Since the **BACKUP** disk was just reformatted, you will be copying all the files from the **EXERCISES** disk onto the **BACKUP** disk.

First, use the * wildcard to copy all the COM files from the **EXERCISES** disk to the **BACKUP** disk.

Use **BACKUP** disk in Drive B: and **EXERCISES** disk in Drive A:.

	What to Do	*What Happens*
Step 1	Obtain an A>.	Nothing.
Step 2	Place **EXERCISES** disk in Drive A: and **BACKUP** disk in Drive B:.	Nothing.
Step 3	Type COPY *.COM B: and press Enter.	See screen that follows.

```
A>COPY *.COM B:
WP.COM
DB.COM
SS.COM
REPLY.COM
        4 File(s) copied

A>
```

**Review
Exercise**

Check the directory of **BACKUP** disk to make sure that the files were copied to the disk.

Now copy all the files that begin with CHAP from the **EXERCISES** disk to the **BACKUP** disk using the following steps.

Use **BACKUP** disk in Drive B: and **EXERCISES** disk in Drive A:.

	What to Do	*What Happens*
Step 1	Obtain an A >.	Nothing.
Step 2	Type COPY CHAP???.* B: and press Enter.	See screen that follows.

```
A>COPY CHAP???.* B:
CHAP1.TXT
CHAP2.TXT
CHAP3.TXT
CHAP12.EXT
        4 File(s) copied

A>
```

Step 3	Check the directory of the **BACKUP** disk to make sure the files were copied.	

Another command that would have performed the same result is A > COPY CHAP*.* B:.

Review Exercises	Copy all the files from **EXERCISES** to **BACKUP** using the COPY commands and wildcard. What command is the easiest to use?

Answer

You can use the COPY command A > COPY *.* B: to copy all the files from Drive A: to Drive B:.

How to Combine Files Using COPY (Concatenating)	When you wish to merge the contents of one file with another, you may do so by separating the files to be added with + signs and designating the file to which the merged files are copied.

Use **Practice** disk in Drive A:.

	What to Do	*What Happens*
Step 1	At an A >	Nothing.
Step 2	Type COPY DATA1.DBF+DATA2.DBF+ DATA3.DBF DATA4.DBF and press Enter.	See screen that follows.

```
A>COPY DATA1.DBF+DATA2.DBF+DATA3.DBF+DATA4.DBF
DATA1.DBF
DATA2.DBF
DATA3.DBF
        1 File(s) copied

A>
```

Notice that DOS copied only one file to the disk. The one file is a combination of the three DBF files.

Review Exercises

1. Use the TYPE command to display the contents of DATA4.DBF.

2. Combine the files DATA3.DBF+DATA2.DBF+DATA1.DBF and store the results in DATA4A.NEW. Display the contents of DATA4A.NEW using the TYPE command.

3. If you use the command COPY DATA?.* DATA4.DBF instead of using the individual filenames and the plus signs as shown in the previous exercise, would the files be the same?

Answers

1. Name
   Address
   Phone number
   Birthdate
   Social Security number

2. Birthdate
   Social Security number
   Phone number
   Name
   Address

3. No. The file would be the same as in Exercise 1 because using the wildcard * causes the files to be copied in alphanumeric order. Ignore the message "Content of destination lost before copy."

How to Use DISKCOPY

DISKCOPY is used extensively for creating backup disks for important software such as your DOS disk, your applications software program disks, and your data files. DISKCOPY creates an exact duplicate of the source diskette. Since DISKCOPY is an external DOS command, you will need a DOS disk for this exercise.

Note: If your computer has only one floppy disk drive, you will be prompted to switch disks during the DISKCOPY process. If your computer has two different types of disk drives, you must use either Drive A: or Drive B: individually during a DISKCOPY, using the command DISKCOPY A: A: or DISKCOPY B: B:. Different disk drives are not identical in size and therefore an exact duplicate cannot be created. DOS will stop the DISKCOPY program and display the following message:

```
Drive types or diskette types
not compatible

Copy process ended

Copy another diskette (Y/N)?
```

Right now, you need to create a backup of the disk entitled EXERCISES that was supplied to you with this text.

Use a DOS disk, the disk labeled **EXERCISES,** and the **Practice** disk.

	What to Do	*What Happens*
Step 1	Obtain an A >, insert DOS in Drive A: and close the drive door.	Nothing.
Step 2	Type DISKCOPY and press Enter.	See screen that follows.

```
A>DISKCOPY

Insert SOURCE diskette in drive A:

Press any key when ready...
```

Step 3	Insert the disk marked **EXERCISES** in A: and press Enter.	See screen that follows.

```
Copying 80 tracks
 9 Sectors/Track, 2 Side(s)

Insert TARGET diskette in drive A:

Press any key when ready . . .
```
▶ *First this appears;*

▶ *then this appears.*

Step 4	Remove the **EXERCISES** disk and insert the **Practice** disk in Drive A: and press Enter.	See screen that follows.

Note: If you receive an error message, make sure your diskettes are the same type.

Tips: 1. DISKCOPY can be used to reformat an old disk that contains files that you no longer need. Be sure to use the directory command to check to see that there are no files on a disk that you want to keep. *Warning:* DISKCOPY wipes out all files previously contained on the target diskette.

2. If the target disk needs to be formatted during the disk copy process, DOS will inform you that it is FORMATTING WHILE COPYING. If the target disk backup was already formatted, DOS will erase all the files on the source disk and then copy all the files from the source disk to the target disk, including any hidden files. After using DISKCOPY, you will have an exact duplicate of the original disk, unless the original (source) disk contained a write-protection feature.

3. If the source disk contains many files, you may need to switch from source to target disk several times as requested by DOS. Just follow the DOS prompt telling you when to remove the source and replace with a target. Always remember that the source is the disk you are copying and the target is the disk you are copying to.

After the DISKCOPY is complete, you will see the following screen:

```
Copy another diskette (Y/N)?n
```

For now, you will only be making the one copy, so you should answer no.

Step 5	Type N.	An A > appears.

There are several other remarks that DOS will give you on occasion when using DISKCOPY. If DOS encounters any unreadable tracks or sectors, or has trouble writing to any tracks or sectors, DOS will send a message to the screen indicating the type of problem encountered, and its location on the target or source disk. At the completion of the copying procedure, it will inform you that the target disk may not be usable.

You can also use the DISKCOPY command with dual-disk drive systems. Using two floppy drives makes disk copying a little easier because you do not have to keep switching the source and target disks in and out of one drive. When using two drives and drive designators with the DISKCOPY command, such as

```
A>DISKCOPY A: B:
```

you would be asked to insert the source disk in Drive A: and the target disk in Drive B: at the beginning of the DISKCOPY. You would not have to touch either disk until the disk copy was finished. Since you would not have to switch disks manually, you could do something else while the computer was busy making the backup.

If the DOS disk is in Drive A: and Drive B: is identical to Drive A:, you may use DISKCOPY as shown in Figure 4.4.

Other Considerations When Using DISKCOPY

If the DOS disk is in Drive A:, you may use DISKCOPY as shown in Figure 4.4.

See Figure 4.5 for the results of DISKCOPY if the DOS disk is in Drive B: and both drives are identical.

Figure 4.4

DISKCOPY results if DOS is in Drive A:.

Command	Result
A > DISKCOPY A: B:	The source drive is A: and the target drive is B:.
A > DISKCOPY B: A:	The source drive is Drive B: and the target drive is Drive A:.
B > A:DISKCOPY A: B:	The source drive is A: and the target drive is B:.
B > A:DISKCOPY B: A:	The source drive is Drive B: and the target drive is Drive A:.
A > DISKCOPY B:	Same as DISKCOPY B: A:.
A > DISKCOPY	The target and source drives are the same. The default drive is the drive you will be using. You will have to switch disks manually. This method is slower than the previous methods where the drive(s) is/are designated.

Figure 4.5

DISKCOPY results if DOS is in Drive B:.

Command	Result
B > DISKCOPY A: B:	The source drive is A: and the target drive is B:.
B > DISKCOPY B: A:	The source drive is Drive B: and the target drive is Drive A:.
A > B:DISKCOPY A: B:	The source drive is A: and the target drive is B:.
A > B:DISKCOPY B: A:	The source drive is Drive B: and the target drive is Drive A:.
B > DISKCOPY	The source drive is Drive B: and the target drive is Drive B:.
A > B:DISKCOPY	The source drive is Drive A: and the target drive is Drive A:.

How to Use DISKCOMP	After making a diskcopy, you should use the DOS DISKCOMP command to make sure that the two disks are identical.	
	What to Do	*What Happens*
Step 1	Obtain an A >.	Nothing.
Step 2	Insert a DOS diskette into Drive A:.	Nothing.
Step 3	Type DISKCOMP and press Enter.	See screen that follows.

```
A>DISKCOMP

Insert FIRST diskette in drive A:

Press any key when ready ...
```

Step 4	Remove the DOS diskette from Drive A: and insert the disk labeled **EXERCISES** and then press any key.	See screen that follows.

```
Comparing 80 tracks
 9 Sectors per track, 2 side(s)

Insert SECOND diskette in drive A:

Press any key when ready . . .
```

Note: The information displayed to the screen will vary according to the DOS version, the type of floppy disk, and the type of disk drive being used.

Step 5	Remove the **EXERCISES** disk from Drive A: and insert the disk labeled **Practice** and then press any key.	See screen that follows.

If the two disks compared are identical, DOS will display the following screen.

```
Compare OK

Compare another diskette (Y/N)?
```

If the two diskettes are not identical, DOS will display the tracks or sectors where the diskettes are not similar. If the diskettes compared are identical, continue with Step 6. If they are not identical, repeat the DISKCOPY procedure in an attempt to obtain a usable copy of the source disk.

Step 6	Press N for No.	An A> appears.

Tip: If the screen becomes cluttered with previous commands, you can clear the screen with the DOS internal command CLS. Use this command as often as you need, so only relevant data are on the screen.

Step 7	At the A>, type CLS and press Enter.	The screen is cleared.

How to Rename a File

If you want to rename a file, you can do so by using the internal DOS command RENAME (REN for short).

Use **Practice** disk in Drive A:.

	What to Do	*What Happens*
Step 1	At the A>	Nothing.
Step 2	Type RENAME DAYDATE.TXT DAYDATE.OLD and press Enter.	See screen that follows.

```
A>RENAME DAYDATE.TXT DAYDATE.OLD

A>
```

Check the directory of **Practice** disk to make sure that the extension for DAYDATE is OLD.

How to Rename a File While Copying It	The following procedure is used when you want to make a backup of a file with another name.

Use **Practice** disk in Drive A:.

	What to Do	*What Happens*
Step 1	At the A>	Nothing.
Step 2	Type COPY DAYDATE.OLD DAYDATE.NEW and press Enter.	See screen that follows.

```
A>COPY DAYDATE.OLD DAYDATE.NEW
        1 File(s) copied
```

A file can be copied from any drive to any other drive by specifying the source and target drive designations before the filenames.

Review Exercises

1. Using **Practice** disk, compare the files DAYDATE.OLD and DAYDATE.NEW. Are they identical?

2. Compare the **EXERCISES** and **Practice** disks. Are they identical?

3. Can you copy and rename multiple files using one command?

4. Using **Practice** disk, copy and rename all the TXT files to the extension OLD. Then copy and rename all the DBF files to the extension BAK.

Answers

1. Yes.

2. No.

3. Yes, wildcards can be used to copy and rename files in the same way that they are used to copy files without renaming them.

How to Delete a Single File Using ERASE	The DOS command ERASE can be used to delete a file. In this exercise, you will delete the file DAYDATE.OLD.	
	Use **Practice** disk in Drive A:.	
	What to Do	*What Happens*
Step 1	Verify that DAYDATE.OLD is on the the disk.	
Step 2	Obtain an A>.	Nothing.
Step 3	Type ERASE DAYDATE.OLD.	See screen that follows.

```
A>ERASE DAYDATE.OLD

A>
```

Step 4	Check the directory to make sure the file was erased.

Note: If DOS responds with the message "File not found," it means that the file you requested to delete was not found on the disk in the default drive.

Check to make sure that you typed in the correct filename and extension. If you made the correct entry, check the directory to see if you spelled the filename correctly when you created the file or copied it from another disk.

How to Erase Selected Files Using ERASE	To erase more than one file at a time, you can use ERASE with wildcards.

Use **Practice** disk in Drive A:.

	What to Do	*What Happens*
Step 1	Obtain an A >.	Nothing.
Step 2	Type ERASE *.OLD and press Enter.	See screen that follows.

```
A>ERASE *.OLD
```

Step 3	Use the DIR command with wildcards to make sure the files were deleted.	A directory list is displayed.

Another Method of Erasing Selective Files Using DELETE	ERASE and DEL can be used interchangeably. When you learn to work with hard disks, you will learn that there are some differences.

Use **Practice** disk.

	What to Do	*What Happens*
Step 1	Obtain an A >.	Nothing.
Step 2	Type DEL DATA?.BAK and press Enter.	See screen that follows.

```
A>DEL DATA?.BAK

A>
```

Note: DEL and ERASE are used interchangeably.

Step 3	Use the DIR command with wildcards to make sure the files were deleted.	A directory list is displayed.

How to Protect Files from Deletion Using the ATTRIB Command	The DOS ATTRIB command can be used to protect files from deletion by changing their read-only flags to the "on" position. Use the ATTRIB command to change the read-only flags of all the .COM files on the **BACKUP** disk to the "on" position.	
	What to Do	*What Happens*

Step 1	Insert the DOS disk in Drive A: and the **BACKUP** disk in Drive B:.	Nothing.
Step 2	Obtain an A>.	Nothing.
Step 3	Type ATTRIB +r B:*.COM and then press the Enter key.	The .COM files on the **BACKUP** disk are changed to read-only. See the screen that follows.

```
A>ATTRIB +r B:*.COM
```

Note: To list the attributes of a file, use the ATTRIB command followed by the filename. For example:

```
A>ATTRIB B:*.COM
```

If you try to delete all of the files on the **BACKUP** disk, all of the files except the .COM files will be deleted.

	What to Do	*What Happens*
Step 1	Obtain an A>.	Nothing.
Step 2	Type DEL B:*.* and press the Enter key.	The message "Are you sure (Y/N)?" appears.

Step 3	Press Y and then press the Enter key.	All except the .COM files are erased from the **BACKUP** disk.

Step 4	Type DIR B: and press the Enter key.	A directory of the **BACKUP** disk is displayed. See the screen that follows.

```
A > DEL B:*.*
Are you sure (Y/N)?Y

A > DIR B:

 Volume in drive B is BACKUP
 Directory of B:\

WP        COM   16707   1-01-80 12:19a
DB        COM   24432   8-26-87  3:58p
SS        COM   21330   8-26-87  3:59p
REPLY     COM      14   9-17-87 12:34p
      4 File(s)      297984 bytes free

A >
```

As you can see, the ATTRIB command is useful in protecting your important files.

Note: You should change all of your DOS files to be read-only, especially the COMMAND.COM file.

Review Exercises

1. If you use the command DEL B:*.COM, what happens?

2. Reset the read-only attribute on the **BACKUP** disk to –r.

Answer

1. A message "Access denied" appears.

***Review
Exercises***

The following review exercises will give you practice in maintaining disks and files.

1. Assuming that all of the files on the **Practice** disk are no longer useful, erase them.

2. Reformat the **Practice** disk and add the VOL label PRACTICE.

3. COPY all of the files from the **EXERCISES** disk to the **BACKUP** disk using COPY.

***Summary
Points***

1. Making backups is an important function of copying, but just as important is the flexibility that copying gives you to move files around. Files are copied either to produce a duplicate of a file or disk or to transfer a file or files from one disk to another.

2. Making backups of your files is important because a number of different problems may occur, causing you to damage your disks or destroy your files.

3. DISKCOPY is the DOS external command used to make an electronic duplicate of a disk. It is convenient for making backups in that you do not have to format the backup disk. DISKCOPY makes a duplicate copy of the source disk and formats the target disk at the same time.

4. DISKCOPY is an external command, the DOS disk must be placed in a drive to initiate the command.

5. DISKCOMP is an external DOS command that allows you to check to see that two disks are identical.

6. The COPY command allows you to copy one or more files or the entire contents of a disk (with the exception of the hidden files) to another formatted diskette.

7. COPY does not destroy the existing contents of a target disk. It merely adds the new files.

8. The COPY command allows you to copy a single file, a selected group of files, or the contents of an entire disk to an other disk(s).

9. If you make a copy of a DOS disk or an applications program disk that you do not own, you are in violation of the copyright laws pertaining to software and can be prosecuted.

10. After you have made a copy of a file, it is wise to check to see that the two files are identical.

11. The wildcards ? and * can be used with the COPY command.

12. DOS will allow you to combine two files and store the results in another file. Files that are merged are called concatenated files.

13. With the COPY command, you can copy a file and rename it simultaneously. The result is the original file and another file with a different name. The RENAME command can be used just to rename a file.

14. The DOS commands ERASE and DEL can be used to delete files.

15. Occasionally it is wise to archive old files—store them away for safekeeping.

16. Repacking files is useful if you have done a lot of copying, adding, and deleting of files.

17. Disk and file maintenance is the process of (1) analyzing the contents of a file or disk to determine whether the file or files are useful or obsolete and (2) updating the current files.

Application Exercises

Perform the following exercises at your computer.

1. Using ERASE and a wildcard designation, erase all the files with the extension TXT from the **BACKUP** disk.

2. Use COPY to copy CHAP1, CHAP2, CHAP3 individually from **EXERCISES** to the **BACKUP** disk, giving the files the extension DOC. (Use the F1 key to help you.)

3. Copy all the CHAP files and DATA files from **BACKUP** disk to **Practice** disk.

4. Rename while copying all the files on the **Practice** disk to the extension OLD. Both original files and backups with the extension OLD will be on the same disk. You should have 14 files.

5. a. Attempt to erase LETTER1.DOC from **Practice** disk. What message did you receive?

   b. Use the internal command CLS to clear the screen.

6. Using wildcards, compare all the DOC and OLD files on **Practice** disk that begin with CHAP.

   a. What command initiates the comparison?

   b. What command was used after "Enter primary file name"?

   c. What command was used after "Enter 2nd file name or drive id"?

7. Using a wildcard, erase all the files with CHAP as a root and OLD as an extension from **Practice** disk.

8. Concatenate (merge) the files DATA1.DBF, DATA2.DBF, and DATA3.DBF on **Practice** disk and store them in DATA4.DBF using command COPY DATA*.DBF DATA4.DBF.

9. Use the TYPE command to display the contents of DATA4.DBF on **Practice** disk. What command could have been used to keep DOS from copying the OLD files to DATA4?

10. Using one command, delete all the files from **Practice** disk.

11. Reformat the **Practice** disk using the volume label PRACTICE.

Comprehension Questions   Answer the following questions.

1. Explain the difference between COPY and DISKCOPY.

2. Describe how to rename a file using COPY.

3. Explain how to use a wildcard as an extension.

4. Use a ? with a filename and explain what it does.

5. Use ?? with a filename and explain what it does.

6. Explain the purpose of F1 and F3 function keys used during copying and deleting files.

7. Describe a use for CLS.

Completion Exercises

Complete the following sentences.

1. The disk that contains the file or files that are to be copied is called the _____ disk.

2. The disk to which the file or files are to be copied is called the _____ disk.

3. Explain what each of the following commands do. Be sure to tell what is done and where the disk is located.

   a. `A>COPY A:LETTER1.TXT B:`

   b. `A>COPY MEMO.* B:`

   c. `A>COPY *.* B:`

   d. `A>COPY SMITH?.BAK B:`

   e. `A>COPY A:SMITH.DOC B:SMITH.BAK`

   f. `A>COPY A:DRAFT1.DOC A:DRAFT2.DOC`

   g. `A>COPY A:CHAP3.DOC B:PART1.DOC`

   h. `A>COPY *.NEW B:*.OLD`

   i. `A>DISKCOPY`

   j. `A>DISKCOPY A: B:`

   k. `A>ERASE LET1.TXT`

   l. `A>ERASE A:LET1.TXT`

   m. `A>ERASE B:LET1.BAK`

   n. `A>ERASE B:*.*`

   o. `A>ERASE A:*.BAK`

   p. `A>ERASE A:REPORT?.TXT`

Matching Exercises

Choose the correct letter from the right-hand column.

1. COPY

a. A key that can recall the last DOS command character by character from left to right

2. DISKCOPY

b. A DOS command that allows you to copy files to a formatted disk

3. F1

c. A key that recalls the last DOS command in its entirety

4. F3

d. A command used to clear the screen at any system prompt

5. A>COPY ????????.???

e. A DOS command that allows you to copy files and format a disk at the same time

6. CLS

f. The same as A>COPY *.*

5

Directories and Subdirectories

When you have completed this chapter, you will be able to

Learning Objectives:

1. Explain what a root directory is.
2. Explain why you classify your files into hierarchical categories called *subdirectories*.
3. Explain how to plan your tree structure (diagram).
4. Explain how subdirectories are named and created.
5. Explain how to move (change) between subdirectories.
6. Explain how to use the TREE commands in DOS to list the tree structure and files contained within each subdirectory.
7. Explain how files are copied to and from subdirectories.
8. Explain how to copy an entire subdirectory.

Performance Objectives:

1. Plan a tree structure.
2. Create subdirectories.
3. Move between directories.
4. Copy to and from subdirectories.
5. Find out the files that exist in each subdirectory of a tree structure.
6. Erase and rename files from subdirectories.
7. Remove subdirectories.
8. Load applications programs into subdirectories.
9. Use XCOPY.

Chapter Overview

In previous chapters, you worked with directories that contain a small number of files. With the advances in computer technology, disks are now capable of containing hundreds, even thousands of files. When a directory contains thousands of files, it can be difficult to locate the file that you want, unless a different type of organization is used.

In previous chapters, the directory that you used is called the *root directory*. The root directory is created during the format procedure and is limited in the number of files it can contain. Since the root directory of most floppy disks is limited to 112 files and finding a file within a directory with that many files is difficult, a further means of categorizing files—called *subdirectories*—was developed. Subdirectories allow you to manage large numbers of files efficiently. You can classify your software such as your applications program files and the data files that pertain to each into individual subdirectories, making them easier to work with.

In Chapter 5, you will be learning how to create and use subdirectories for floppy disk management. What you learn in this chapter you can apply to hard disk management discussed in Chapter 6. In the past, subdirectories were not widely used on floppy disks because of their limited storage capacity. However, floppy disks now have greater storage capacity, making the use of subdirectories more common on floppy disk drive systems.

Problems with File Organization

One difficulty in managing files is that there is no particular method by which files are listed on a directory. Although files are listed on the directory according to date and time created, the more current files are listed at the bottom of the directory while the older files appear at the top. As you delete a large file from the center of a directory, a new file may replace it at that location on the directory. Thus, the directory from top to bottom rarely represents an accurate list in order from old to current files, nor does it list the files in alphabetical order. They are stored rather like files placed randomly in a file drawer, without any filing system. When you return to retrieve a file stored this way, you have to search through the entire contents of the file drawer until you find the file you want. When you have many files, the process can take a long time.

What are Subdirectories?

Because of the way that files are stored on a root directory and because of the limited files that a root directory can contain, you need to create subdirectories. A subdirectory is a file that contains a list of files that you have grouped together under one heading. For example, suppose you have a disk with the following contents:

15 word processing files

20 spreadsheet files

19 database management files

Instead of having all these files on the root directory arranged in no logical order, you can create three subdirectories (headings) and place each of the three different types of files into a corresponding subdirectory.

Hierarchical Organization

The organization applied to disk management is a hierarchy with subdirectories branching from the root directory. This type of organization is similar to the type of hierarchy used in large university library systems. In a large university library system, the main library (root directory) may have a card catalogue listing the general books (files) contained within that particular library and a listing of the other branch libraries (subdirectories) that are more specific in nature. In a root directory, you may have individual files (general books) and a list of subdirectories (branch libraries).

Another main library may contain no books (files) at all, but just a listing of the more specific libraries (subdirectories) available. For example, a main library card catalogue (root directory) may list several branch libraries (subdirectories) that are divided into specific areas of study, such as medicine, law, business, physics, education, and history.

Like subdirectories, branch libraries may contain some books (files) and a list of other more specific departments of that library (further subdirectories). For example, the law library (subdirectory), which is a branch of the main library (root directory), may contain two more specific departments (subdirectories): civil and criminal. Therefore, the civil and criminal departments are subdirectories of the law library, which is a subdirectory of the main library. This hierarchical process of breaking down from the general to the specific can continue almost indefinitely. (See Figure 5.1.)

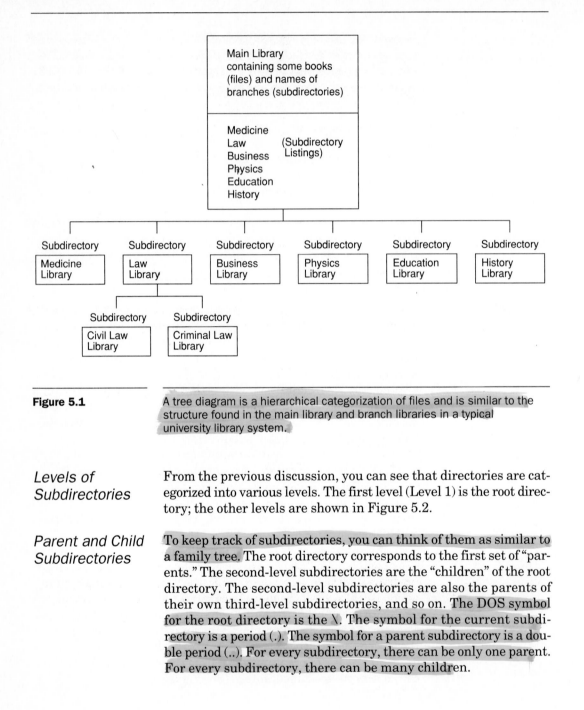

Figure 5.1   A tree diagram is a hierarchical categorization of files and is similar to the structure found in the main library and branch libraries in a typical university library system.

Levels of Subdirectories

From the previous discussion, you can see that directories are categorized into various levels. The first level (Level 1) is the root directory; the other levels are shown in Figure 5.2.

Parent and Child Subdirectories

To keep track of subdirectories, you can think of them as similar to a family tree. The root directory corresponds to the first set of "parents." The second-level subdirectories are the "children" of the root directory. The second-level subdirectories are also the parents of their own third-level subdirectories, and so on. The DOS symbol for the root directory is the \. The symbol for the current subdirectory is a period (.). The symbol for a parent subdirectory is a double period (..). For every subdirectory, there can be only one parent. For every subdirectory, there can be many children.

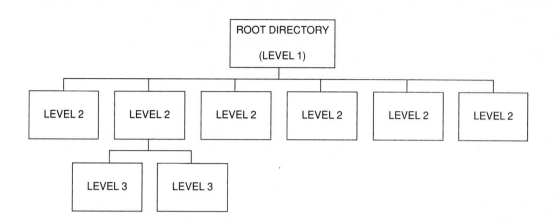

Figure 5.2   This figure shows three levels of a tree diagram. The number of levels is limited only by the amount of space you have on your disk.

Using Subdirectories

To use subdirectories, you need to be able to

1. Create them.

2. Move from one to another.

3. Create a system prompt that displays your location within the tree.

4. Copy files to them.

5. Copy files from them.

6. Delete files from them.

7. Rename files within them.

8. Remove them.

9. List the tree structure and its contents.

Creating Subdirectories

A subdirectory can be created using the DOS "Make directory" (MKDIR or MD) command. To make a second-level subdirectory, you must be in the root directory (parent directory). For example, to create the subdirectories LAW, BUSINESS, and MEDICINE, you need to be in the root directory: see Figure 5.3.

Figure 5.3
To create second-level subdirectories, you must be in the root directory.

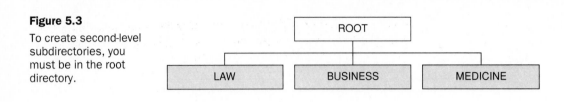

To create two third-level subdirectories (CIVIL and CRIMI-NAL) with LAW as the parent subdirectory, you must be in the LAW subdirectory, as shown in Figure 5.4.

Figure 5.4
To create a third-level subdirectory, you must be in the second-level parent subdirectory.

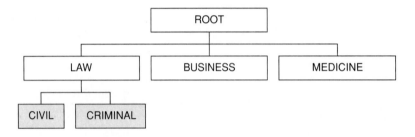

Moving Among Subdirectories

Once subdirectories have been created, you can move to them using the change directory (CHDIR or CD) commands. Movement can be either away from the root directory or toward the root directory. To move across the tree, you must first move to a common parent and then to the desired child subdirectory.

Changing the System Prompt

If you are moving among subdirectories, a regular DOS prompt will not tell you your location within the tree. The only way to determine your location would be to use the DIR command. You can, however, change your system prompt using a DOS command, causing it to display your location within the tree structure. Changing the system prompt to reflect your location within the tree is accomplished by typing the command PROMPT PG at any system prompt:

```
A>PROMPT $P$G
```

DOS also allows you to customize a system prompt, as you will see in the Hands-On Exercises.

*Copying to
and from
Subdirectories*

You can copy a file or files to or from a subdirectory just as you did with the files in the root directory of individual disks. The easiest method is to move to the directory that contains the files you wish to copy and then use the COPY command. For example, you could move to the subdirectory CRIMINAL and copy one or all of the files to the subdirectory APPLIED. (See Figure 5.5.)

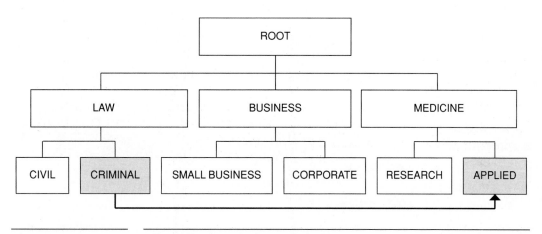

Figure 5.5   Copying files from CRIMINAL to APPLIED.

Files can be copied

1. From the root directory to any subdirectory within a single disk.

2. From one subdirectory to any other subdirectory within one disk.

3. From a subdirectory to a root directory within one disk.

4. From a subdirectory in one disk to a subdirectory on another disk.

*Deleting and
Renaming
Files Within
Subdirectories*

Files can be erased or renamed within subdirectories in the same way that they are erased and renamed in root directories. The important consideration when deleting files is that you are in the correct subdirectory because you can use the same filenames in various subdirectories. Each subdirectory could possibly contain one or more of the same filenames used in other subdirectories; therefore, be sure you have located the correct file.

Removing a Subdirectory

Sometimes a classification of files become obsolete, and you may wish to free up disk space. Not only do files become obsolete but also subdirectories become obsolete. To remove a subdirectory, you first need to delete all the files contained within that subdirectory and any subsequent subdirectories and their files. In essence, you must delete everything from a subdirectory before you can remove it.

Once all files and lower directories have been removed, you may then remove that subdirectory with the DOS command RMDIR or RD. For example, to remove the subdirectory LAW, you need to do the following:

1. Delete all files within that subdirectory, including lower directories (CIVIL and CRIMINAL) and their files.

2. Move to the parent directory and use the command RD LAW.

Obtaining a List of Subdirectories and Files

If you ever wish to obtain a list of the directories on a disk, including each parent directory and child directories within the parent directory, you can use the DOS external command TREE.COM. For example, the directory path listing for Figure 5.5 is obtained as follows:

```
A>TREE B:
```

```
DIRECTORY PATH LISTING FOR VOLUME FILES
Path: \LAW
Sub-directories:      CIVIL
                      CRIMINAL

Path: \LAW\CIVIL
Sub-directories:      None

Path: \LAW\CRIMINAL
Sub-directories:      None

Path: \BUSINESS
Sub-directories:      SMALL_BS
                      CORP

Path: \BUSINESS\SMALL_BS
Sub-directories:      None

Path: \BUSINESS\CQRP
Sub-directories:      None

Path: \MEDICINE
Sub-directories:      RESEARCH
                      APPLIED

Path: \MEDICINE\RESEARCH
Sub-directories:      None

Path: \MEDICINE\APPLIED
Sub-directories:      None
```

TREE.COM can also be used with the /F option to list all the files contained within the subdirectories. You can also send the results to the printer with >PRN following the TREE command.

Before you begin working on an unfamiliar disk, you should first list or print the contents of the disk using the TREE command. This practice will allow you to be sure that you are using the correct disk and provide you with valuable information about where application programs and/or data files are stored.

Copying an Entire Subdirectory

Up until now, you have been using the COPY command to copy single and multiple files among disks. One of the limitations in using the COPY command is that you cannot copy any more files, at a single time, than your target disk can hold. In addition, the COPY command cannot copy subdirectories themselves but only files. With the release of version 3.2, DOS incorporated the ability to copy large quantities of files and their subdirectories. The command that supports this activity is XCOPY (extended copy). XCOPY allows you to transfer a whole subdirectory system from one disk (floppy or hard) to another.

XCOPY has three disadvantages. The first is that it cannot copy a file to a disk if the file is larger than the total bytes available on that disk. The second is that it does not copy hidden files. The third is that it requires more floppy disk space to store the same amount of information as BACKUP. In Chapter 6, you will learn to back up a hard disk using the DOS command BACKUP. BACKUP, like XCOPY, copies all files and subdirectories to floppy disks. However, BACKUP stores the files and subdirectory information on the floppy disks as one massive file. In other words, BACKUP compresses or packs together many files into one large file. This large file cannot be copied using the COPY command. It requires a special DOS command called RESTORE.

When you need to have access to individual files from your floppy disk back ups, the XCOPY command is preferable to the BACKUP command because XCOPY stores each file as an individual file and allows you to copy subdirectories. It provides an alternative to BACKUP and COPY.

Hands-On Activities

In this section, you will be using the following inverted tree diagram (directory structure) in creating, deleting, copying to and from, and moving among subdirectories. Refer to the diagram in Figure 5.6 as you perform the exercises.

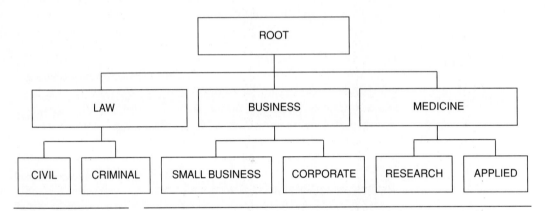

Figure 5.6   A directory structure with second-level and third-level subdirectories.

Use the **Practice**, **EXERCISES**, and **BACKUP** disks for these exercises. You do not need to use blank disks for this purpose, but it is easier for you to see what you are doing.

How to Make a Subdirectory

To create a subdirectory when you are in the root directory, use the DOS internal commands MKDIR or MD, which stand for "Make directory." At a system prompt, type the "Make directory" command followed by the name you wish to call that directory. For example, to create the subdirectory LAW you would use the command A > MKDIR LAW or A > MD LAW.

The same guidelines used to name a file are applicable to naming subdirectories, except that you do not use an extension.

Use **Practice** disk in Drive A:.

	What to Do	*What Happens*
Step 1	Insert **Practice** disk into Drive A:.	Nothing.
Step 2	Perform a DIR of **Practice** disk.	See screen that follows.

```
A>DIR

 Volume in drive A is PRACTICE
 Directory of A:\

File not found

A>
```

Note: You should always perform a DIR to be sure that you are in the proper directory.

Step 3	Type MD LAW and press Enter. (You have just created a second-level subdirectory.)	An A> appears.
Step 4	Perform a DIR of **Practice** disk to make sure the subdirectory was created.	See screen that follows.

```
A>MD LAW

A>DIR

 Volume in drive A is PRACTICE
 Directory of A:\

LAW       <DIR>         5-13-91 12:30p
    1 File(s)    1457152 bytes free

A>
```

Notice that this directory listing contains the <DIR> LAW. This means that you now have a more specific directory (subdirectory) where you can store files that relate to the subdirectory's name.

Create the other second-level subdirectories shown in the tree diagram.

Step 5	Type MD BUSINESS and press Enter.	An A> appears.
Step 6	Type MD MEDICINE and press Enter.	An A> appears. See screen that follows.

Note: You have just created two more second-level subdirectories.

```
A>MD BUSINESS

A>MD MEDICINE

A>
```

Step 7	Perform a DIR of **Practice** disk to make sure the subdirectories were were created.	See screen that follows.

```
A>DIR

 Volume in drive A is PRACTICE
 Directory of A:\

LAW       <DIR>        5-13-91 12:30p
BUSINESS  <DIR>        5-13-91 12:31p
MEDICINE  <DIR>        5-13-91 12:31p
     3 File(s)    1456128 bytes free

A>
```

Notice that each directory created uses up several bytes of storage.

*How to Move
to Lower
Subdirectories*

The DOS command for moving to a directory is CHDIR or CD, followed by the name of the subdirectory. CHDIR and CD stand for "change directory." To move from the root directory to the subdirectory you have just created called LAW, type in the command CD LAW as shown:

```
A>CD LAW
```

and then press Enter. (See Figure 5.7.)

Figure 5.7

Moving from the root directory to the subdirectory LAW using CD LAW.

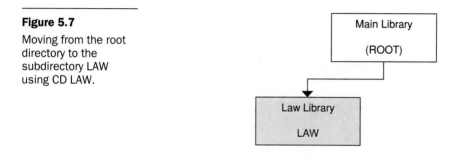

	What to Do	*What Happens*
Step 1	Type CD LAW and press Enter. (You have just moved to a second-level subdirectory.)	An A> appears. See screen that follows.

```
A>CD LAW

A>
```

To make sure of the subdirectory you are within, use the DOS DIR command.

Step 2

Perform a DIR of **Practice** disk to make sure that you are in the subdirectory A:\LAW.

See screen that follows.

```
A>DIR

 Volume in drive A is PRACTICE
 Directory of A:\LAW

 .            <DIR>        5-13-91  12:30p
 ..           <DIR>        5-13-91  12:30p
      2 File(s)     1456128 bytes free

A>
```

▶*Current directory*
▶*Parent Directory*

The single-period (.) directory <DIR> represents the current directory. The double-period (..) directory <DIR> represents the parent directory. By looking at the contents of A:\LAW directory, you can determine that there are no files within this subdirectory (none are listed) and that you can only move back to the parent directory because there are no subdirectories below this one. (They would have been listed by name, as you will see later.)

How to Create a DOS Prompt with Subdirectory Listings

Currently, the DOS prompt does not tell you your location within the tree. You can change the prompt to give you this information.

The basic PROMPT command to show your location in a tree system is as follows:

`A>PROMPT $P$G`

The command PROMPT tells DOS that you are changing the system prompt and anything that follows the PROMPT command will become the new system prompt. There are several special options called metastrings that allow you to customize the prompt. All metastrings begin with a $ (dollar sign). The following is a list of special characters and what they produce when used within the metastring.

Character	Result
_ (Underscore)	Creates a new line (skips to the next line)
b	Creates a vertical bar (¦)
d	Displays the date
g	Displays the > sign
h	Causes the cursor to backspace
l	Displays the < sign
n	Lists the current disk drive
p	Lists the current disk drive and subdirectory location
q	Displays the equal sign (=)
t	Displays the time
v	Lists the version of DOS

You may also write any text following the PROMPT command. For example, if you used the command

```
A>PROMPT My computer $G
```

the system prompt would look like the following:

```
My computer >
```

The prompt command by itself lists only the drive letter followed by the > sign.

Some examples of combining metastrings and text are shown in Figure 5.8 as follows:

Figure 5.8

Prompt Command	Result
PROMPT	A >
PROMPT PG	A:\>
PROMPT The time is: T_PG	The time is: 0:04:24.13
	A:\>
PROMPT Good Morning PG	Good Morning A:\>
PROMPT Good Afternoon	Good Afternoon

Note: It is always a good idea to use the PG metastring within a prompt so that you will know where you are working.

For now, you need to create a prompt that lists your location in the tree system.

What to Do	What Happens
Step 1	Type PROMPT PG and press Enter.	See screen that follows.

```
A>PROMPT $P$G

A:\LAW>
```

As you can see, the prompt now shows you that you are located within the subdirectory LAW, as shown by \LAW. In a later chapter, you will learn how to insert this command in a file so that this prompt will always automatically list your subdirectories in the DOS prompt.

How to Make Third-Level Subdirectories

From the LAW library subdirectory and following our tree diagram, you can now create the two third-level subdirectories: CIVIL and CRIMINAL.

	What to Do	What Happens
Step 1	At the A:\LAW>	
Step 2	Type MD CIVIL and press Enter. (You have just created a third-level subdirectory.)	An A:\LAW appears.
Step 3	Type MD CRIMINAL and press Enter. (You have just created another third-level subdirectory.)	An A:\LAW appears.
Step 4	Perform a DIR of **Practice** disk to make sure the subdirectories were created.	See screen that follows.

```
A:\LAW>MD CIVIL

A:\LAW>MD CRIMINAL

A:\LAW>DIR

 Volume in drive A is PRACTICE
 Directory of A:\LAW

.             <DIR>        5-13-91  12:30p
..            <DIR>        5-13-91  12:30p
CIVIL     <DIR>        5-13-91  12:30p
CRIMINAL <DIR>        5-13-91  12:30p
  4 File(s)        1455104 bytes

A:\LAW>
```

▶ *Current subdirectory*
▶ *Parent directory (root)*
▶ *Third-level subdirectory*
▶ *Third-level subdirectory*

The parent directory is the root directory (first-level directory). The current subdirectory is a second-level subdirectory. By looking at A:\LAW > and the directory, you can determine the following:

1. The current directory is \LAW.

2. \LAW has two child subdirectories, CIVIL and CRIMINAL.

3. The double period represents the parent directory of \LAW and is the root directory.

How to Move to a Third-Level Subdirectory

To move from the subdirectory LAW to the subdirectory CIVIL, you use the same command as you used to move from the root directory to the subdirectory LAW. (See Figure 5.9.) The command in this case is

```
A:\LAW>CD CIVIL
```

Figure 5.9

Moving from the subdirectory LAW to the subdirectory CIVIL using CD CIVIL.

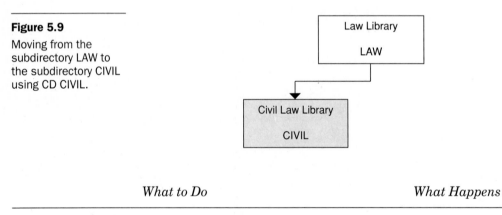

	What to Do	*What Happens*
Step 1	At A:\LAW > type CD CIVIL and press Enter.	See screen that follows.

```
A:\LAW>CD CIVIL

A:\LAW\CIVIL>
```

Once subdirectories have been created, you can move through several subdirectories with one command. To move from the root directory to the subdirectory called CIVIL, which is a subdirectory of LAW, you would use the command CD LAW\CIVIL and press Enter. (See Figure 5.10.)

Figure 5.10

Moving from the root directory to the CIVIL subdirectory using one CD command (CD LAW\CIVIL).

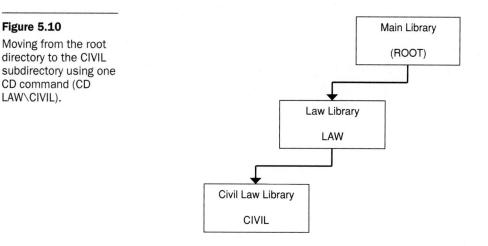

How to Move Back to a Parent Directory

Just like moving to child subdirectories, moving to parent subdirectories can be accomplished in individual steps or in one step. For example, if you were in the third-level subdirectory CIVIL and you wanted to move to its parent directory (LAW) you would type the command CD .. and press Enter. (See Figure 5.11.)

Figure 5.11

Moving from the subdirectory CIVIL to the subdirectory LAW using CD ..

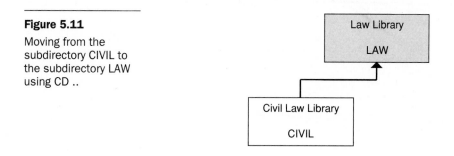

	What to Do	*What Happens*
Step 1	Type CD .. and press Enter.	See screen that follows.

```
A:\LAW\CIVIL>CD ..

A:\LAW>
```

CD stands for "Change directory" and the double period (..) stands for the parent directory. *Note:* A space must be typed after CD and before the two periods.

Once in the LAW subdirectory, you could move to its parent directory, the root directory with the same command. Type CD .. and press Enter. (See Figure 5.12.)

Figure 5.12

Moving from the LAW subdirectory to the root directory using CD ..

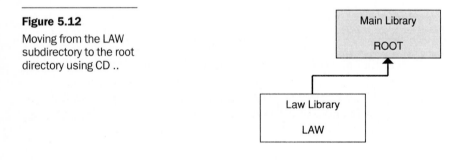

	What to Do	*What Happens*
Step 2	Type CD .. and press Enter.	See screen that follows.

```
A:\LAW>CD ..

A:\>
```

How to Move Through Multiple-Parent Subdirectories with One Command

If you wanted to move up two directories, you could use the double period (..) twice within the same command. For example, if you want to move from the CIVIL subdirectory to the root directory, you type the command CD ..\.. and then press Enter. (See Figure 5.13.)

Figure 5.13

Moving up two parent directories from the CIVIL subdirectory using CD .. \ ..

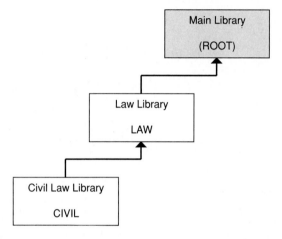

	What to Do	*What Happens*
Step 1	Type CD LAW\CIVIL and press Enter (to move out to CIVIL).	An A:\LAW\CIVIL appears.
Step 2	Type CD ..\.. and press Enter (to move back to the root directory).	See screen that follows.

```
A:\>CD LAW\CIVIL

A:\LAW\CIVIL>CD ..\..

A:\>
```

The \ is used to separate directory names. This command tells DOS to move to the parent directory and then to the next parent directory. If you wanted to move up more than two directories, just use as many sets of double periods as needed.

How to Move from Any Subdirectory to the Root Directory

The CD \ command can be used to return you to the root directory from any subdirectory. Note that CD stands for *change directory*; the symbol \ stands for the root directory. Do not confuse the \ symbol with the / symbol.

	What to Do	*What Happens*
Step 1	Type CD LAW\CIVIL and press Enter (to move out to CIVIL).	An A:\LAW\CIVIL appears.
Step 2	Type CD \ and press Enter (to move back to the root directory).	See screen that follows.

```
A:\> CD LAW\CIVIL

A:\LAW\CIVIL > CD \

A:\>
```

Note: Anytime you want to return to the root directory, simply use the CD \ command. To list only the subdirectories in the current directory, use the DIR *. command.

Review Exercises	1. Perform the following steps to review changing directories.	

	What to Do	*What Happens*
Step 1	At the A:\>	
Step 2	Type CD LAW\CRIMINAL and press Enter.	An A:\LAW\ CRIMINAL> appears.
Step 3	Type CD .. and press Enter. (You have just moved back to the second-level subdirectory <LAW>.)	An A:\LAW> appears.
Step 4	Type CD .. and press Enter. (You have just moved back to the first-level directory or root.)	An A:\> appears.
Step 5	Type CD LAW\CIVIL and press Enter. (You have just moved from the root directory to a third-level subdirectory, using one command.)	An A:\LAW\ CIVIL> appears.
Step 6	Type CD \ and press Enter. (You have just moved from the third-level directory <CIVIL> to the first-level or root directory.	An A:\> appears. See screen that appears.

```
A:\>CD LAW\CRIMINAL

A:\LAW\CRIMINAL>CD ..

A:\LAW\>CD ..

A:\>CD LAW\CIVIL

A:\LAW\CIVIL>CD \

A:\>
```

2. Create the rest of the tree structure on **Practice** disk as shown in Figure 5.14, using SMALL_BS to represent SMALL BUSINESS and CORP to represent CORPORATE, and return to the root directory using CD\.

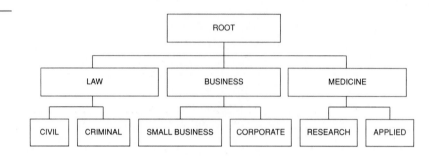

3. Create the entire tree structure shown in Figure 5.14 again on the **BACKUP** disk and return to the root directory using CD\.

4. Copy all the TXT files from the root directory on the **EXERCISE** disk to the root directory on the **Practice** disk.

How to Copy to a Subdirectory

The easiest method to use to copy to a subdirectory is to move to the source directory and then using the COPY command specify the target drive and/or subdirectories as needed. The following sections describe

1. Copying from a root directory to a subdirectory within the same disk.

2. Copying from one subdirectory to another within the same disk.

3. Copying from one subdirectory to another subdirectory located in a different drive.

4. Copying from a subdirectory to a root directory.

How to Copy from the Root Directory to a Subdirectory Within the Same Disk

Suppose that you wanted to copy the file MEDREC1.TXT from the root directory to the subdirectory APPLIED. You would first move to the root directory and make sure that the file exists. Then you would use the command COPY MEDREC1.TXT \MEDICINE\ APPLIED. (See Figure 5.15.)

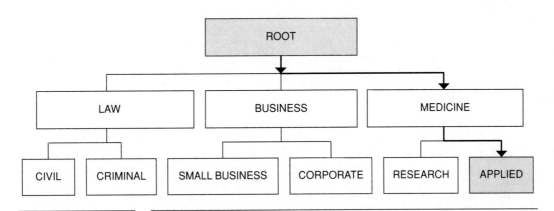

Figure 5.15   Copying from the root directory to a third-level subdirectory (APPLIED).

Use **Practice** disk in Drive A:.

	What to Do	*What Happens*
Step 1	Move to the root directory.	An A:\> appears.
Step 2	Type COPY MEDREC1.TXT \MEDICINE\APPLIED and press Enter.	See screen that follows.

```
A:\>COPY MEDREC1.TXT \MEDICINE\APPLIED
          1 File(s) copied

A:\>
```

How to Copy from One Subdirectory to Another Within the Same Disk

To copy the same file (MEDREC1.TXT) from APPLIED to CRIMINAL, you would first move to APPLIED, then use the COPY command

`COPY MEDREC1.TXT \LAW\CRIMINAL`

(See Figure 5.16.)

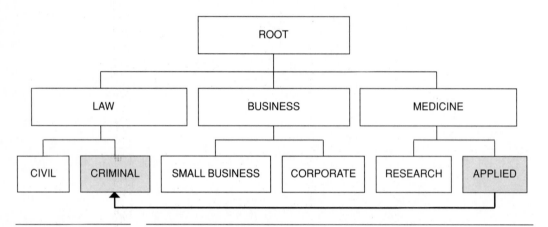

Figure 5.16

Copying from a third-level subdirectory (APPLIED) to another third-level subdirectory (CRIMINAL).

Use **Practice** disk in Drive A:.

	What to Do	*What Happens*
Step 1	Move to the APPLIED subdirectory.	An A:\ MEDICINE \APPLIED> appears.
Step 2	Type COPY MEDREC1.TXT \LAW \CRIMINAL and press Enter.	See screen that follows.

```
A:\MEDICINE\APPLIED>COPY MEDREC1.TXT \LAW\CRIMINAL
        1    File(s) copied

A:\MEDICINE\APPLIED>
```

How to Copy from One Disk to Another with Subdirectories

If you wish to copy a file from the root directory of one disk to a subdirectory of another disk, the procedure is as follows:

1. Move to the root directory of your source disk.

2. Use the DIR command to list contents of that directory.

3. Use the COPY command and the drive designator of the target drive. (See Figure 5.17.)

For example, if you wanted to copy the file MEDREC1.TXT from the root directory of the disk in Drive A: to the subdirectory RESEARCH in the target disk in Drive B:, you would use the command

```
A:\>COPY MEDREC1.TXT B:\MEDICINE\RESEARCH
```

Use **Practice** disk in Drive A: and **BACKUP** disk in Drive B:.

	What to Do	*What Happens*
Step 1	Move to the root directory of Drive A:.	An A:\> appears.
Step 2	Type COPY MEDREC1.TXT B:\MEDICINE\ RESEARCH and press Enter.	See screen that follows.

```
A:\>COPY MEDRIC1.TXT B:\MEDICINE\RESEARCH
        1 File(s) copied

A:\>
```

Step 3	Make sure that the file was copied.

Note: If you were copying a file from a subdirectory on the source drive, the only difference would be that you would have to move to the source subdirectory before using the preceding command.

If you do not first move to the source drive and source subdirectories before using the COPY command, you will have to specify both within the COPY command prior to the source filename.

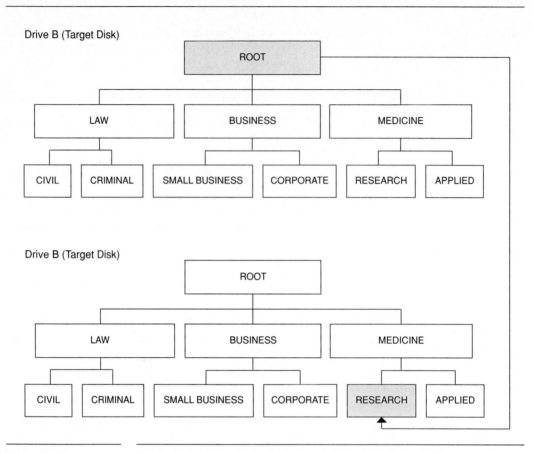

Drive B (Target Disk)

Drive B (Target Disk)

Figure 5.17   Copying a file from the root directory in Drive A: to the subdirectory
RESEARCH in the target disk in Drive B:.

DOS keeps track of your location on each disk drive so that when
you switch between drives, you will be returned to the subdirectory
you were last using. For example, if you were in the LAW/CIVIL
subdirectory in Drive A: and then switched to Drive B:, when you
returned to Drive A:, you would be at the A:\LAW\CIVIL> prompt.
DOS also uses this feature when copying files between drives.
Therefore, make sure that you know where DOS is going to copy
your files if you do not list subdirectories during copy commands.

Review Exercises

1. Create the following files on **Practice** disk, using COPY CON.

Filename	Contents
a. `OVERVIEW.LAW`	The scales of justice are evenly balanced.
b. `CASE1.CVL`	Case No. 101, *Jones vs. Jones*
c. `CASE2.CRM`	Case No. 201, *State of California vs. Jones*

2. Make sure that all three files have been created and are present in the root directory of **Practice** disk. *Hint:* Use DIR and TYPE commands.

3. Copy OVERVIEW .LAW to the subdirectory LAW, CASE1.CVL to the subdirectory CIVIL, and CASE2.CRM to the subdirectory CRIMINAL.

Erasing/Deleting and Renaming Files Within Subdirectories

Files can be erased and renamed within subdirectories just as within root directories. Just be sure that you are in the appropriate subdirectory. Also, if you are renaming and copying files at the same time, do not forget to list the target subdirectory and drive designator when needed.

How to Remove Directories

Removing directories is a four-step process using the DEL and RD commands. The steps in order to remove a directory are as follows (*Note:* the root directory of any disk cannot be removed):

1. Move to the directory that you wish to remove. Bring up a directory listing to determine the files and subdirectories contained.

2. Delete all files within the current subdirectory and subsequent lower directories. (If useful files exist, copy them to another directory first.)

3. Starting with the lowest subdirectory, delete each directory with the RD (REMOVE DIRECTORY) DOS command until you have deleted all subordinate directories.

4. Change to the parent directory of the directory you wish to delete and then delete the desired directory.

If you were going to remove the LAW subdirectory from **Practice** disk, the following procedures would have to be followed.

1. Transferring to Subdirectory

	What to Do	*What Happens*
Step 1	Obtain an A:\>.	Nothing.
Step 2	Insert **Practice** disk into Drive A:.	Nothing.
Step 3	Type CD\LAW and press Enter to move to the desired directory.	A:\LAW> appears.
Step 4	Type DIR and press Enter.	See screen that follows.

```
A:\>CD LAW

A:\LAW>DIR

 Volume in drive A is PRACTICE
 Directory of A:\LAW

 .              <DIR>     5-13-91  12:30p
 ..             <DIR>     5-13-91  12:30p
 CIVIL          <DIR>     5-13-91  12:32p
 CRIMINAL       <DIR>     5-13-91  12:32p
 OVERVIEW  LAW      44    5-13-91  12:48p
     5 File(s)      1446400 bytes free

A:\LAW>
```

2. Saving Useful Files to Another Directory

	What to Do	What Happens
Step 1	Type DEL OVERVIEW.LAW. (OVERVIEW.LAW is obsolete.)	File is deleted.
Step 2	Type CD CIVIL to change directory.	A:\LAW\CIVIL> appears.
Step 3	Type COPY CASE1.CVL \ and press Enter. (This file is still useful.)	Copies file to root directory.
Step 4	Type ERASE CASE1.CVL and press Enter.	File is deleted.
Step 5	Type CD .. and press Enter.	Moves back to LAW directory.
Step 6	Move to the Criminal subdirectory.	
Step 7	Copy CASE2.CRM to the root directory and erase all the files from the subdirectory. Be sure to erase MEDREC1.TXT.	

Tip: In Step 3, the \ was used to represent the root directory. You can also use A:\ to represent the root directory. Using A: alone is not acceptable.

3. Removing Lower Subdirectories

Since there are no subdirectories lower than < CIVIL > and < CRIMINAL >, we can begin deleting lower subdirectories with them.

	What to Do	What Happens
Step 1	Obtain an A:\LAW >.	Nothing.
Step 2	Type RD CIVIL and press Enter.	Civil is removed.
Step 3	Type RD CRIMINAL and press Enter.	Criminal is removed.

4. Removing Desired Subdirectory

	What to Do	*What Happens*
Step 1	Obtain an A:\LAW>.	Nothing.
Step 2	Check the directory to make sure the subdirectories were deleted.	
Step 3	Type CD .. and press Enter.	Moves to parent (root) directory.
Step 4	Type RD LAW and press Enter.	Subdirectory LAW has been removed.

Loading Applications Programs into Subdirectories

Applications programs are normally located in separate subdirectories. They are separated into subdirectories because subdirectories allow each application to have its own storage area for the program and data files it uses. For example, most computer users do not wish to mix their word processing files with their database or spreadsheet files. By keeping each application program and its data files separate in a subdirectory, the files are easier to locate.

In the following exercise, you will learn how to copy an applications program into its own subdirectory and then move into the subdirectory and use the program. Most applications are loaded into subdirectories on hard disks. However, in this exercise, you will be using a floppy disk instead. In a later chapter, you will learn a shortcut to call up a program on the hard disk using a special file called a batch file.

Instead of having to create subdirectories and to copy applications program files from a floppy disk onto a hard disk manually, most applications programs available today have their own installation programs that create their own subdirectories and copy all of the files into the appropriate subdirectories automatically. The most common steps to install an applications program is to type INSTALL C: at an A> with the install disk in Drive A:.

The first step you will do is to prepare a disk with the appropriate subdirectories.

	What to Do	*What Happens*
Step 1	Format the **Practice** disk with the volume label PRACTICE.	The disk is formatted.
Step 2	Copy the *.COM files from the **BACKUP** disk to the **Practice** disk.	The COM files are copied.
Step 3	Using the **Practice** disk in Drive A:, create three subdirectories within the root directory. Call them WORDP, DATAB, and SPREADS.	The Subdirectories are created.
Step 4	Copy the WP.COM file from the root directory to the subdirectory WORDP.	The WP.COM file is copied
Step 5	Copy the DB.COM file from the root directory to the subdirectory DATAB.	The DB.COM file is copied
Step 6	Copy the SS.COM file from the root directory to the subdirectory SPREADS.	The SS.COM file is copied.

Now that each subdirectory contains its own mock applications program, you will move to each subdirectory and load each program.

Load the WP.COM file first using the following steps.

	What to Do	*What Happens*
Step 1	Move to the WORDP subdirectory.	An A:\WORDP> appears.
Step 2	Obtain a directory listing to make sure that the file WP.COM exists.	The Directory is listed.
Step 3	Type WP and press Enter.	The program appears.
Step 4	Press 9 to exit the mock program.	The DOS prompt returns.

Note: DOS may request that you insert a DOS disk in Drive A: when exiting these mock programs. If so, put the DOS disk in Drive A: and press a key to return to an A:.

Review
Exercises

1. Move to the DATAB subdirectory and load the DB.COM file. Try each of the title selections to see what happens. Read the screen for instructions. To exit the program, press Q to Quit.

2. Move to the SPEADS subdirectory and load the SS.COM file. Press the / key to access the main menu. This spreadsheet and main menu is similar to many typical spreadsheet programs. Press Q when the main menu is displayed to quit.

Using XCOPY

For this exercise, you will be copying the contents of the **BACKUP** disk to the **Practice** disk. By using XCOPY, you can add the entire tree structure and files from the **Practice** disk to the **BACKUP** disk.

XCOPY has several options that are used to determine what files and what subdirectories are copied during the procedure. A list of these options and their results is as follows:

Option	Results
/A	Copies only files that have had their file attribute of archive turned on.
/D:mm-dd-yy	Copies only the files with the creation dates that are identical or more recent than the date following the /D.
/E	Creates subdirectories on target disk even if the subdirectories made will be empty.
/M	Copies only files that have been modified since the last time the files have been archived.
/P	Causes XCOPY to pause before each file is copied and requests confirmation that each file should be copied.
/S	Copies all files from source disk directory and subsequent lower directories to the target disk except for subdirectories that will be empty.
/V	Verifies each file as being copied successfully.
/W	Waits for source disk to be placed in disk drive.

	What to Do	*What Happens*
Step 1	Obtain an A:\>.	Nothing.
Step 2	Place the DOS disk in Drive A: and **BACKUP** disk in Drive B:.	Nothing.
Step 3	Type XCOPY A:*.* B:\ /S /E /W	The Message "Press any key to begin copying file(s)" appears.
Step 4	Remove the DOS disk from Drive A: and insert **Practice** disk, then press any key.	Copies the entire contents of **Practice** to **BACKUP**.
Step 5	Place the DOS disk in Drive A: and use the TREE B: /F > PRN command to print the contents of the **BACKUP** disk to the printer to verify that all the files and subdirectories were copied.	The contents of the **BACKUP** disk is printed out. The results should appear as in the "Directory Path Listing" that follows.

Note: If you do not have a printer, use the TREE B: /F command to list the contents of the **BACKUP** disk to the screen.

Figure 5.18

```
A:\>TREE B: /F

DIRECTORY PATH LISTING FOR VOLUME BACKUP

Files:              WP       .COM
                    DB       .COM
                    SS       .COM
                    REPLY    .COM
                    CONTINUE .BAT
                    MENU     .BAT
                    COMMAND  .DAT
                    DATA1    .DBF
                    DATA2    .DBF
                    DATA3    .DBF
                    CHAP1    .DOC
                    CHAP2    .DOC
                    CHAP3    .DOC
                    CHAP12   .EXT
                    CHAP1    .TXT
                    README   .ANS
                    README   .DOC
                    README   .SC3
                    README   .BAT
                    README   .AN2
                    README   .SC1
                    README   .SC2
                    README   .AN3
                    README   .AN1
                    RETRIEVE .SCR
                    MENU2    .SCR
                    MOVIE2   .LST
                    MOVIE    .LST
                    MENUFER  .BAT
                    ANSWER   .BAT
                    CHAP2    .TXT
                    CHAP3    .TXT
                    MYNAME   .TXT
                    DAYDATE  .TXT
                    SCHEDULE .TXT
                    MEDREC1  .TXT


Path: \LAW

Sub-directories:    CIVIL
                    CRIMINAL

Files:              None


Path: \LAW\CIVIL

Sub-directories:    None

Files:              None


Path: \LAW\CRIMINAL

Sub-directories:    None

Files:              None


Path: \BUSINESS

Sub-directories:    CORP
                    SMALL_BS

Files:              None
```

```
Path: \BUSINESS\CORP

Sub-directories:      None

Files:                None


Path: \BUSINESS\SMALL_BS

Sub-directories:      None

Files:                None


Path: \MEDICINE

Sub-directories:      APPLIED
                      RESEARCH

Files:                None


Path: \MEDICINE\APPLIED

Sub-directories       None

Files:                None


Path: \MEDICINE\RESEARCH

Sub-directories:      None

Files:                MEDREC1 .TXT


Path: \WORDP

Sub-directories:      None

Files:                WP      .COM

Path: \DATAB

Sub-directories:      None

Files:                DB      .COM


Path: \SPREADS

Sub-directories:      None

Files:                SS      .COM

A:\>
```

As mentioned before in Chapter 4, there are several file utility programs such as PCTools and Norton Utilities that help you copy delete and undelete, rename, and change the attributes of files. These programs also allow you to view your tree structure in a graphic form as follows:

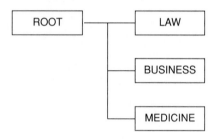

Summary Points

1. Since disks—especially hard disks—can contain thousands of files, it can be difficult to find files on the main directory.

2. The main directory that is created when a disk is formatted is called the *root directory*. The root directory is limited in the number of files it can contain. Most floppy disks are limited to 112.

3. Since the root directory is limited, a further means of categorizing files, called *subdirectories,* was developed.

4. One difficulty in file organization is that there is no particular method in which files are stored on a directory.

5. Subdirectories are necessary because of the way that files are stored on a disk and because of the limited files that a root directory can contain.

6. The organization that is applied to disk management is a hierarchical organization with subdirectories branching from the root directory.

7. Directories are categorized into various levels. The first level (Level 1) is the root directory. Level 2 is the first level of subdirectories, and so on.

8. A subdirectory structure can be thought of as a family tree, with the root directory being the first set of parents. The second-level subdirectories are the children of the root directory, but the parents of the third-level directories.

9. The DOS symbol for the root directory is the \.

10. The DOS symbol for the current subdirectory is the period (.).

11. The DOS symbol for the parent subdirectory is a double period (..).

12. For every subdirectory, there can be only one parent.

13. For every subdirectory, there can be many children.

14. A subdirectory can be created using the "Make directory" (MKDIR or MD) command.

15. To make a second-level directory, you must be in the root directory.

16. To create a third-level directory, you must be in the second-level subdirectory.

17. The command to move among subdirectories is the "Change directory" (CHDIR or CD) command.

18. To move across the tree, you must first move to a common parent and then to the desired child subdirectory.

19. The DOS system prompt can be changed allowing it to display your location within the tree structure.

20. Changing the system prompt to reflect your location within the tree is accomplished by typing the command PROMPT PG.

21. The easiest method to use to copy to or from a subdirectory is to move to the directory that contains the files you wish to copy and then use the COPY command.

22. Files can be erased or renamed within subdirectories in the same way that they are erased and renamed in root directories.

23. It is important to be in the proper subdirectory when deleting files because you can use the same filenames in various subdirectories.

24. To remove a subdirectory, you first need to delete all the files contained within that subdirectory and any subsequent subdirectories and their files. In essence, you must delete everything from a subdirectory before you can remove it.

25. The command to remove a subdirectory is (RMDIR or RD).

26. An alternative to copy and backup is XCOPY.

27. Applications program files are usually placed into their own subdirectories.

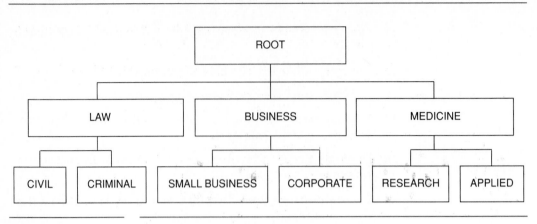

Figure 5.19   Tree diagram for Application Exercises.

Application
Exercises

The following exercises will give you practice in maintaining disks and files. Refer to the tree diagram in Figure 5.19.

1. Using **Practice** disk, create the second-level subdirectories LAW, BUSINESS, and MEDICINE.

2. Using **Practice** disk, create the third-level subdirectories CIVIL, CRIMINAL, SMALL_BS, CORP, APPLIED, and RESEARCH.

4. Copy the files CHAP1.TXT, CHAP2.TXT, CHAP3.TXT, and MEDREC1.TXT from the **EXERCISES** disk to the root directory of **Practice** disk.

5. Copy CHAP1.TXT, CHAP2.TXT from the root directory to the subdirectory \BUSINESS\CORP on **Practice** disk.

6. Copy the file MEDREC1.TXT from the root directory to the subdirectory \MEDICINE\APPLIED on the **Practice** disk.

7. Copy MEDREC1.TXT from the subdirectory APPLIED to the subdirectory BUSINESS on the **Practice** disk.

8. Draw the diagram and list the files contained within the subdirectories, if any.

9. Delete the second level subdirectories WORDP, SPREADS, and DATAB on **Practice** disk.

10. Delete all of the COM and TXT files from the root directory on **Practice** disk.

11. Use XCOPY to copy all of the files and subdirectories from the **BACKUP** disk to the **Practice** disk.

12. Draw the diagram and list the files contained within the sub-directories on the **Practice** disk, if any.

13. Use the TREE command to list only the subdirectories on **BACKUP** disk.

14. Draw the tree structure of **BACKUP** disk.

Comprehension Questions

Answer the following questions.

1. Why are subdirectories created?

2. How can you change from a root directory to a second-level sub-directory?

3. How can you copy from a root directory to a second-level sub-directory?

4. Explain how to create a third-level subdirectory.

5. How can you move from a third-level subdirectory to a root directory?

6. Explain how to remove a subdirectory that contains files.

7. What is the difference between DIR . and DIR ..?

Completion Exercises

Complete the following sentences.

1. A _____ is a global listing of the contents of a disk without regard to organization.

2. The _____ directory is either the root directory or the next closest directory to the root directory.

3. Explain what each of the following commands do. Be sure to tell what is done and where the disk is located.

a. `A>MD LAWLBRY`

b. `A>CD LAWLBRY`

c. `A>COPY CVL.TXT A:\LAWLBRY`

d. `A>COPY CVL.TXT B:\LAWLBRY`

e. `A>RD LAWLBRY`

f. `A>CD ..`

g. `A>CD \`

Matching Exercises

Choose the correct letter from the right-hand column.

1. MD

    a. A command used to move to the root directory from any subdirectory

2. CD

    \
    b.   A   command that causes the prompt to display your location within a tree structure

3. RD

    c. A command used to create a subdirectory

4. LAW<DIR>

    d. A subdirectory

5. PROMPT

    PG
    e.   A   command used to remove a subdirectory once all files and/or subsequent directories have been removed

6. .

    f. DOS symbol for the root directory

7. ..

    g. DOS symbol for a current subdirectory

8. \

    h. DOS symbol for a parent subdirectory

6

Hard
Disks

When you have completed this chapter, you will be able to

Learning Objectives:

1. Explain the difference between a hard disk and a floppy disk.

2. Explain why a hard disk holds more information than a floppy disk.

3. Explain why subdirectories are important to hard disk organization.

4. Explain why FDISK is used.

5. Explain the difference between BACKUP and RESTORE.

6. Describe how to format a hard disk.

Performance Objectives:

1. Back up and restore files with a particular extension.

2. Create subdirectories on a hard disk.

3. Move among directories on a hard disk.

4. Copy to and from subdirectories on a hard disk.

5. Find out the files that exist in each subdirectory of a tree structure on a hard disk.

6. Erase files from subdirectories of a hard disk.

7. Remove subdirectories on a hard disk.

Chapter Overview

In the previous chapter, you learned to work with subdirectories on a floppy disk system. In this chapter, you will learn to apply what you learned in previous chapters to hard disks. Working with hard disks is similar to working with floppy disks except that hard disks can hold more files, making the use of subdirectories a necessity. Another distinction is that instead of the default drive being the A: drive, it is most commonly the C: drive. A C > tells you that DOS is looking in the hard disk. Even if you do not have a hard disk, you need to become familiar with hard disk systems.

What are Hard Disks?

When you use a number of applications software program disks, you have to switch disks every time you change programs. With a hard disk installed, you can store all your DOS, all your applications software programs, any other programs (such as games or utility programs), and any data files that you wish to keep on your hard disk.

A hard disk is a storage device capable of holding large amounts of information. Hard disks are similar to floppy disks in that they store information in a similar manner. They differ from floppy disks in that they consist of rigid platters instead of flexible disks and hold considerably more information than floppy disks.

The number of platters found in a hard disk drive determine the amount of information that the drive can store. Each side of a platter normally contains 2.5 million bytes of information or more. In other words, a two-platter hard disk drive can hold approximately 10 megabytes (million bytes) of information, while a four-platter disk drive can hold 20 megabytes (million bytes) of information. (See Figure 6.1.)

Figure 6.1

A comparison of a 10-megabyte disk drive and a 20-megabyte disk drive.

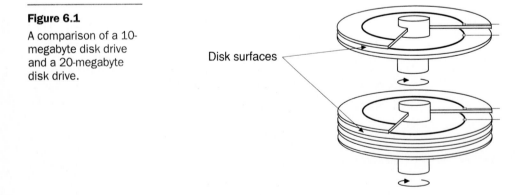

Disk surfaces

The standard hard disk drive used on microcomputers is known as a Winchester drive. Winchester drives are usually internally mounted within a computer and are sealed to prevent damage caused by dust particles. They are sealed to protect them from dust particles because the clearance between the rigid platters, used for information storage, and the read/write heads that transfer information to and from those platters is less than the size of a smoke particle. Therefore, if these drives were not sealed, smoke or dust particles could get between the read/write heads and the platters, causing loss of information and damage to both surfaces. (See Figure 6.2.)

Figure 6.2

Fingerprints, smoke particles, or hair can cause hard disks to crash.

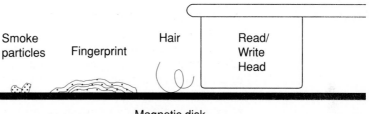

With the clearance between the heads and the platters being as small as they are, hard drives are susceptible to a phenomenon known as a *disk crash*. A disk crash is caused when a head comes in contact with a platter, destroying valuable information. The read/write head normally floats above the surface of the rotating platter, unlike a phonograph needle that touches the surface of a record. In a Winchester drive, any contact between platters and read/write heads causes some degree of damage. The damage can be as drastic as ruining a complete disk. This type of damage is caused when the read/write head comes in contact with (crashes) the platter in the area of the platter where system files are stored. If a hard drive crashes into data or application software files, information is lost. If it crashes while the heads are over the hard disk system files, the disk no longer has the information on it necessary for disk drive booting. The disk will need to be reformatted.

The way to keep a hard drive from crashing is to handle the computer with care, making sure not to bump or jar it at any time, especially during operation. If you need to move a computer that has a hard disk in it, you should park the read/write heads before transporting it. Most newer hard drives have self-parking mechanisms. These drives will automatically move the read/write head assemblies away from the disk surfaces when the power is turned off. This ensures a greater degree of safety for your data over user-activated parking programs.

If you do not have a self-parking hard drive, you will need to install a disk parking program such as PARK.COM or SHIPDISK-.COM on your hard drive. After one of these programs has been installed on your hard disk, you can activate it by typing in the filename and pressing the Enter key. You should immediately turn the computer off after the program has parked the heads. As soon as your computer's power is turned back on, the park program becomes disabled until called again.

Types of Hard Drives

Hard drives are available in many different sizes and speeds. Hard drive sizes range from 20 megabytes to 200 or more megabytes. The average personal computer uses one or more hard drives with at least 20 megabytes per hard drive. The type and quantity of applications programs you intend to use determines the size requirement of your hard drives. Hard drives are also rated in respect to how fast they can access and store information. The term for a hard drive's speed is *average access time*. A fast access time is 15 to 20 milliseconds. Software programs that use very large data files such as video and graphics programs require the fastest hard drives available. If you are using simple word processing programs, you will not need a hard drive of this type. Normally, the larger a hard drive, the faster its access time.

Hard drives also are available in different physical sizes. When hard drives were first introduced to the PC market, they were 10 megabyte drives with each platter diameter equal to the size of a 5 1/4-inch floppy disk. When larger drives were required, manufacturers stacked more disks into one physical drive. As technology advanced, the size of the disks decreased to 3 1/2-inches in diameter. This decrease in hard disk size allowed computer systems to decrease in overall size.

How Information is Stored

Advancements in hardware technology have constantly improved the accuracy of the read/write heads, allowing the number of tracks and sectors per platter side to be increased. The increased number of tracks and sectors enables a larger volume of information storage. After startup, the disks are spun at a speed of 3,600 rpm (revolutions per minute). The air currents built up due to the spinning platters causes the heads to float off the platters during operation. The platters are connected to a spindle, causing them to spin in unison. The read/write heads move in and out over the platters while they are spinning. Two read/write heads exist per platter; one per side.

Using a 20-megabyte drive, information is stored in the following manner:

1. DOS begins writing onto the first track, first side of the first platter. It continues writing on that track until it is finished.

2. When the first track of the first side is full, DOS then proceeds to the first track of the second side of the first platter.

3. When that track is full, DOS proceeds to the first track of the first side of the second platter, then onto the first track of the second side of the second platter.

After you have filled up the first track of all four sides of the two platters, DOS will return to the second track of the first side of the first platter and repeat the preceding steps. This procedure repeats itself from the outside of the disk to the inside, at which point the disk is full.

If you connect the same track on all four sides of both platters, you have created what is known as a *cylinder*. On hard disk drives, DOS refers to cylinder location more often than to track and sector location. During the format process, you will see DOS calling out not the tracks and sectors but cylinders. (See Figure 6.3.)

Figure 6.3

The difference between sectors (on floppy disks) and cylinders (on hard disks).

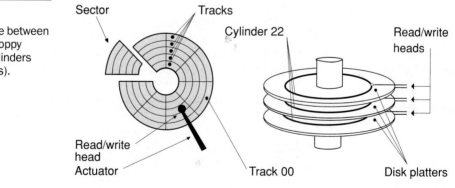

Why Use a Hard Disk Drive?

The primary reasons for using a hard disk drive are its large storage capacity and increased speed. It also provides you with organizational benefits and allows you to work more productively. By having the capacity to store a large number of files on one disk drive, you have the added convenience of not having to switch from one floppy disk to another when you move from one applications software program to another.

An important benefit of using a hard disk drive is the speed at which files can be copied onto or removed from the disk. It takes approximately half the time to perform the same task of reading or writing files when compared to a floppy disk drive. Being contained within the computer, the hard disk drive is also protected from mishandling.

Preparing a Hard Disk for Use

Normally, the dealer from which you purchase your hard disk will format the hard disk and install the DOS COMMAND.COM for you. The only reason you may have to know the steps in formatting a hard disk is if

1. Your dealer did not format the disk for you.

2. Your hard disk crashed during operation and you have to reformat it.

WARNING!

Do not attempt to format a hard disk unless it is the first time the disk has ever been used or if you have already backed up all the existing files.

Before Formatting a Hard Disk

Before formatting a hard disk the first time, you must use the DOS command FDISK to specify how much of the hard disk will be used by DOS and how many sections (partitions) the hard disk will be divided up into. In addition to DOS, a user may wish to use another operating system such as UNIX or CP/M. A user might want to use DOS and UNIX or CP/M on the same computer because he or she might have applications programs that require two of these systems. Normally, IBM PC and PC-compatible users initialize their whole hard disk to be used with DOS. Unless a hard disk is initialized with the FDISK external DOS command, that drive will be unavailable to use. It may physically exist within the computer, but will not be recognized until the hard disk is prepared.

In addition to specifying how much of the hard drive will be used for DOS, FDISK also allows you to partition your hard disk into several sections. With current technology, 40-megabyte (million bytes) hard drives are becoming commonplace. Because of the size of these hard disk drives, proper disk management becomes laborious. Partitioning the disk into smaller segments (such as 20-megabyte segments) makes managing the disk easier. Once partitioned, you can specify each 20-megabyte section as an individual disk such as C: and D:.

Note: Some hard drives require a special procedure called a low-level format prior to being able to create a DOS partition. Low-level format instructions are found in DOS manuals within the DEBUG section. Only special or unusual hard drives require a low-level format.

Determining the DOS Version for Your Hard Drive

Up until DOS version 4.0, a hard drive could not be partitioned larger than 32 megabytes in size, although the physical capacity could be larger. If the physical size of a hard drive were larger than 32 megabytes, you would have to partition the disk drive into separate drives. For example, if you had a 40 megabyte hard drive, you would partition it into two drives C: and D:. Either drive could be 0 to 32 megabytes in size. The normal partitioning of a 40 megabyte drive would be 32 megabytes for drive C: and 8 megabytes for drive D:. The larger drive would be used for programs that required a large amount of storage capacity.

With the release of DOS version 4.0, disk drives could be partitioned into drives as large as 256 megabytes. Once a disk drive has been partitioned, changing a partition size is virtually impossible without reformatting the entire hard drive.

If your hard drive is larger than 32 megabytes and you wish to partition it into one drive, you must use at least DOS 4.0. However, many users still prefer using several small partitions instead of one large partition for organizational purposes.

Another reason for installing DOS 4.0 on your hard drive is that version 4.0 can directly access RAM sizes in excess of 640 kilobytes. If you are not planning to use DOS 4.0, however, make sure that the version of DOS that you are planning to use on your hard drive supports all the hardware in your system.

Using FDISK

The DOS FDisk command is used to partition a hard drive. By typing FDISK C: at an A> with DOS in Drive A:, you will be presented with the following screen:

```
IBM Personal Computer
Fixed Disk Setup Program Version X.XX
(C)Copyright IBM Corp. 1983

FDISK Options

Choose one of the following:

1.Create DOS Partition
2.Change Active Partition
3.Delete DOS Partition
4.Display Partition Data

Enter choice: [1]

Press Esc to return to DOS
```

▶ *No. 1 is current choice, but you can change to any other number.*

Refer to the DOS manual for instructions on how to use FDISK to create a DOS partition before formatting your hard disk.

Formatting a Hard Disk

Once a DOS partition has been created with FDISK, DOS recognizes the existence of a hard disk Drive C: (possibly C: and D:). You can then format it for file storage. A hard disk should not be formatted unless one of the two following situations occurs:

1. You have just purchased the hard disk and it has not yet been formatted.

2. After you have stored files on it, part of that disk has become damaged due to a disk crash. If such an event occurs, you must first save the information from the hard disk onto another type of storage (floppy disks) using the DOS commands COPY or (hard disk) BACKUP. BACKUP is covered later in this chapter.

The command normally used to format a hard disk is

A>FORMAT C:/S/V

and press Enter.

Note: When you format Drive C:, you should always format it with the system /S option so you can boot the computer from the hard disk. The /V enables you to label the hard disk. A DOS disk needs to be in Drive A: when using this command.

WARNING! Do not use the FORMAT command to format a hard disk or you may lose important files.

After a hard drive has been formatted, the next step is to make sure that DOS transferred all three system files (IBMBIO.COM, IBM-DOS.COM, and COMMAND.COM) to the root directory before you can use the hard drive to boot the system. Some versions of DOS do not transfer COMMAND.COM to a disk during a DOS system disk format (FORMAT C: /S).

If COMMAND.COM is not found on the root directory, copy it to the root directory from the DOS disk. The DOS version of these three system files must be identical. If they are different, the computer cannot boot from the hard drive. DOS will give you a message that says that the command interpreter is not found. If this happens, place a DOS disk in Drive A: and boot the system. Then copy the COMMAND.COM file into the hard drive root directory.

If you do not have a floppy disk version of DOS identical to the two hidden system files on the hard drive, you must replace all of the system files by using the DOS SYS command (A>SYS C:). The DOS SYS command is an external DOS command that transfers the two hidden files and, in some versions, COMMAND.COM to the target drive. This can only happen if there is enough room on the target drive to accept the files.

An example of when you might have to use the SYS command is as follows: Suppose you had been using your computer and by accident deleted all of the files in the hard drive's root directory by typing DEL *.* at a C:\>. If the COMMAND.COM file was not protected from deletion by using the ATTRIB +r flag, the COMMAND.COM file would be deleted along with all the others. At this point, your hard drive is not able to boot DOS.

In addition to deleting all of your files, you may not have the same version of DOS available to you on a floppy disk that you had on your hard disk. If you copied the incompatible version of COMMAND.COM to the hard drive root directory, you still would not be able to boot the system.

To remedy this situation, you would insert your DOS disk into Drive A: and boot your system. At the A>, you would type SYS C: and press the Enter key. This procedure replaces the two hidden system files on the hard drive with the new DOS hidden files from your floppy DOS disk. You would then need to copy COMMAND.COM from your floppy disk to the root directory of your hard disk.

You now have the version of DOS installed that is on your floppy disk. If the DOS version on your floppy disk is newer than the version that was on your hard drive, there might not be enough room on your hard drive to allow you to update to the newer version. If this happens, you must find a version identical to the one you originally had on your hard drive and copy the COMMAND.COM file back to the root directory.

After a hard-drive has been formatted and the DOS system files have been installed, you should create a subdirectory called DOS and copy all of the DOS files from your floppy disks to the subdirectory DOS. This procedure ensures that DOS is always available to you on your hard drive. In addition, it is a good idea to change the read-only attribute of the DOS files so that they cannot be deleted.

Customizing Your Hard Disk

After your hard drive has been partitioned, formatted as a system disk, and had all of the DOS commands copied into the DOS sub-directory, you need to customize your system to handle all specialized hardware and software requirements.

The two files that help you customize your hard disk are the CON-FIG.SYS and AUTOEXEC.BAT files. It is necessary for you to create both files and place them in the root directory of your hard disk.

CONFIG.SYS

CONFIG.SYS stands for "configure your system." It is used to specify how your computer will utilize its hardware. There are many different types of commands that can be used. Some of them are as follows:

Command	Why Used
BUFFERS	Specifies the amount of RAM dedicated to handling the transfer of data to and from your disk drives.
FILES	Specifies the number of files that can be opened and used in RAM at any one time.
LASTDRIVE	Specifies the number of hard disks available to DOS.
DEVICE	Specifies any special device, such as a mouse, to be used by the computer.

The contents of a CONFIG.SYS file may be similar to the following:

```
BUFFERS = 20
FILES = 20
LASTDRIVE = F:
DEVICE = MOUSE.SYS
DEVICE = HIMEM.SYS
```

BUFFERS.   In this example, twenty buffers refers to DOS setting aside 20 buffers (512 bytes per buffer) in RAM for transferring files to and from disks. This means that DOS can then transfer files at a faster rate.

FILES.   Twenty files means that DOS can use 20 files at the same time. For instance, WordPerfect 5.0 uses its main program WP.COM and several overlay programs to act as the entire applications program. At the same time, WordPerfect allows you to work on two different files by switching between them using the Shift F3 key combination. In addition to WordPerfect using all of these files at the same time, DOS itself has to be loaded in the computer's memory. For this reason, you need to specify a large number of files that can be opened at any one time when using WordPerfect. The reason for not specifying more than 20 files open at any one time is that DOS sets aside a certain amount of RAM for each file that can be opened. Therefore, if you have a small amount of RAM available, you need to be careful when specifying the number of files that can be opened. Always refer to your applications program documentation for appropriate file and buffer allocation.

LASTDRIVE.   If LASTDRIVE = F:, then DOS will recognize the ability to use as many as six drives (A through F). If you have a large hard drive partitioned into three drives, (C, D, E), then you will have to specify LASTDRIVE as E. If in addition to these three drives, you use a virtual disk (an area of RAM that is set aside to emulate a disk drive), then you would have to specify the last drive as F where the virtual disk will be labeled F:. To create a virtual disk, refer to your DOS manual.

DEVICE.   If you are going to use a mouse, you may need to include the DEVICE = MOUSE.SYS command in the CONFIG.SYS file. In addition to adding this command line, you will need to copy the MOUSE.SYS file from your mouse program disk to the root directory on your hard drive. In doing so, DOS will now understand how to use this piece of hardware.

Some other devices that have to be specified are external disks, specialized monitor software, and memory allocations. For example, HIMEM.SYS is a software file that enables DOS to use your computer's memory above one megabyte. HIMEM.SYS, like MOUSE.SYS, needs to be copied into the root directory of your hard disk.

AUTOEXEC.BAT   Batch files are files that contain several DOS commands that can be automatically executed by typing in the batch file filename. A special batch file is AUTOEXEC.BAT. AUTOEXEC.BAT stands for "automatically execute during system boot." Whenever DOS is loaded into memory, it looks for a CONFIG.SYS file and then an AUTOEXEC.BAT file. If either or both are found, DOS will perform whatever commands they contain. A simple AUTOEXEC.BAT file for a hard disk is as follows:

```
ECHO OFF
TIME
DATE
PROMPT $P$G
CLS
MENU
```

This simple file tells DOS to do the following:

Command	What It Does
ECHO OFF	Turns off the command from being displayed to the screen. Only displays the results.
TIME	Displays the time prompt just as when you type in TIME at a DOS prompt.
DATE	Displays the date prompt just as when you type in DATE at a DOS prompt.

PROMPT PG   Sets the system prompt to display the cur-
                          rent drive and subdirectory being used.

CLS   Clears the screen.

MENU   Loads a menu program called MENU.

Several other DOS commands that are used in the AUTOEXEC
.BAT file and their functions are as follows:

PATH   Specifies the subdirectories to search for
                          COM, EXE, and BAT files. For example, it is
                          always a good idea to specify the root direc-
                          tory and the DOS subdirectory in the PATH
                          command so that whenever you use an
                          external DOS command, you do not have to
                          tell DOS where to find the DOS files. The
                          command to use is PATH C:\;C:\DOS.

APPEND   Specifies the subdirectories to search for files
                          other than COM, EXE, and BAT files. For
                          example, if you kept your data files in the
                          subdirectory C:\DATA, you would use the
                          command APPEND C:\DATA in your
                          AUTOEXEC.BAT file so that DOS will
                          always look in the subdirectory DATA when
                          looking for nonexecutable files.

ASSIGN   Allows you to tell DOS that one drive equals
                          another. For example, B = A tells DOS that
                          when it is told to look in Drive B:, it should
                          look in Drive A: instead.

SUBST   Tells DOS to substitute a subdirectory for a
                          disk drive. SUBST A: C:\TEMP, for exam-
                          ple, tells DOS to use the subdirectory
                          C:\TEMP whenever it is supposed to use
                          Drive A:.

MODE   Tells DOS to redirect output from one device
                          to another or change the number of columns
                          used on the monitor. For example, MODE
                          LPT1:=COM1: tells DOS to redirect the
                          printer output and send the information to
                          the serial port. This command is commonly
                          used when a laser printer is attached to the
                          serial port of a computer.

because it avoids DOS the menu system is good

At the end of your AUTOEXEC.BAT file, you should usually list the command for loading a menu system or an applications program. You can create AUTOEXEC.BAT and CONFIG.SYS files on floppy disks if you do not have a hard disk. Be sure that the files are located on the disk that is used to boot the system.

DOS version 4.0 has a special user interface called the DOSSHELL. The DOSSHELL utilizes a graphic user interface with pull-down menus, instead of prompting you with just a plain C:\>. The DOSSHELL assists you in copying, renaming, and deleting files, creating and deleting subdirectories, and loading applications programs. It also provides you with the choice to return to the system prompt. If DOS 4.0 has been installed on your hard disk and you want to use the DOSSHELL interface, type DOSSHELL at the C:\> or place the command DOSSHELL in your hard disk's AUTOEXEC.BAT file. The DOSSHELL interface was designed to be used with a mouse, but you can access the commands by using the Alt key and letter representations on the main menu. For example, to access the file selection Menu item, you would press Alt F. (See Figure 6.4.)

Figure 6.4
DOS Shell screen.

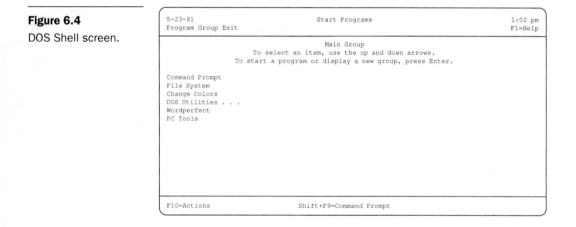

```
5-23-91                          Start Programs                        1:02 pm
Program Group Exit                                                     F1=Help
┌──────────────────────────────────────────────────────────────────────────┐
│                               Main Group                                    │
│                  To select an item, use the up and down arrows.             │
│               To start a program or display a new group, press Enter.       │
│                                                                            │
│ Command Prompt                                                             │
│ File System                                                                │
│ Change Colors                                                              │
│ DOS Utilities . . .                                                       │
│ Wordperfect                                                                │
│ PC Tools                                                                   │
│                                                                            │
│                                                                            │
│                                                                            │
│                                                                            │
│ F10=Actions              Shift+F9=Command Prompt                          │
└──────────────────────────────────────────────────────────────────────────┘
```

Installing Applications Program Software

As mentioned in Chapter 5, applications software programs should be placed into their own subdirectories. They are usually placed there automatically using an INSTALL program that accompanies the application files. Install programs usually create the appropriate subdirectories and copy the system files automatically. In addition, most INSTALL programs will prompt you for confirmation of your computer's hardware and whether you wish it to use its default subdirectory name. It will also prompt you if you need to switch disks during the installation. Always read the install procedures that accompany your applications program before attempting to install your program. Each applications program will also specify hardware requirements and CONFIG.SYS commands to be used in your CON-FIG.SYS file. If a program does not have its own install program, create a subdirectory in which to store the applications files and copy them from the floppy disk(s) using the steps that you learned in previous chapters for copying files.

If you wish to have an applications program load itself during the system boot, you should list the appropriate applications program subdirectory and filename at the end of the AUTOEXEC.BAT file. For example, if you wanted to load WordPerfect and WordPerfect was stored in the subdirectory WP51, you would use the following commands in the AUTOEXEC.BAT file:

`C:`	Checks that you are in the C: drive.
`CD \`	Makes sure that you are in the root directory.
`CD WP51`	Changes to the WP51 subdirectory.
`WP`	Loads WP.COM, the main program file.
`CD \`	Returns you to the root directory after WordPerfect is finished.

Backing Up a Hard Disk

The BACKUP command is used to create a duplicate of the hard disk on multiple floppy disks or magnetic tape. Prior to beginning the BACKUP procedure, you will need to obtain several formatted data floppy disks. The amount of bytes used on the hard disk will determine the number of floppy disks needed.

Back up hard disk with floppy disks

Tips:

1. Be sure to format enough floppy disks before you begin the backup procedure. Once the backup procedure has begun, you cannot format any new disks if you run out. Some DOS versions such as 3.3 automatically format the backup disks during the backup procedure.

2. Each disk should be labeled on the outside with a number starting with 1 and continuing until all the disks that will be used during the procedure are numbered. Be sure to keep these disks in order because during the backup procedure DOS will ask you to insert each disk as numbered.

A number of options can be used with BACKUP:

/S   backs up all subdirectories starting with the spe-
              cific or current directory on the disk and all lower
              subdirectories.

/M   backs up all files that have been modified since the
              last time that you backed up.

/A   adds the files being backed up onto the existing
              backup disks without writing over existing files.

/D   backs up any file changed or created after a spe-
              cific date.

The options that you choose depend on what files you wish to back
up; for example,

C>BACKUP C:\ A: /S   backs up all the files on the
                              hard drive to target disks.

C>BACKUP C: A: backs up all the files in the
                              root directory.

C>BACKUP C:\ A: /S /M   backs up all the files that
                              have been modified since the
                              last backup.

C>BACKUP C:\ A: /S /M /A   backs up all the files that
                              have been modified since the
                              last backup and copies them
                              to the target disks without
                              erasing the existing files on
                              the target disks.

C>BACKUP C:\ A: /S /A /D:1/01/88   backs up all the files created
                              since 1/01/88 and adds them
                              to the target disks without
                              erasing the existing files on
                              the target disks.

You can also back up a specific subdirectory or subdirectories of the hard disk and/or specific files within those subdirectories.

`C>BACKUP C:\LAW A:`   backs up only the files in the subdirectory LAW.

`C>BACKUP C:\LAW A: /S`   backs up the files within the subdirectory LAW and any lower subdirectories (child subdirectories).

`BACKUP C:\LAW\*.TXT A: /S /A /M`   backs up any TXT files within the LAW subdirectory and lower subdirectories that have been modified since the last backup, and adds them to the target disks without erasing the existing files on the target disk.

Tip: Combine the options and the subdirectory names within the BACKUP command to achieve the type of backup you desire.

When the BACKUP command is entered as shown:

`C>BACKUP C:\ A: /S`

and you press Enter, the following screen appears:

```
C:\>BACKUP C:\ A: /S

Insert backup diskette 01 in drive A:

Warning! Files in the target drive
A:\ root directory will be erased
Strike any key when ready
```

As you can see, DOS is requesting you to insert Diskette 01 in Drive A:. Make sure that there are no files on this disk that you will want at a later time, since they will be erased.

When you depress any key, the following screen appears:

```
*** Backing up files to drive A: ***
Diskette Number: 01
```

Files from the hard disk are listed on the left-hand side of the screen. For example,

```
\IBMBIO.COM
\IMBDOS.COM
\COMMAND.COM
\AUTOEXEC.BAT
\CONFIG.BAK
\SCRNX.BAK
\CONFIG.SYS
```

The rest of the files continue to list until the following message appears:

```
Insert backup diskette 02 in drive A:

Warning! Files in the target drive
A:\ root directory will be erased
Strike any key when ready
```

At this point, you would remove Diskette number 01 and insert Diskette number 02. The following screen appears.

```
*** Backing up files to drive A: ***
Diskette Number: 02
```

DOS will continue to list the files being transferred to the floppy disk until the disk is full, in which case DOS will ask you to insert another disk. DOS will continue asking for new disks until the process is finished. When the backup process is finished, DOS will return you to the C>.

Restoring Files to the Hard Disk

If a hard disk crashes, reformat your hard disk and then use the backup medium (disks or magnetic tape) to copy the tree structure and files back onto the hard disk.

After a hard disk is reformatted, you would normally use the DOS command RESTORE to copy the contents of the hard disk drive from backup floppy disks back onto the hard disk drive. Another use for BACKUP and RESTORE is to protect yourself against information loss resulting from a disk crash. In other words, BACKUP creates a copy of the contents of the hard disk and should be used regularly. RESTORE is used only if the contents of the hard disk are lost or if the hard disk needs to be reformatted due to a disk crash.

If a hard disk crash[...]
files, you could spend [...]
data and/or recopy all t[...]

The command used [...]

```
A>RESTORE A: C: /S
```

and press Enter.

The /S option is used i[...]
command. It causes al[...]
copied back onto the ha[...]
subdirectory and its chi[...]
disk by using the \SUB[...]

When you use the [...]
appears:

```
Insert backup diskett[...]
Strike any key when r[...]
```

You can follow the s[...]

Tip: If you insert a disk out o[...]
mand, DOS will inform [...]
request you to insert th[...]
always number your bac[...]

Using XCOPY to Back Up Files

As you learned in Chap[...]
their subdirectories fror[...]
used to copy a part of or[...]
disks. The benefit of usi[...]
individual files from the[...]
XCOPY takes up more fl[...]
a hard disk to a floppy d[...]
one floppy disk. For ex[...]
floppy disk and your ha[...]
not subdivide the 400k f[...]
must be smaller than th[...]

You can also use X[...]
they were damaged, del[...]

[...] is a simple inverted tree structure.
[...]ctures on hard disks are not that simple.
[...] realistic diagram of what a hard disk
[...]It was arrived at by analyzing the types
[...]users intend to place on their hard disks.
[...]consideration the fact that several users
[...]e. Individual user data files are normally
[...]bdirectory of a specific software program
[...]elow the software program subdirectory

```
ROOT DIRECTORY

DOS      <DIR>
WORDP    <DIR>
SPREADS  <DIR>
DATAB    <DIR>
COMM     <DIR>
UTIL     <DIR>

...EADS    DATAB   COMM    UTIL
...LES     FILES   FILES   FILES
```

same software program, each user should
er own data files in individual subdirec-
tions software program subdirectories.
e individual user subdirectories can be
wn respective categories.
just how complex the directory structure
me with multiple users and multiple soft-
h the root directory is fixed in the number
ld, the number of files that can be stored
limited only by available hard disk space.

Any disk, including hard disks, has a limited number of bytes allotted for the root directory. Because first-level subdirectories are contained within the root directory, the number of subdirectories are limited. For this reason, it is advisable not to create unnecessary subdirectories.

Movement Within a Tree

As you learned in Chapter 5, you can create a DOS prompt that tells you your location within a subdirectory system. For example, if you were in the subdirectory OFFMEMOS on a hard disk and wanted to copy a file to another subdirectory, the DOS prompt would be as follows:

C:\WORDP\MMATE\JANE\OFFMEMOS >

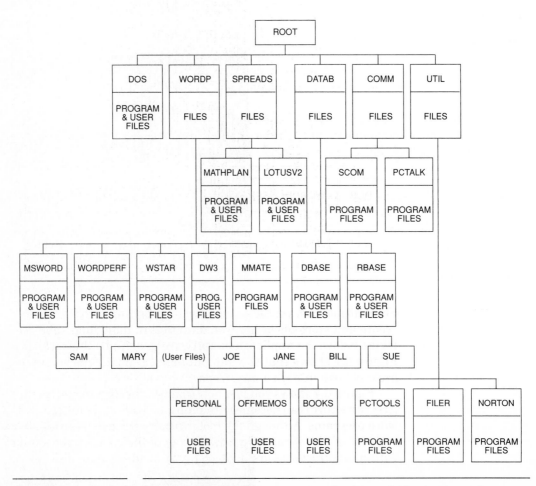

Figure 6.6   Sketching out your directory structure is also useful in planning and organizing your hard disk.

The listing of the subdirectories shows the path taken from the root directory to the subdirectory OFFMEMOS.

C:	stands for the default drive.
\WORDP	stands for the second-level subdirectory WORDP.
\MMATE	stands for the child subdirectory MMATE of WORDP.
\JANE	stands for the child subdirectory JANE of MMATE.
\OFFMEMOS	stands for the child subdirectory OFFMEMOS of JANE.

Figure 6.7

A comparison showing user-files found in either a software program subdirectory or within their own subdirectory below the software program subdirectory.

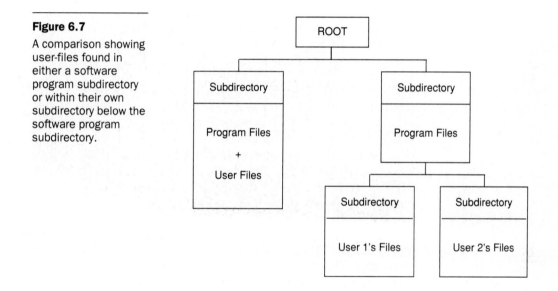

In the future, this type of listing of subdirectories will be referred to as a *path*. Paths can sometimes be cumbersome to type out. In Chapter 7 you will learn how to create a batch file that will move you to the subdirectory OFFMEMOS without having to type the entire path each time you wish to move to that subdirectory.

Hands-On Activities

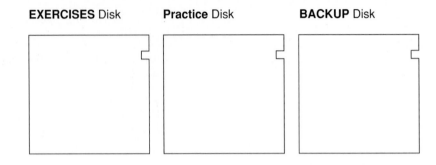

EXERCISES Disk   **Practice** Disk   **BACKUP** Disk

Since it is risky to practice on hard disks that may contain important files, you will perform only a simple backup exercise and check the directory of a backup disk.

How to Use BACKUP and RESTORE

BACKUP and RESTORE can be used to copy selective sections of a hard disk drive onto floppy disks or other types of storage systems. As with the COPY commands, you can use wildcards to specify selective files to backup. Also if the /S is not used in conjunction with the BACKUP command, only the current directory will be backed up. For example, if you were to back up only the files with a BAT extension within the root directory of a hard disk, you would follow the steps below:

Note:

In the following exercises, you will be using the DOS external commands located on your computer's hard drive instead of a DOS floppy disk. Therefore, you need to make sure that the DOS external command files are either in the root directory of the hard disk or in a subdirectory that has been listed within a PATH command in the AUTOEXEC.BAT file. If the AUTOEXEC.BAT file does not contain a path command and the DOS files are not in the root directory, type a PATH command, at any DOS prompt, that includes the subdirectory where the DOS files are located.

Use **Practice** disk in Drive A:.

	What to Do	*What Happens*
Step 1	Obtain a C:\>.	Nothing.
Step 2	Insert **Practice** disk in Drive A:.	Nothing.
Step 3	Type BACKUP C:\ *.BAT A: and press Enter.	See screen that follows.

```
C:\>BACKUP C:\ *.BAT A:

Insert backup diskette 01 in drive A:

Warning! Files in the target drive
A:\ root directory will be erased
Strike any key when ready
```

Step 4	Press any key.	See screen that follows.

Your screen will vary, depending on the number of BAT files found on your root directory. The messages will remain the same, but the files will vary from hard disk to hard disk.

```
*** Backing up files to drive A: ***
Diskette Number: 01
More files will be listed if they exist.

\AUTOEXEC.BAT

C:\>
```

▶*The other BAT files will vary.*

This exercise shows you how to use a simple BACKUP command. Since most of you do not have multiple disks, the *.BAT was used as a backup option so that only the BAT files from the root directory are copied onto your disk.

How to Check a Backup Disk Directory

You will know if you have a **BACKUP** disk if you look at the directory and see a file labeled BACKUPID.@@@. This file is located at the top of the directory.

Use **Practice** disk in Drive A:.

What to Do	*What Happens*
Step 1 Obtain an A:\>.	Nothing.
Step 2 Type DIR /P and press Enter.	Screen will vary depending on the number of BAT files found in your root directory.

```
A:\>DIR /P

 Volume in drive A is BACKUP  001
 Directory of A:\

BACKUP   001      353   5-23-91 11:34a
CONTROL  001      447   5-23-91 11:34a
LAW           <DIR>     5-13-91  1:11p
BUSINESS      <DIR>     5-13-91  1:11p
MEDICINE      <DIR>     5-13-91  1:11p
WORDP         <DIR>     5-13-91  1:22p
DATAB         <DIR>     5-13-91  1:22p
SPREADS       <DIR>     5-13-91  1:22p
    8 File(s)    1384960 bytes free

A:\>
```

▶ *Time and date backup disk created. Other fields may also be displayed.*

Summary Points

1. Hard disks require the use of subdirectories for organization.

2. The default drive of a hard disk drive is most commonly drive C:. A C > tells you that DOS is looking in the hard disk.

3. A hard disk is a storage device capable of holding large amounts of information.

4. Hard disks are similar to floppy disks in that they store information in a similar manner. They differ from floppy disks in that they consist of rigid platters, instead of flexible disks, and hold considerably more information than floppy disks.

5. The number of platters found in a hard disk drive determine the amount of information that the drive can store.

6. The standard hard disk drive used on microcomputers is known as a *Winchester drive.*

7. A disk crash is caused when a read/write head comes in contact with a disk platter.

8. Either PARK or SHIPDISK should be used to park the read/write heads of your hard disk before you turn your computer off and before you move it.

9. On hard disk drives, DOS refers to cylinder location. On floppy disks, it refers to track and sector location.

10. Hard disks require DOS 2.0 or greater. DOS 3.0 and above provides more DOS commands that are available for hard disk operations.

11. FDISK is a DOS command that provides for the initial access of a hard disk. It can also separate the hard disk into smaller disk drives by means of an electrical partition.

12. BACKUP allows you to create an identical copy of a hard disk including all files and subdirectories.

13. RESTORE allows you to replace the information stored onto the backup medium back onto the hard disk.

14. Hard disk users store their applications software programs and DOS on their hard disks. Some users even store data files.

15. The listing of subdirectories is known as a *path.* Paths can sometimes be cumbersome to type out. Batch files can be created that will move you within subdirectories without having to type the entire path each time you wish to move to a subdirectory.

***Application
Exercises***

These exercises can be done as reinforcement of directory and sub-directory use on floppy disk systems. Unless otherwise directed, these exercises should be performed on floppy disk-based systems.

Use the **BACKUP** disk as the source disk and the **Practice** disk (representing the hard disk) as the target disk. Refer to the tree structure in Figure 6.8.

1. Reformat the **Practice** disk with the volume label PRACTICE.

2. Create all the second-level subdirectories shown: DOS, WORDP, SPREADS, DATAB, COMM, UTIL.

3. Create third-level subdirectories: MMATE, LOTUSV2, DBASE.

4. Create fourth-level subdirectories under MMATE: JOE, JANE.

5. Create fifth-level subdirectories under JANE: PERSONAL, OFFMEMOS, BOOKS.

6. Copy from **BACKUP** disk all the DBF files to DBASE on the **Practice** disk.

7. Copy from **BACKUP** disk all the DOC files to BOOKS on the **Practice** disk.

8. Copy MOVIE.LST from **BACKUP** disk to OFFMEMOS on the **Practice** disk.

9. Use the DOS external command TREE.COM to obtain a listing of the subdirectories and files on the **Practice** disk. Redirect the output to the printer. *Note:* This exercise cannot be performed if your computer's disk drives are different sizes.

Figure 6.8

Tree diagram for Application Exercises.

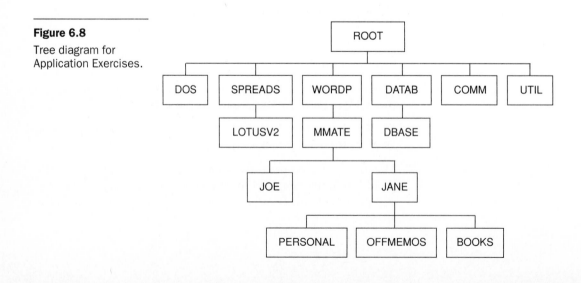

Comprehension Questions

Answer the following questions.

1. Explain the difference between a hard disk and a floppy disk.

2. Explain why a hard disk holds more information than a floppy disk.

3. Explain why subdirectories are important to hard disk organization.

4. Explain why FDISK is used.

5. Describe how to format a hard disk.

6. Use the diagram in Figure 6.9 and answer the questions that follow.

   a. What are the steps to move to WSTAR from the root directory?

   b. How would you change the C> to C:\WORDP> when you are in the root directory?

   c. Explain two methods of copying a file LETTER1.DOC from a floppy disk to a subdirectory WSTAR.

   d. Explain two methods of copying a file from a hard disk subdirectory to the root directory.

Figure 6.9

Tree diagram for Comprehension Question 6.

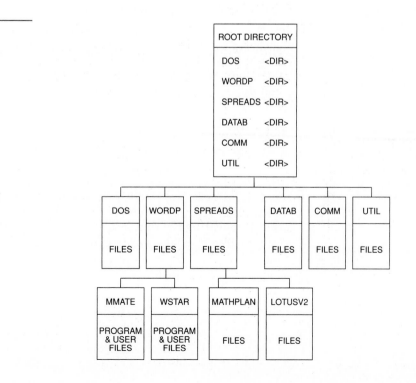

7. Explain why you would use a DOS partition.

8. Explain what each of the following commands do.

    a. `A>COPY DATA1.DBF C:\DATAB`

    b. `C>COPY C:\DATAB\DATA1.DBF A:`

    c. `A>FDISK C:`

    d. `A>FORMAT C: /S/V`

    e. `C>BACKUP C:\ A: /S`

    f. `A>RESTORE A: C: /S`

    g. `C>BACKUP C:*.COM A:`

    h. `C:\>SHIPDISK`

    i. `C>COPY C:\DATAB C:\BACKDB`

    j. `A>ERASE C:\DATAB`

    k. `C>ERASE DATAB`

9. Explain the difference between BACKUP and RESTORE.

Completion Exercises

Complete the following sentences.

1. A _____ is caused when a read/write head comes in contact with a platter, causing loss of valuable information.

2. If you need to move a computer that has a hard disk in it, you should _____ the read/write heads before transporting it.

3. On a hard disk, DOS refers to _____ instead of tracks and sectors.

4. A hard disk should always be formatted with the _____ command.

5. _____ should be used to back up a hard disk. _____ is used only in the event of a disk crash or when duplicating the contents from one hard disk onto another from the floppy disk copies created by the former command.

Matching Exercises

Choose the correct letter from the right-hand column.

1. SHIPDISK

    a. A command that cannot be used with hard disks

2. DISKCOPY

    b. A listing of subdirectories

3. FDISK

    c. A command to create an identical copy of the contents of a hard disk

4. BACKUP

    d. A command used before the FORMAT command

5. RESTORE

    e. A command to replace the information stored onto the backup medium back onto the hard disk

6. PATH

    f. A command used to park a hard disk

7

Batch
Files

When you have completed this chapter, you will be able to

Learning Objectives:

1. Explain what a batch file is.

2. Explain why batch files are used.

3. Explain what batch files contain.

4. Explain what an AUTOEXEC.BAT file is.

Performance Objectives:

1. Create several batch files.

2. Create an AUTOEXEC.BAT file.

Chapter Overview

Many of the activities that you learned to perform in previous chapters can now be simplified through the use of batch files. Batch files provide a powerful tool for increasing productivity. In this chapter, you will learn how to create and use batch files. Batch files enable you to do the following kinds of activities more efficiently:

1. Change subdirectories without having to type in a lengthy subdirectory path

2. Display the contents of one or more text files, using a single command

3. Send the contents of multiple text files to the printer

4. Delete, copy, and rename one or more files with one command

5. Create a self-booting applications program disk

6. Access a menu system for hard disk management

What is a Batch File?

A batch file is a text file that contains a series of DOS commands. The commands are stored in the file in the order in which you wish to have them carried out. For example, if you wanted to clear the screen and display a directory of a disk, you could create a batch file that would accomplish both these tasks by placing the CLS and DIR commands within the file. The commands within the file would be listed as

```
CLS
DIR
```

If the DIR preceded the CLS within the batch file, the directory command would be carried out first.

How Are Batch Files Created?

Batch files can be created using the DOS editor EDLIN or by using COPY CON. Other methods can be used, but these two can be used within DOS. In this chapter, you will create batch files using COPY CON. To create a batch file using COPY CON,

1. Type COPY CON followed by any filename and the extension BAT, and then press the Enter key.

2. List each DOS command on a separate line.

3. Depress F6 or Ctrl-Z followed by the Enter key to save the file.

What Commands Are Stored in Batch Files?

Any command that can be given to DOS at a system prompt can be stored in batch files. These commands include all the DOS external and internal commands, the filename of any applications program, and a number of special batch commands.

A sample of the special DOS batch processing commands, and what each does, is as follows:

Command	What It Does
ECHO ON	Displays to the screen the commands being executed within the batch file.
ECHO OFF	Prevents the commands being executed within the batch file from displaying to the screen.
ECHO (Message)	Displays the message following the ECHO command, regardless of whether the ECHO OFF command has been used before this command.
FOR IN DO	Allows you to carry out a command in a batch file more than once.
GOTO (Label)	Allows you to redirect the batch file to execute commands out of sequence.
IF (Condition)	Allows you to specify a command if a condition is met.
IF NOT (Condition)	Allows you to specify a command if a condition is not met.
SHIFT	Moves the list of parameters you type with a batch command one position to the left. For example, suppose you type three parameters: %1,%2,%3. After a SHIFT command is used, %1 is dropped off, %2 moves into the position of %1, and %3 moves into the position of %2. Parameters are discussed later in this chapter.

PAUSE

Pauses the execution of the batch file until a key is depressed on the keyboard. When PAUSE is used in a batch file, it causes the message "Strike a key when ready" to appear.

REM

Allows you to document your batch files with remarks about their operations. These remarks do not display to the screen if the ECHO is turned off.

How Are Batch Files Executed?

Batch files can be executed at a DOS prompt by typing the filename and pressing ENTER. Since batch files are usually located in the root directory of a disk or within a subdirectory that you might create especially for batch files, you should use a command that tells DOS where to look for these files. This command is called the PATH command. Without specifying a PATH, you would have to move to the subdirectory where the batch file was located or specify the directory location of the batch file within a command line to execute the batch file. For example,

C:\PATH

C:\;C:\BATFILES;C:\DOS
is a path command that tells DOS to search the root directory and the subdirectories BATFILES and DOS if it cannot locate the file within the current subdirectory.

C:\

is the root directory.

C:\BATFILES

is the subdirectory that was created to contain batch files.

C:\DOS

is the subdirectory that was created to contain the DOS external commands. This subdirectory is listed within the PATH command to enable you to use any external DOS command at any system prompt.

Tip: If a COM or EXE file with the same filename exists, the COM or EXE file will be called up before the batch (BAT) file. DOS looks for files in the following order: COM, EXE, BAT, and data files.

What is an AUTOEXEC.BAT File?

An AUTOEXEC.BAT file is a special type of batch file that is automatically executed when you boot your computer. This batch file is placed in the root directory of a disk. An AUTOEXEC.BAT file on a floppy disk system enables you to create a self-booting applications program disk that asks you the date and time and loads the applications program of your choice. On hard disk systems, the AUTOEXEC.BAT file is used to specify a path, ask you the date and time, and then load a hard disk menu or file management program.

Hands-On Activities

In the following exercises, you will create a number of batch files that include many of the DOS internal, external, and special batch file processing commands. In addition, you will learn to create a self-booting program disk and an AUTOEXEC.BAT file used to call up a menu on a hard disk. You will be performing these exercises on the disk labeled PRACTICE. Refer to the tree structure in Figure 7.1 as you perform these exercises.

Note: Be sure you have created this structure on the **Practice** disk before performing the following exercises.

Figure 7.1

The diagram for Hands-On Activities.

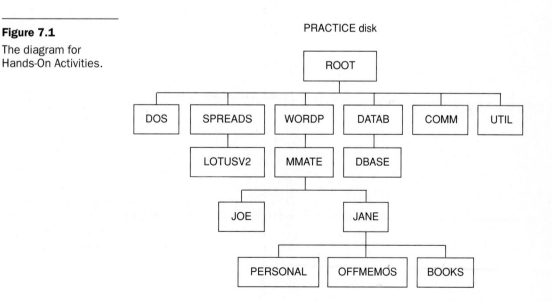

PRACTICE disk

| *How to Use the PATH Command* | In this exercise, you will create a PATH command that instructs DOS to look in the root directory of Drive A: if it cannot find a file. You will also set the system prompt to display your location within the tree structure. |

Use **Practice** disk in Drive A:.

What to Do	*What Happens*
Step 1	Type PATH A:\ and press Enter.	Nothing.
Step 2	Type PROMPT PG and press Enter.	The system prompt displays your location.

```
A>PATH A:\

A>PROMPT $P$G

A:\>
```

▶ *Tells DOS where to look for COM, EXE, and BAT files.*
▶ *Lists your location within the subdirectory with the system prompt.*

A Simple Batch File

You will create a simple batch file using COPY CON that does the following:

Command	Result
CLS	Clears the screen.
ECHO	Types a message.
PAUSE	Pauses and displays a message.
DIR	Displays the current directory.

In this exercise, the ECHO will remain on. This means that all of the commands will be displayed on the screen, followed by the results.

Use the **Practice** disk in Drive A:.

	What to Do	*What Happens*
Step 1	Obtain an A:\>.	Nothing.
Step 2	Type COPY CON SIMPLE.BAT and press the Enter key.	
Step 3	Type CLS and press the Enter key.	
Step 4	Type ECHO This is a Message on the Echo line. and press the Enter key.	
Step 5	Type PAUSE and press the Enter key.	
Step 6	Type DIR and press the Enter key.	
Step 7	Press F6 or Ctrl-Z and press the Enter key.	The file is saved.

How to Execute a Batch File

To execute a batch file you need only type in the filename for the batch file. However, if you are in a subdirectory other than the one that contains the batch file and the last path command used did not list the subdirectory, you must also list the drive and subdirectory before the filename to execute the batch file.

	What to Do	*What Happens*
Step 1	Obtain an A:\>.	Nothing.
Step 2	Type SIMPLE and press the Enter key.	The first three commands are executed.
Step 3	Press any key to continue.	The final command is executed and an A:\> appears.

In this exercise you will create the same batch file using COPY CON, but add the command ECHO OFF so the commands will not be displayed on the screen.

Command	Result
ECHO OFF	Stops the commands from being displayed.
CLS	Clears the screen.
ECHO	Types a message.
PAUSE	Pauses and displays a message.
DIR	Displays the current directory.

	What to Do	*What Happens*
Step 1	Obtain an A:\>.	Nothing.
Step 2	Type COPY CON SIMPLE.BAT and press the Enter key.	
Step 3	Type ECHO OFF and press the Enter key.	
Step 4	Type CLS and press the Enter key.	
Step 5	Type ECHO This is a Message on the Echo line. and press the Enter key.	
Step 6	Type PAUSE and press the Enter key.	
Step 7	Type DIR and press the Enter Key.	
Step 8	Press F6 or Ctrl-Z and press the Enter key.	The file is saved.

Next, you will execute the batch file.

	What to Do	*What Happens*
Step 1	Obtain an A:\>.	Nothing.
Step 2	Type SIMPLE and press the Enter key.	The first four commands are executed.
Step 3	Press any key to continue.	The last command is executed and an A:\> appears.

Creating a Batch File That Loads an Applications Program

In this exercise you will create a batch file that moves from the root directory to the subdirectory WORDP, loads the mock word processing program WP.COM automatically, and returns to the A:\> prompt.

Use **Practice** disk in Drive A:

	What to Do	*What Happens*
Step 1	Copy the WP.COM file from the **BACKUP** disk to the subdirectory WORDP on the **Practice** disk.	The file is copied.
Step 2	Obtain an A:\>.	Nothing.
Step 3	Type COPY CON WP.BAT and press the Enter key.	
Step 4	Type ECHO OFF and press the Enter key.	
Step 5	Type CD WORDP and press the Enter key.	
Step 6	Type WP and press the Enter key.	
Step 7	Type CD \ and press the Enter key.	
Step 8	Press F6 or Ctrl-Z and then the Enter key to save the file.	

Note: Be sure to complete Step 1.

Load the application WP.COM file using the batch file WP.BAT.

	What to Do	*What Happens*
Step 1	Obtain an A:\>.	Nothing.
Step 2	Type WP and press the Enter key.	The mock program appears.
Step 3	Press 9 to exit the mock program.	An A:\> appears.

Review Exercises

1. Copy the file DB.COM from the **BACKUP** disk to the subdirectory DATAB\DBASE on the **Practice** disk.

2. Copy the file SS.COM from the **BACKUP** disk to the subdirectory SPREADS\LOTUSV2 on the **Practice** disk.

3. Create a batch file that loads the DB.COM file from the root directory.

4. Create a batch file that loads the SS.COM file from the root directory.

5. Call up DB.COM and SS.COM and use the mock programs. Note that to exit SS.COM, press the / key followed by Q; to exit DB.COM, press Q.

6. Copy the DBF files from **BACKUP** to the subdirectory DATAB\DBASE on the **Practice** disk.

How to Create a Batch File That Displays a Number of Files

If you needed to type out the contents of several files a number of times during the day or week, you might create a batch file to do this type of activity for you. In this exercise, you will create a batch file to automatically display DATA1.DBF, DATA2.DBF, and DATA3.DBF when executed.

Use the **Practice** disk in Drive A:.

	What to Do	*What Happens*
Step 1	Type COPY CON TYPE3TXT.BAT and press Enter.	Nothing.
Step 2	Type CD \DATAB\DBASE and press Enter.	Nothing.

Step 3	Type TYPE DATA1.DBF and press Enter.	Nothing.
Step 4	Type PAUSE and press Enter.	Nothing.
Step 5	Type TYPE DATA2.DBF and press Enter.	Nothing.
Step 6	Type PAUSE and press Enter.	Nothing.
Step 7	Type TYPE DATA3.DBF and press Enter.	Nothing.
Step 8	Type CD \ and press Enter.	Nothing.
Step 9	Press F6 or Ctrl-Z and then Enter.	See screen that follows.

```
A:\>COPY CON TYPE3TXT.BAT
CD\DATAB\DBASE
TYPE DATA1.DBF
PAUSE
TYPE DATA2.DBF
PAUSE
TYPE DATA3.DBF
CD\
^Z
          1 File(s) copied

A:\>
```

▶ *Changes directory to DBASE.*
▶ *Displays the contents of DATA1.DBF.*
▶ *Pauses batch file execution.*
▶ *Displays contents of DATA2.DBF.*
▶ *Pauses batch file execution.*
▶ *Displays contents of DATA3.DBF.*
▶ *Changes to the root directory.*
▶ *Ends input.*

Review Exercises

1. Display the contents of the batch file TYPE3TXT.BAT.

2. Execute the batch file TYPE3TXT.BAT.

3. What caused the message "Strike a key when ready" to appear?

4. How would you send the files within the batch file to the printer?

Answers

3. The PAUSE command.

4. Use the > PRN. For example, TYPE DATA1.DBF > PRN.

How to Use
Parameters

In the previous exercise, you knew the files that you wished to have displayed when you were creating the batch file. If you did not know the filenames of the files until the batch file was going to be executed, you could use parameters. Parameters are symbols that allow you to pass values from one memory location to another.

This exercise is the same as the previous exercise, except that it uses parameters. In this case, %1, %2, and %3 are the parameters that stand for "file 1," "file 2," and "file 3." File 1 is passed to %1, file 2 is passed to %2, and file 3 to %3.

Use **Practice** disk in Drive A:.

	What to Do	*What Happens*
Step 1	Type COPY CON TYPE3RP.BAT and press Enter.	Nothing.
Step 2	Type CD \DATAB\DBASE and press Enter.	Nothing.
Step 3	Type TYPE %1 and press Enter.	Nothing.
Step 4	Type PAUSE and press Enter.	Nothing.
Step 5	Type TYPE %2 and press Enter.	Nothing.
Step 6	Type PAUSE and press Enter.	Nothing.
Step 7	Type TYPE %3 and press Enter.	Nothing.
Step 8	Type CD \ and press Enter.	Nothing.
Step 9	Depress F6 or Ctrl-Z and press Enter.	

How to Execute a Batch File That Contains Parameters

When executing a batch file with parameters, you need to type in the batch file filename, followed by the names of the files that will stand for the parameters %1, %2, %3, and so on. Each filename is separated from the others by a space.

Use the **Practice** disk in Drive A:.

	What to Do	*What Happens*
Step 1	Type TYPE3RP DATA1.DBF DATA2.DBF DATA3.DBF and press Enter.	See screen that follows.

```
A:\>TYPE3RP.BAT DATA1.DBF DATA2.DBF DATA3.DBF


A:\>CD \DATAB\DBASE


A:\DATAB\DBASE>TYPE DATA1.DBF
Your Name    ------THIS FILE WAS NOT CREATED BY YOU.
Your Address


A:\DATAB\DBASE>PAUSE
Strike a key when ready . . .

A:\DATAB\DBASE>TYPE DATA2.DBF
(XXX) XXX-XXXX        ------YOUR PHONE NUMBER.
        ------THIS FILE WAS NOT CREATED BY YOU.
A:\DATAB\DBASE>PAUSE
Strike a key when ready . . .


A:\DATAB\DBASE>TYPE DATA3.DBF
August 12, 1957 ----THIS FILE WAS NOT CREATED BY YOU.
123-45-6789


A:\DATAB\DBASE>CD \


A:\>
```

▶ Lists batch filename plus %1 %2 %3 parameters.

▶ First command from batch file executes. Changes to DBASE subdirectory.

▶ Second command executes. Displays contents of DATA1.DBF.

▶ Third command executes. Pauses file execution. Strike any key.

▶ Fourth command executes. Displays contents of DATA2.DBF: phone number.

▶ Fifth command executes. Pauses file execution.

▶ Sixth command executes. Displays contents of DATA3.DBF.

▶ Seventh command executes. Changes to root directory. Batch file is done.

Using parameters allows you to pass any files within the specified subdirectory in any order.

*Review
Exercises*

1. Compare the output of this batch file that uses parameters with the output of the previous batch file that listed the three files that were to be displayed.

2. Use the batch file TYPE3RP, again switching DATA3.DBF with DATA1.DBF. Compare the results with Review Exercise 1's results.

*How to Use Sets
with Replaceable
Parameters*

You can perform an activity more than once using the FOR IN DO special DOS batch file command. This command is used in the following way:

```
FOR %%p IN (SET) DO <COMMAND>
```

FOR %%p IN	FOR each item that falls within a particular set
(SET)	Any number of items that make up a unit; for example, DATA1.1DBF, DATA2.DBF, DATA3 .DBF, and DATA4.DBF make up the set *.DBF within the subdirectory \DATAB\DBASE.
DO	Perform the command following the DO on each of the items in the set.

When using sets, you can use parameters, individual filenames, or wildcards to specify the set.

In this exercise, you will create a batch file that displays all the DBF files from the subdirectory \DATAB\DBASE.

Use **Practice** disk in Drive A:.

	What to Do	*What Happens*
Step 1	At an A:\>, type COPY CON WILDRP.BAT and press Enter.	Nothing.
Step 2	Type ECHO OFF and press Enter.	Nothing.
Step 3	Type CD \DATAB\DBASE and press Enter.	Nothing.
Step 4	Type FOR %%p IN (%1) DO TYPE %%p and press Enter.	Nothing.

Step 5	Type CD \ and press Enter.	Nothing.
Step 6	Depress F6 or Ctrl-Z and then Enter.	See screen that follows.

```
A:\> COPY CON WILDRP.BAT
ECHO OFF
CD \DATAB\DBASE
FOR %%P IN (%1) DO TYPE %%P
CD \
^Z
        1 File(s) copied

A:\>
```

▶Starts input.
▶Tells DOS not to display commands.
▶Changes directory to DBASE.
▶Types each item of %1.
▶Changes to root directory.
▶Ends the input.

Review Exercises

1. Activate the batch file WILDRP.BAT. What command is used?

2. Why was ECHO OFF used in the first line of the batch file?

3. Why was PAUSE not used?

Answers

1. Use WILDRP *.DBF. (DBF represents the %1 parameter.)

2. Whenever ECHO OFF is used, the batch file commands will not display while the batch file is executing. Only the results of the commands are displayed.

3. Whenever you want only the contents of the file to be displayed, the PAUSE should not be used because it causes the message "Strike a key when ready" to appear.

How to Use a Batch File to Copy Files

If you were planning to copy and rename multiple files within a sub-directory, you could create a batch file to perform this activity.

In this exercise, you will copy and rename all the DBF files within the subdirectory DBASE with the extension BAK.

Use **Practice** disk in Drive A:.

	What to Do	*What Happens*
Step 1	Type COPY CON COPYREN.BAT and press Enter.	Nothing.
Step 2	Type CD \DATAB\DBASE and press Enter.	Nothing.
Step 3	Type COPY *.DBF *.BAK and press Enter.	Nothing.
Step 4	Type CD \ and press Enter.	
Step 5	Depress F6 or Ctrl-Z and press Enter.	See screen that follows.

```
A:\> COPY CON COPYREN.BAT
CD \DATAB\DBASE
COPY *.DBF *.BAK
CD \
^Z
        1 File(s) copied

A:\>
```

▶ *Starts input.*
▶ *Changes directory to DBASE.*
▶ *Copies all DBF files to BAK.*
▶ *Changes to the root directory.*
▶ *Ends input.*
▶ *File created.*

Review Exercises

1. Execute the batch file.

2. How many files were copied?

3. Why was ECHO OFF not used?

Answers

2. 3 files.

3. You wanted to see the command that DOS will be performing. (If it was wrong, you could press Ctrl-C to stop the batch file from executing.)

How to Create a Batch File to Erase Selected Files

A batch file can be created that will erase a number of selected files. You should be very careful when using a batch file for this purpose. In this exercise, you will delete the files that you just copied and renamed (all the files with the extension BAK).

Use **Practice** disk in Drive A:.

	What to Do	*What Happens*
Step 1	Type COPY CON DELFILES.BAT and press Enter.	Nothing.
Step 2	Type ECHO OFF and press Enter.	Nothing.
Step 3	Type DIR %2 and press Enter.	
Step 4	Type ECHO This batch file is about and press Enter.	The words "ECHO This batch file is about" are typed on the screen.
Step 5	Type ECHO to erase all the %1 files and press Enter.	"ECHO to erase all the %1 files" is typed on the screen.
Step 6	Type ECHO from the subdirectory %2. and press Enter.	"ECHO from the subdirectory %2" is typed on the screen.
Step 7	Type ECHO Press Ctrl-C to Abort or and press Enter.	"ECHO Press Ctrl-C to Abort or" is typed on the screen.

Step 8	Type PAUSE and press Enter.	Nothing.
Step 9	Type CD %2 and Enter.	Nothing.
Step 10	Type ERASE *.%1 and press Enter.	Nothing.
Step 11	Type CD \ and press Enter.	Nothing.
Step 12	Type DIR %2 and press Enter.	Nothing.
Step 13	Depress F6 or Ctrl-Z and then Enter.	See screen that follows.

```
A:\COPY CON DELFILES.BAT
ECHO OFF
DIR %2
ECHO This batch file is about
ECHO to erase all the %1 files
ECHO from the subdirectory %2.
ECHO Press Ctrl-C to Abort or
PAUSE
CD %2
ERASE *.%1
CD \
DIR %2
^Z
          1 File(s) copied

A:\>
```

► *Turns off commands to display to the screen.*
► *Lists the directory of the parameter %2.*
► *Displays the message to the screen.*

► *Stops the execution so you can use Ctrl-C if you wish.*
► *Changes to the subdirectory.*
► *Erases the files specified by the parameter %1.*
► *Changes back to the root directory.*
► *Lists the directory of the %2 parameter.*
► *Ends the input.*
► *File created.*

► *Batch file ended.*

To execute the batch file, type in the filename DELFILES followed by an extension of your choice, followed by the subdirectory path where the files are to be erased. For example,

```
A:\>DELFILES BAK \DATAB\DBASE
```

Note: BAK is the parameter %1 and will be inserted into the batch file wherever the %1 parameter is listed. \DATAB\DBASE is %2 and will be inserted wherever the %2 parameter is listed.

How to Use the AUTOEXEC.BAT File to Create Self-Booting Disks

When you purchase applications program disks from manufacturers, the disks are not permitted to contain DOS, due to copyright laws. Two ways that self-booting disks can be made are

1. Format a blank disk using the /S option, copy the applications program files to that disk, and then create on that disk an AUTOEXEC.BAT file that contains the filename that loads the program.

2. Use the SYS DOS command to add the DOS system files to the applications program disk and then create on that disk an AUTOEXEC.BAT file that contains the filename that loads the program.

Tip: Some applications programs disks do not have enough free disk space to permit the system files to be added. In this case, you cannot create self-booting disks.

Once you have the system files and the applications programs on the same disk, you can create an AUTOEXEC.BAT file.

In this exercise, we will use the first method of creating a self-booting disk. To find out how to use SYS, refer to your DOS manual.

	What to Do	*What Happens*
Step 1	Insert a DOS disk in Drive A:.	Nothing.
Step 2	Format **Practice** disk with the system /S and volume label PRACTICE.	**Practice** disk is formatted.
	Use **Practice** disk in Drive A:.	
Step 3	Obtain an A>.	Nothing.
Step 4	Type COPY CON AUTOEXEC.BAT and press Enter.	Nothing.
Step 5	Type PATH A:\ and press Enter.	Nothing.
Step 6	Type PROMPT PG and press Enter.	Nothing.
Step 7	Type TIME and press Enter.	Nothing.
Step 8	Type DATE and press Enter.	Nothing.

Step 9	Type WP and press Enter.	Nothing.

Step 10	Depress F6 or Ctrl-Z and Enter.	See screen that follows.

```
A>COPY CON AUTOEXEC.BAT
PATH A:\
PROMPT $P$G
TIME
DATE
WP
^Z
        1 File(s) copied

A>
```

▶ *Tells DOS to look in root directory.*
▶ *Sets prompt to display subdirectories.*

▶ *Tells DOS to execute the batch file WP.*

Step 11	Copy all of the COM files from the **BACKUP** disk to the **Practice** disk.	

Step 12	Perform a warm boot (Ctrl-Alt-Del).	See screen that follows.

```
A>PATH A:\


A>PROMPT $P$G


A:\TIME
Current time is 17:09:50.13
Enter new time:
A:\DATE
Current date is Tue 5-23-1991
Enter new date:


A:\>WP
```

▶ *Tells DOS to look in the root directory if it cannot find the file in the current directory.*
▶ *Changes the prompt to list your location within the tree structure.*

▶ *Asks you to enter the current time.*

▶ *Asks you to enter the current date.*

▶ *Loads the program that has the file-name WP.COM (or EXE or BAT); then the word processing menu appears.*

If the word processing screen appears, you have a self-booting disk. At this point, you would normally use the applications program. Since this is a demonstration program, depress 9 to exit.

Summary Points

1. Batch files are a powerful tool for increasing productivity.

2. A batch file is a text file that contains a series of DOS commands. The commands are stored in the file in the order in which you wish to have them carried out.

3. Batch files can be created using the DOS editor EDLIN or by using COPY CON. Other methods can be used, but these are the two methods within DOS.

4. Any command that can be given to DOS at a system prompt can be stored in a batch file. These commands include all the DOS external and internal commands, the filename of any applications program, and a number of special batch commands.

5. Batch files are executed at a DOS prompt by typing the filename and pressing Enter.

6. Since batch files are usually located in the root directory of a disk or within a subdirectory that you might create especially for batch files, you should use a command that tells DOS where to look for these files. This command is called the PATH command.

7. An AUTOEXEC.BAT file is a special type of batch file that is automatically executed when you boot your computer. This batch file is placed in the root directory of a disk.

8. An AUTOEXEC.BAT file on a floppy disk system enables you to create a self-booting applications program disk that asks you the date and time and loads the applications program of your choice.

9. On hard disk systems, the AUTOEXEC.BAT file is used to specify a path, ask you the date and time, and then load a hard disk menu or file management program.

Application Exercises

Do the following exercises at your computer.

1. Create an AUTOEXEC.BAT file on the **Practice** disk that does the following:

   a. Turns the echo off

   b. Changes the prompt to display your location within the tree structure

   c. Sets the path so that DOS will look in the root directory if it cannot find the file it is looking for in the current directory

   d. Displays the version of DOS that is being used

   e. Prompts you for the correct TIME and DATE

   f. Lists the files within the root directory screen by screen

   g. Pauses the batch file.

   h. Loads the applications program DB.COM

2. Boot the computer with the **Practice** disk in Drive A:. Was the DB program activated? How did you leave the DB program?

3. Using COPY CON, create a file called HELLO.TXT on **Practice** disk. The contents of HELLO.TXT should read,

   ```
   Good Morning. It is nice to see you again.
   ```

4. Create a BAT file called MESSAGE.BAT on **Practice** disk that when activated lists the contents of the HELLO.TXT file.

5. Create a BAT file called MAKE.BAT on **Practice** disk that would make the following tree structure:

6. Execute the MAKE batch file on the **Practice** disk. Did it work without giving you the message "Invalid directory"?

7. Use the DOS external command TREE to list the subdirectories and all the files on the **Practice** disk and send the results to the printer. Were the root directory and its files listed? If not, list them also.

Comprehension Questions

For these comprehension questions, refer to the tree structure in Figure 7.2.

1. Is it possible to create a BAT file that would remove all third-level subdirectories without first deleting all files and subdirectories below?

2. If an AUTOEXEC.BAT file is not in a root directory, will it be activated during a system boot?

3. If you wanted to create a BAT file within the < PERSONAL > subdirectory that would move you to the < DBASE > subdirectory on activation, what would be the contents of the file?

4. Could this BAT file be placed in other subdirectories and still perform the same objective?

Figure 7.2

Tree diagram for Comprehension Questions.

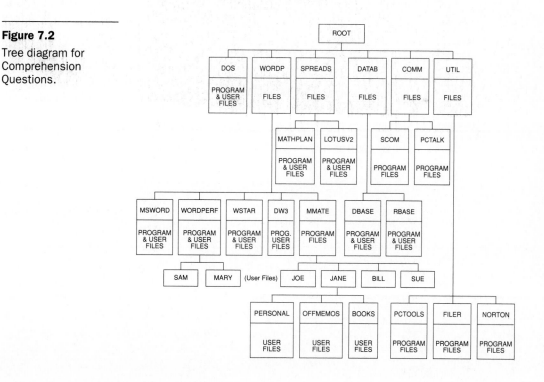

Completion Exercises

Complete the following sentences.

1. A _____ file is a file that contains a series of DOS commands.

2. _____ or _____ is used to save a batch file.

3. %1, %2, and %3 are called _____.

4. _____ is a special batch file.

5. The special batch command _____ allows you to carry out a command more than once in a batch file.

6. Explain what each of the following commands do:

    a. PATH C:\;C:\DOS;C:\UTIL

    b. FOR %%p IN (%1 %2 %3) DO COPY %%p A:\

    c. FOR %%p IN (%1) DO ERASE %%p

    d. FOR %%p IN (CASE?.*) DO REM %% *.BAK

Matching Exercises

Choose the correct letter from the right-hand column.

1. PAUSE

    a. Tells DOS that if it does not find a file within the current subdirectory, look in the subdirectory entitled DOS

2. REM

    b. Keeps the DOS commands within a batch file from being displayed onto a monitor as they are being called up

3. PATH C:\;C:\DOS

    c. Displays on the screen a message to the user if ECHO is set to ON

4. ECHO OFF

    d. Prompts the user to press a key when ready

8

EDLIN— The DOS Editor

When you have completed this chapter, you will be able to

Learning Objectives:

1. Explain what an editor is.

2. Describe the purpose of an editor.

Performance Objectives:

1. Create a file using EDLIN.

2. List the contents of a file using EDLIN.

3. Insert text in a file using EDLIN.

4. Delete text from a file using EDLIN.

5. Copy text within a file using EDLIN.

6. Move text within a file using EDLIN.

7. Search for a word or words within a file using EDLIN.

8. Replace a word or words within a file using EDLIN.

9. Save the changes made during editing using EDLIN.

Chapter Overview

In the previous chapters, you created files using COPY CON. COPY CON provides an easy way to create short batch files that do not have to be edited. When creating larger files, a means of making corrections or revisions is needed. DOS provides its own editor, called EDLIN, to be used for this purpose. In this chapter, you will learn to use some of the common EDLIN editing commands.

What is an Editor?

An editor is a program that allows you to create a file or alter an existing file. Several types of editors are used:

1. Editors that are used with program languages such as Turbo Pascal or Turbo C

2. More sophisticated editors, known as word processors or word processing applications software, such as WordStar, Multimate, WordPerfect, and MicroSoft Word

3. Limited editors such as the DOS editor EDLIN and SideKick, an add-on program that can be used for editing purposes

Why is EDLIN Used?

Although some of the first two types of editors can be used to edit batch files, we will limit our discussion to EDLIN because EDLIN is a built-in DOS editor.

How is EDLIN Used?

EDLIN was created primarily as a tool to edit batch files and short text files. It is part of the DOS disk-resident command structure. To access EDLIN, you must have a disk with the EDLIN.COM file on it.

What Can You Do with EDLIN?

Once you have entered EDLIN by typing in EDLIN followed by the filename and extension of an existing file or a file you wish to create, EDLIN prompts you for an action. The EDLIN prompt is the asterisk (*). At the EDLIN prompt, you can type in any of the following letters. Each letter represents an EDLIN command.

Command	What It Does
L	Lists the contents of the file you are editing. (The number of lines listed and their location within the file depend on several items.)
I	Inserts a line(s) of text. (Either at the current position or at a specified location.)
D	Deletes a line or several lines of text from the file.

C   Copies a line or series of lines to another position within the file.

M   Moves a line or series of lines to another position within the file.

R   Replaces a string of text (characters) with another string.

S   Searches the file, or a specific number of lines within the file, for a specific string of text.

T   Transfers a specific line(s) to another file.

W   Writes edited lines to a specified file.

E   Exits and saves the edited file with the current changes.

Q   Quits EDLIN without saving any of the changes.

Hands-On Activities

In the following exercises, you will learn how to create and edit files using EDLIN. The advantage of using EDLIN over COPY CON is that you can change any part of the file without retyping the whole file. EDLIN can, however, be used to edit files created using COPY CON.

The advantage of EDLIN over other editors is that EDLIN is convenient in that it is one of the files supplied to purchasers of DOS.

How to Create a Batch File Using EDLIN

You will be creating the file AUTO.BAT, which contains the following:

```
ECHO OFF
TIME
DATE
PAUSE
WP
```

This exercise has no purpose other than to show you how to create a short batch file using EDLIN.

Use **DOS** disk in Drive A: and **BACKUP** in Drive B:.

	What to Do	*What Happens*
Step 1	At an A>	Nothing.
Step 2	Type EDLIN B:AUTO.BAT and press Enter.	See screen that follows.

```
A>EDLIN B:AUTO.BAT
New file

*
```

▶*Means you are creating a new file.*
▶*EDLIN prompt for a command.*

Step 3	Type I and press Enter to begin inserting text.	See screen that follows.

```
*I

    1:*
```

▶*This is where you will begin entering text.*

Step 4	Type ECHO OFF and press Enter.	2:* appears.
Step 5	Type TIME and press Enter.	3:* appears.
Step 6	Type DATE and press Enter.	4:* appears.
Step 7	Type PAUSE and press Enter.	5:* appears.
Step 8	Type WP and press Enter.	6:* appears.
Step 9	Depress Ctrl-C to end the input process.	See screen that follows.

```
New file
*I
      1:*ECHO OFF
      2:*TIME
      3:*DATE
      4:*PAUSE
      5:*WP
      6:*^C
*
```

Now you should save the file and exit using the E command.

Step 10	At the EDLIN command prompt *	
Step 11	Type E and press Enter.	An A> appears.

To make sure that the file is correct, use the TYPE command to display its contents. For example,

A>TYPE B:AUTO.BAT

```
A:>TYPE AUTO.BAT
ECHO OFF
TIME
DATE
PAUSE
WP

A>
```

How to Insert a Line in an Existing File

Suppose you wanted to add a few lines to the file AUTO.BAT. EDLIN allows you to go back into the file and edit text.

Current File Contents	Desired File Contents
ECHO OFF	ECHO OFF
TIME	CLS
DATE	VER
PAUSE	DATE
WP	TIME
	CLS
	DB

Use **DOS** disk in Drive A: and **BACKUP** in Drive B:.

What to Do	*What Happens*
Step 1 Type EDLIN B:AUTO.BAT and press Enter.	See screen that follows.

```
A>EDLIN B:AUTO.BAT
End of input file
*
```

▶ *Means that a file exists.*
▶ *EDLIN prompt for a command.*

You should now list the contents of the file using the L command. The following are the different ways you can use the L command to list the contents of a file.

Command	Result
L (at the opening prompt)	Lists the first 23 lines. If fewer lines exist, all the lines in the file will be listed.
L (at any location in a file)	Lists the next 23 lines, beginning with the current line.
12L	Lists 23 lines, beginning with Line 12.
2,13L	Lists only Lines 2 through 13.

Step 2	Type L and press Enter to list the contents of the file (first 23 lines.) EDLIN can only display 23 lines at a time. If the text you wish to change is beyond Line 23, list a number near and preceding the desired line, followed by typing L and pressing Enter.	See screen that follows.

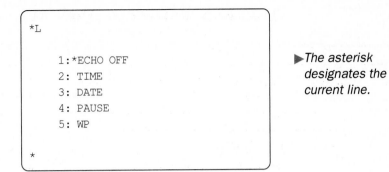

```
*L

    1:*ECHO OFF
    2: TIME
    3: DATE
    4: PAUSE
    5: WP


*
```

▶The asterisk
designates the
current line.

When using the I (insert) command, you need to specify a line at which input should begin. If you press 4I, EDLIN will begin inserting text at Line 4. If no line number is designated, EDLIN will begin inserting text with the current line (the line marked with the *, when you list the file).

To update the file, you first need to add the lines CLS and VER.

Step 3	Type 2 I and press Enter.	2:* appears.
Step 4	Type CLS and press Enter.	3:* appears.
Step 5	Type VER and press Enter.	4:* appears.
Step 6	Depress Ctrl-C.	See screen that follows.

```
End of input file
*L

    1:*ECHO OFF
    2: TIME
    3: DATE
    4: PAUSE
    4: WP
*2I
    2:*CLS
    3:*VER
    4:*^C


*
```

To make sure that the additions were made, list the file using the EDLIN command L as shown.

| Step 7 | Type L and press Enter. | See screen that follows. |

```
*L
     1: ECHO OFF
     2: CLS
     3: VER
     4:*TIME
     5: DATE
     6: PAUSE
     7: WP
   *
```

►*The current line has changed.*

How to Delete a Line

The delete command D can be used to delete one or more lines. If you press D and Enter without specifying a line, EDLIN deletes the current line. If you list a single line number before the D, EDLIN deletes only that line. If you want to delete several lines, you list the beginning and ending lines that you want deleted, separated by a comma, and then D, followed by pressing Enter. For example, to delete Lines 2 through 7, the delete command would look like this: * 2,7D and press Enter.

Now that you have inserted the lines CLS and VER, you should delete the line PAUSE.

What to Do	*What Happens*
Step 1	Type L and press Enter to list the file.	See screen that follows.

```
*L
     1: ECHO OFF
     2: CLS
     3: VER
     4:*TIME
     5: DATE
     6: PAUSE
     7: WP
   *
```

►*The current line.*

Step 2	Type 6D and press Enter to delete Line 6.	See screen that follows.

```
*6D
*
```

Tip: If you had not specified a line prior to the D command, EDLIN would have deleted Line 4 because Line 4 is the current line.

List the file by using L.

Step 3	Type L and press Enter.	See screen that follows.

```
*L

    1: ECHO OFF
    2: CLS
    3: VER
    4: TIME
    5: DATE
    6:*WP

*
```
▶*The current line.*

▶*EDLIN command prompt.*

How to Edit Without Using INSERT

To edit a single line, just press the letter of the line you wish to edit, followed by Enter. For example, to edit Line 14 the command would be

```
*14
```

and press Enter.

In this exercise, you will change WP to DB.

What to Do	*What Happens*
Step 1 Type 6 and press Enter to edit Line 6.	
Step 2 Type DB and press Enter.	See screen that follows.

```
*L
     1: ECHO OFF
     2: CLS
     3: VER
     4: TIME
     5: DATE
     6:*WP
*6
     6:*WP
     6:*DB
*
```

Tip: You can also use the arrow keys if you want to keep part of the line intact without having to retype it.

List the file by using L.

Step 3 Type L and press Enter.	See screen that follows.

```
*L

     1: ECHO OFF
     2: CLS
     3: VER
     4: TIME
     5: DATE
     6:*DB

*
```

How to Move a Line of Text

Moving a line or series of lines is accomplished by typing the line or line numbers you wish to copy, a comma and then the command M followed by pressing Enter. For example, if you wanted to copy Line 14 to Line 3, the command would be 14,14,3M and press Enter. And if you wanted to copy Lines 14 through 17 and place them in front of Line 3, you would use the command 14,17,3M and press Enter.

To complete the file update, there are only two things left to do. First, you need to move Line 4 (TIME) so that it follows (DATE).

List the file.

What to Do	*What Happens*
Step 1 Type L and press Enter.	See screen that follows.

```
*L

    1: ECHO OFF
    2: CLS
    3: VER
    4: TIME
    5: DATE
    6:*DB

*
```

| **Step 2**   Type 4,4,6M and press Enter. | See screen that follows. |

```
*L

    1: ECHO OFF
    2: CLS
    3: VER
    4: DATE
    5:*TIME
    6: DB
*4,4,6M
*
```

List the file.

Step 3	Type L and press Enter.	See screen that follows.

```
*L

    1: ECHO OFF
    2: CLS
    3: VER
    4: DATE
    5:*TIME
    6: DB

*
```

How to Copy a Line

To copy a line to another line, simply list the command in the following way:

```
Line,Line,LineC
```

For example,

4	The first line you will copy.
4	The last line you will copy.
6C	Where the line(s) are copied to.

Tip: If only one line is being copied, the line number must appear twice.

The last thing you need to do is copy the CLS to precede DB.

List the file.

	What to Do	*What Happens*
Step 1	Type L and press Enter.	See screen that follows.

```
*L

        1: ECHO OFF
        2: CLS
        3: VER
        4: DATE
        5:*TIME
        6: DB


*
```

Step 2   Type 2,2,6C and press Enter.   See screen that follows.

```
*2,2,6C
*
```

List the file.

Step 3   Type L and press Enter.   See screen that follows.

```
*L

        1: ECHO OFF
        2: CLS
        3: VER
        4: DATE
        5: TIME
        6:*CLS
        7: DB


*
```

How to
Search Text

To search, you must do the following:

1. List the range of lines that you wish EDLIN to search.

2. List the S command followed by the characters that you are searching for. The characters must be written as they appear in the file, including both uppercase and lowercase distinctions.

Tip: EDLIN will search the file until it finds the first occurrence of the string of characters. By placing a ? between the range and the S command, EDLIN will ask you if the string of characters it has found is the correct one. If it is, press Y for yes. If it is not, press N for no and EDLIN will continue searching the range for the next occurrence of the string of characters.

In this exercise, you will search for CLS.

List the file.

What to Do	*What Happens*
Step 1	Type L and press Enter.	See screen that follows.

```
*L

    1: ECHO OFF
    2: CLS
    3: VER
    4: TIME
    5: DATE
    6:*CLS
    7: DB

*
```

| **Step 2** | Type 1, ? SCLS and press Enter. | See screen that follows. |

```
*1, ? SCLS
      2:CLS
O.K.?
```

▶*EDLIN prompts you with a flashing cursor.*

If this is not the string of characters you are looking for, then you would continue the search by pressing N.

Step 3   For now, press Y to exit the search.   An * follows.

How to Replace Text

To search for a string of characters and replace the string with another string of characters, you must do the following:

1. List the range of lines that you wish EDLIN to search.

2. List the R command followed by the characters that you are searching for and replacing. The characters must be written as they appear in the file, including the use of both uppercase and lowercase.

3. Press F6 followed by the letters of the new string of characters that will replace the old string.

4. Press Enter to activate the search and replace.

Tip: You can place the ? between items 1 and 2 in the previous list to stop EDLIN and have it ask you if the string of characters found should be replaced by the new string of characters, just as it did with the search command.

In this exercise, you will replace CLS with PAUSE.

List the file.

What to Do	*What Happens*
Step 1 Type L and press Enter.	See screen that follows.

```
*L

    1: ECHO OFF
    2:*CLS
    3: VER
    4: DATE
    5: TIME
    6: CLS
    7: DB

*
```

| **Step 2**   Type 1, ? RCLS, depress F6, type PAUSE, and press Enter. | See screen that follows. |

```
*1, ? RCLS^ZPAUSE
    2:*PAUSE
O.K.?
```

▶ *If CLS should be replaced by PAUSE in Line 2, press Y for yes.*

| **Step 3**   Type Y and press Enter. | See screen that follows. |

```
O.K.?Y
    6: PAUSE
O.K.?
```

| Step 4 | Type Y and press Enter. | See screen that follows. |

```
O.K.?Y
*
```

List the file.

| Step 5 | Type L and press Enter. | See screen that follows. |

```
*L

1: ECHO OFF
2: PAUSE
3: VER
4: DATE
5: TIME
6: *PAUSE
7: DB

*
```

| Step 6 | Type E and press Enter to save the file and exit EDLIN. | Returns to the DOS system prompt. |

Review Exercises

1. Using the search procedure, search for the second occurrence of PAUSE in the file AUTO.BAT.

2. Using the replace procedure, replace both occurrences of the PAUSE to CLS in the file AUTO.BAT.

Summary Points

1. An editor is a program that allows you to create a file or alter an existing file.

2. EDLIN is a built-in DOS editor. To access EDLIN, you must have a disk with the EDLIN.COM file on it.

3. The * is the EDLIN prompt.

4. An advantage of using EDLIN is that you can change any part of the file without retyping it. EDLIN can be used to edit files created by COPY CON.

5. EDLIN can be used to

   a. List the contents of the file you are editing.

   b. Insert a line or lines of text.

   c. Delete a line or several lines of text.

   d. Copy a line or series of lines to another position within a file.

   e. Move a line or series of lines to another position within a file.

   f. Replace a string of text.

   g. Search the file for a specific string.

   h. Transfer a specific line(s) to another file.

   i. Write edited lines to a specified file.

   j. Exit and save the edited file with current changes.

   k. Quit EDLIN without saving any of the changes.

Application Exercises

1. Edit the file AUTO.BAT file on **BACKUP** using EDLIN so that when activated it uses the following DOS commands:

```
ECHO OFF
PROMPT $P$G
TIME
DATE
REM   (A comment you wish to place in the file)
PAUSE
ECHO   (Place a comment you wish to display to the screen.)
PAUSE
MENU
```

2. Use MENU2.SCR from **BACKUP** to change the words OPENING MENU to your name or personalized menu. *Hint:* Use the arrow keys so that you will not write over the lines. If you do, obtain another copy of MENU2.SCR from your **EXERCISES** disk.

3. Use MENU.BAT from **BACKUP** to do the following, using EDLIN:

   a. Display the contents of the file to the printer.

   b. Switch Lines 15 through 16 with Lines 27 through 28.

   c. Switch :F1 with :F3 using the replace command (R).

   d. Using the search command (S), find out how many occurrences of the string GOTO there are.

   e. Call up the MENU and see if all the function keys call up the correct applications programs listed next to them.

4. Create the file MOVIE.LST with EDLIN on the **BACKUP** disk.

   The contents of MOVIE.LST is

```
12345678901234567890
3       The Goodbye Girl
2       Trading Places
2       Verdict
7       Animal House
7       Police Academy
8       Amadeus
8       Casablanca
4       Guess Who's Coming to Dinner
4       It Happened One Night
5       Pinocchio
6       Seven Brides for Seven Brothers
6       The Black Swan
1       Gone with the Wind
2       Splash
9       Annie Hall
9       In the Heat of the Night
9       Samson and Delilah
```

▶ *This line is a ruler, not included in the file.*

5. Copy the file MOVIE2.LST from **EXERCISE** disk to **BACKUP** disk. Edit the file MOVIE2.LST using EDLIN so that its contents will be identical to the following list. Use all the editing commands you learned.

```
12345678901234567890
1      Gone with the Wind
2      Splash
2      Trading Places
2      Verdict
3      The Sound of Music
3      The Goodbye Girl
4      Guess Who's Coming to Dinner
4      Mr. Roberts
4      It Happened One Night
5      Alice in Wonderland
5      Dumbo
5      Pinocchio
6      Seven Brides for Seven Brothers
6      The Black Swan
7      Animal House
7      Pal Joey
7      Police Academy
8      Amadeus
8      Casablanca
9      Annie Hall
9      In the Heat of the Night
9      Samson and Delilah
10     Boys Town
10     Goodbye Charlie
10     Murder by Death
11     For Your Eyes Only
11     The Graduate
11     The Man with the Golden Gun
12     The Jewel of the Nile
12     Romancing the Stone
13     Aliens
13     Born Free
13     Star Wars
14     My Fair Lady
14     The Wonderful World of the B. Grimm
15     Mickey Christmas Carol
15     The Sword in the Stone
```

▶ *This line is a ruler, not included in the file.*

```
15    The Three Caballeros
15    Yogi's First Christmas
16    Never Say Goodbye
16    Quiet Man
16    The Flame and the Arrow
17    Mary Poppins
17    That's Entertainment I
17    That's Entertainment II
18    Rocky
18    The Adventures of Robin Hood
18    Thunderball
19    Swiss Family Robinson
19    The Ten Commandments
20    It's a Wonderful Life
20    The Best Years of Our Life
20    The Miracle on 34th Street
21    Parent Trap
21    Tom Thumb
21    20,000 Leagues Under the Sea
```

6. a. Using **BACKUP** disk, create the file MAIN.BAT, using CLS and ECHO, that contains the following menu. Use asterisks to create the frame.

```
*****************************************
*                                       *
*          MAIN MENU                    *
*       1. WP                           *
*       2. SS                           *
*       3. DB                           *
*       4. QUIT                         *
*                                       *
*                                       *
*       ENTER OPTIONS FROM 1 - 4        *
*                                       *
*****************************************
```

b. With COPY CON, create four batch files.

Batch filename	Contents
1.BAT	WP
	MAIN
2.BAT	SS
	MAIN
3.BAT	DB
	MAIN
4.BAT	CLS

    c. Execute the file MAIN.BAT (Be sure that WP.COM, SS. COM, and DB.COM are on **BACKUP** disk when you execute MAIN.BAT.)

Comprehension Questions

Answer the following questions.

1. Describe three types of editors.

2. Explain what each of the following commands do.

    a. `A>EDLIN B:PERSONAL.LTR`

    b. `A>EDLIN B:AUTOEXEC.BAT`

      `*L`

    c. `*3I`

    d. `*4D`

    e. `1,1,8M`

    f. `5,6,9C`

    g. `1, ? SOFF`

    h. `1, ? R:F2^Z:F1`

Completion Exercises

1. To use EDLIN, you must type in _____ followed by the filename and extension of an existing file or a file you wish to create.

2. The command 12L means _____.

3. The _____ command would be used if you wish to list only Lines 2 through 14.

4. The _____ is used to designate the "current line" when using EDLIN.

5. Moving a line or a series of lines is accomplished by typing the line or line numbers you wish to move, a comma, and then the command _____.

6. When copying, the 6 in the command 4,4,6C means _____.

7. When searching for a string of characters, you can place a _____ between the range and the S command, and EDLIN will ask you if the string of characters it has found is the correct one.

**Matching
Exercises**

Choose the correct letter from the right-hand column.

1. *I   a. Ends input to a file created with EDLIN

2. *^C   b. Lists a file created with EDLIN

3. *E   c. EDLIN prompt

4. *L   d. Exits EDLIN without saving the changes

5. *   e. Saves and exits a file created with EDLIN

6. *Q   f. Inserts a line

9

Sorting, Locating, and Redirecting Input/Output

When you have completed this chapter, you will be able to

Learning Objectives:

1. Explain what a filter is.

2. Explain what how commands are linked together with pipes.

3. Describe how the DOS filter MORE can assist in reading long directories and files that will not fit onto one screen.

4. Explain how the DOS filters can be used to sort directories and lists within files.

5. Explain how DOS filters can be used to find files and specific text within a file.

Performance Objectives:

1. Use the filter MORE to display portions of a directory to a screen.

2. Use the filter SORT to list a directory in alphabetical order.

3. Use the FIND filter to locate a file in a directory.

4. Combine the DOS filters with redirection to send a directory list to a file.

5. Sort the contents of a file.

6. Find a specific string of characters within a file.

7. Combine SORT and FIND to obtain a more specific list of the contents of a file.

Chapter Overview

In this chapter, you will learn how to sort the contents of a directory or a file, find a string of characters within a directory or file, save a sorted directory to a file, list parts of a directory or file to the screen, and redirect the output of a command such as DIR. All these activities are achieved by using three DOS commands: MORE, SORT, and FIND. These files, called *filters,* can be used alone or linked together using pipes. They can also be used together with other DOS commands that redirect input or output.

What are Filters?

When you list the directory of a disk, you notice that the files do not display in any order. By using a filter, you can control what files you wish to display (FIND), the order in which they display (SORT), and how much is displayed—the whole directory or a screen at a time (MORE).

Filters are files that allow you to take input from a DOS file such as DIR and select the output. They can also take input from user-created files and display selected output to a screen or printer.

Command	What It Does
MORE	Sends the contents of a directory or a file to the screen a screenful at a time and waits until you instruct it to continue. It is similar to using the DIR /P, except that it can be used with the TYPE command.
SORT	Sorts a directory or the contents of a file alphabetically and numerically. You can also specify on what column to begin the sort or reverse sort.
FIND	Finds a specific string of characters within a directory or the contents of a file. It can be used to display the line number of each line of the directory or file where the string was found. It can be used to display the line number and the line where it encountered the string. It can also list all the lines where it did not find the string of characters.

What are Pipes?

When you wish to sort a directory, you need to link together the two DOS commands DIR and SORT. The character used to link these two files together is called a *pipe* (¦). A pipe is used to take the output of one DOS command and use that output as the input for the second DOS command. For example,

```
A>DIR ¦ SORT
```

In this example, DIR and SORT are piped together. The result is a sorted directory of Drive A:. Since filters are DOS external commands and reside on a DOS disk, the previous example could only be used if the SORT.EXE file was located in the root directory of Drive A:.

If the SORT.EXE file is located within another drive such as Drive B:, you can use the command DIR ¦ B:SORT to obtain a sorted directory of Drive A:.

What is Redirection?

If you wanted to send the output from the previous example to the printer, you would use PRN, following the command as you did in previous chapters. The > sign causes the redirection to the printer. This type of redirection is called *output redirection*. Any time the output of a command is redirected, a > sign is used. The opposite is *input redirection*. The < sign is used to tell a DOS command to take its input from the file that follows the < sign. For example,

```
A>SORT<FILENAME.EXT
```

In this example, the input file is FILENAME.EXT. The SORT command will receive its input from FILENAME.EXT.

The output from this command is displayed to the screen. The output can be redirected to the printer as follows:

```
A>SORT<FILENAME.EXT>PRN
```

Hands-On Activities

In this section, you will use MORE, SORT, and FIND on both directories and files. While using MORE, SORT, and FIND, you will designate your source file (input redirection) and determine where your output is to be sent (output redirection).

How to Use MORE with Directories

In this exercise, you will display a screenful of the **BACKUP** disk root directory at a time.

Reformat the **BACKUP** disk with the label "Backup," and copy all the files from the **EXERCISES** disk to the **BACKUP** disk. Then use the **BACKUP** disk in Drive B: and the **DOS** disk in Drive A:.

	What to Do	*What Happens*
Step 1	At a B>, type DIR ¦ A:MORE and press Enter.	A screenful is displayed.
Step 2	Press any key to continue viewing the directory a screenful at a time.	You see the next screenful.

How to Send a Sorted Directory List to a File	You may want to sort the contents of your directory to make it easier to read and store the sorted contents in a file so that you can refer to it later.

Use the **BACKUP** disk in Drive B: and the **DOS** disk in Drive A:.

What to Do	*What Happens*
Step 1	Obtain a B>. Type DIR ¦ A:SORT > DIRECTOR.LST and press Enter.	DOS returns you to a B>.

If you wish to see the contents of the sorted file, you must use the TYPE command as you did in the previous chapter.

Review Exercises

1. Send the contents of the file DIRECTOR.LST to the printer.

2. Send the contents of the sorted directory of **BACKUP** disk to the file SORTDIR.DOC.

How to List Specific Files Using FIND and SORT

When your directories are hard to read, you may wish to find specific files, sort them, and display them to the screen.

Use the **BACKUP** disk in Drive B: and the **DOS** disk in Drive A:.

What to Do	*What Happens*
Step 1	Obtain a B>. Type DIR ¦ A:FIND "COM" ¦ A:SORT and press Enter.	See screen that follows.

```
B>DIR ¦ A:FIND "COM" ¦ A:SORT
COMMAND    DAT        5   8-31-87  12:48p
DB         COM    24432   8-26-87   3:58p
REPLY      COM       14   9-17-87  12:34p
SS         COM    21330   8-26-87   3:59p
WP         COM    16707   1-01-80  12:19a
```

Tip: When you searched for COM, notice that not only were all the COM files located, but any files that began with COM.

If you wish to store the contents of this list in a file, use the output redirection character > and a filename following the SORT command. Anytime you use output redirection to a file, DOS will create a file with the specified name if one does not already exist. If one does exist, the old file will be written over.

Review Exercises

1. Store the contents of the previous sort in a file named FIND COM.LST.

2. Send FINDCOM.LST to the printer.

How to Sort the Contents of a File

Sorting the contents of a file is similar to sorting the contents of a directory, except that the input comes from a user-created file and not a DOS command. Some of the options that you can use with the SORT command are as follows:

Option	What It Does
/R	Sorts the file in reverse.
/+n	Sorts the file beginning with a particular column. The symbol +n stands for any positive integer.

In the following example, the contents of the file can be sorted by the numbers on the left or by the title of the movie. The title starts on the seventh column. The /+n allows you to designate this column.

The contents of MOVIE.LST is

```
3      The Goodbye Girl
2      Trading Places
2      Verdict
7      Animal House
7      Police Academy
8      Amadeus
8      Casablanca
4      Guess Who's Coming to Dinner
4      It Happened One Night
5      Pinocchio
6      Seven Brides for Seven Brothers
6      The Black Swan
1      Gone with the Wind
2      Splash
9      Annie Hall
9      In the Heat of the Night
9      Samson and Delilah
```

The normal format of the SORT is

```
SORT [/R] [/+n]
```

In this exercise, you will be sorting the contents of file MOVIE.LST in reverse order.

Use **BACKUP** disk in Drive B: and **DOS** disk in Drive A:.

What to Do	*What Happens*
Step 1 Obtain a B>. Type A:SORT /R <MOVIE.LST and press Enter.	See screen that follows.

```
B>A:SORT  /R <MOVIE.LST
9    Samson and Delilah
9    In the Heat of the Night
9    Annie Hall
8    Casablanca
8    Amadeus
7    Police Academy
7    Animal House
6    The Black Swan
6    Seven Brides for Seven Brothers
5    Pinocchio
4    It Happened One Night
4    Guess Who's Coming to Dinner
3    The Goodbye Girl
2    Verdict
2    Trading Places
2    Splash
1    Gone with the Wind
```

*How to Sort
the Contents
of a File on
a Specified
Column*

If you wanted to sort the contents of MOVIE.LST by the first letter of the movie titles, you would use the /+n option. Since the title begins on Column 7, you would use 7 as the integer for the +n option.

Use **BACKUP** disk in Drive B: and **DOS** disk in Drive A:.

What to Do	*What Happens*
Step 1	At the B >, type A:SORT /+7 <MOVIE.LST and press Enter.	See screen that follows.

```
B>A:SORT  /+7 <MOVIE.LST

8    Amadeus
7    Animal House
9    Annie Hall
8    Casablanca
1    Gone with the Wind
4    Guess Who's Coming to Dinner
9    In the Heat of the Night
4    It Happened One Night
5    Pinocchio
7    Police Academy
9    Samson and Delilah
6    Seven Brides for Seven Brothers
2    Splash
6    The Black Swan
3    The Goodbye Girl
2    Trading Places
2    Verdict
```

Review Exercises

1. Obtain the following results by sorting the file MOVIE.LST.

```
1    Gone with the Wind
2    Splash
2    Trading Places
2    Verdict
3    The Goodbye Girl
4    Guess Who's Coming to Dinner
4    It Happened One Night
5    Pinocchio
6    Seven Brides for Seven Brothers
6    The Black Swan
7    Animal House
7    Police Academy
8    Amadeus
8    Casablanca
9    Annie Hall
9    In the Heat of the Night
9    Samson and Delilah
```

2. Sort the directory of **BACKUP** disk by date (Column 24), and display the results to the printer.

Answers

1. B>A:SORT /+1 <MOVIE.LST

2. B>DIR ¦ A:SORT /+24 >PRN

How to Use the FIND Filter

The FIND filter is used to locate a specific string of characters within a DIR listing or within a file. FIND is also capable of listing the location (line number) where it found the string(s). This filter will search through a file for a string of characters the user specifies.

Some options that can be used with FIND are as follows:

Option	What It Does
/V	Displays the lines that do not match the criterion.
/C	Displays only the number of lines that contain the string.
/N	Displays each line and its line number where the string was found.

The format of the FIND command is

```
FIND [/V] [/C] [/N] string {filename}
```

How to List the Lines That Contain a Character(s)

In this exercise, you will find all the lines that contain the lower-case letter "h" within the file MOVIE.LST.

Use **BACKUP** disk in Drive B: and **DOS** disk in Drive A:.

What to Do	*What Happens*
Step 1	Obtain a B>. Type A:FIND "h" <MOVIE.LST and press Enter.	See screen that follows.

```
B>A:FIND "h" <MOVIE.LST
3     The Goodbye Girl
4     Guess Who's Coming to Dinner
4     It Happened One Night
5     Pinocchio
6     Seven Brides for Seven Brothers
6     The Black Swan
1     Gone with the Wind
2     Splash
9     In the Heat of the Night
9     Samson and Delilah
```

How to List the Number of Lines Containing Specific Character(s)

In this example, you will obtain a list of the number of lines that contain the lowercase letter "h."

Use **BACKUP** disk in Drive B: and **DOS** disk in Drive A:.

What to Do	*What Happens*
Step 1	Obtain a B>. Type A:FIND /C "h" <MOVIE.LST and press Enter.	See screen that follows.

```
B>A:FIND /C "h" <MOVIE.LST
10
```

How to List the Lines and Numbers of All Lines Containing a Character(s)	In this exercise, you will obtain a list of the lines that contain the lowercase letter "h" and the line number of each line.	
	Use **BACKUP** disk in Drive B: and **DOS** disk in Drive A:.	
	What to Do	*What Happens*
Step 1	Obtain a B>. Type A:FIND /N "h" < MOVIE.LST and press **Enter**.	See screen that follows.

```
B>A:FIND /N "h" <MOVIE.LST
[1]3    The Goodbye Girl
[8]4    Guess Who's Coming to Dinner
[9]4    It Happened One Night
[10]5   Pinocchio
[11]6   Seven Brides for Seven Brothers
[12]6   The Black Swan
[13]1   Gone with the Wind
[14]2   Splash
[16]9   In the Heat of the Night
[17]9   Samson and Delilah
```

Review Exercises

1. Obtain a list of all the lines from MOVIE.LST that do not contain the lowercase letter "h." Use option /V.

2. Display the lines and the line numbers of MOVIE.LST that contain the uppercase letter "G."

3. How many lines contained the uppercase letter "G"? What are their line numbers?

Answers

1. A:FIND /V "h" <MOVIE.LST

2. A:FIND /N "G" <MOVIE.LST

3. Three, and they are 1, 8, and 13.

*How to Find
and Sort Lines
Containing
a Given
Character(s)*

In this exercise, you will be finding all the lines that contain the lowercase letter "h" and then sort those lines by the title of the movie.

Use **BACKUP** disk in Drive B: and **DOS** disk in Drive A:.

What to Do	*What Happens*
Step 1	Obtain a B>. Type A:FIND "h" ¦ A:SORT /+7 < MOVIE.LST and press Enter.	See screen that follows.

```
B>A:FIND "h" ¦ A:SORT /+7<MOVIE.LST
1    Gone with the Wind
4    Guess Who's Coming to Dinner
9    In the Heat of the Night
4    It Happened One Night
5    Pinocchio
9    Samson and Delilah
6    Seven Brides for Seven Brothers
2    Splash
6    The Black Swan
3    The Goodbye Girl
```

*Summary
Points*

1. By using filters, you can control what files you wish to display (FIND), the order in which they display (SORT), and how much is displayed—the whole file or a screen at a time (MORE).

2. Filters are files that allow you to take input from a DOS command such as DIR and select the output. They can also take input from user-created files and display selected output to a screen or printer.

3. Three filter commands are MORE, SORT, and FIND.

4. The character (¦) is used to link two or more commands together. It is called a *pipe*. A pipe is used to take the output of one DOS command and use that output as the input for another DOS command.

5. The > sign redirects output to a printer. This type of redirection is called *output redirection*.

6. Any time the output of a command is redirected, a > sign is used. The opposite is input redirection. The < sign is used to tell a DOS command to take its input from the file that follows the < sign.

Application Exercises

Do the following exercises at your computer. For all exercises, use **BACKUP** disk in Drive B: and **DOS** disk in Drive A:.

1. Use MOVIE.LST to obtain the following output, using the FIND and SORT commands:

```
9       Annie Hall
9       In the Heat of the Night
9       Samson and Delilah
```

2. Use MOVIE.LST to obtain the following output:

```
3       The Goodbye Girl
6       The Black Swan
```

3. Using MOVIE.LST, what letter is missing from the FIND command?

```
B>A:FIND " " ¦ A:SORT /+1<MOVIE.LST
2       Splash
6       Seven Brides for Seven Brothers
6       The Black Swan
9       Samson and Delilah
```

4. Explain what the following command does when you use it with MOVIE.LST.

```
B>A:FIND "S" ¦ A:SORT /+6<MOVIE.LST
```

5. Explain what the following command does when you use it with **Practice** disk:

```
B>DIR ¦ A:FIND "TXT" ¦ A:SORT /+23
```

6. Use **Practice** disk to create a file called INVENT.LST with the following contents.

```
PART No. 176     SPARK PLUG        3.47
PART No. 183     GENERATOR        27.93
PART No. 842     CONDENSER         3.24
PART No. 963     RADIATOR         47.83
```

7. Sort the contents of the file INVENT.LST.

8. Use the FIND command to locate Part No. 842.

Comprehension Questions

Answer the following questions.

1. Explain what the following does:

   B>A:MORE<MOVIE2.LST

2. Explain what the following does:

   B>A:FIND "The" ¦ A:MORE<MOVIE2.LST

3. Explain what the following does:

   B>A:FIND "e" ¦ A:SORT /+8 ¦ A:MORE<MOVIE2.LST

4. What does redirection mean?

5. What is a filter?

6. What is a pipe?

Completion Exercises

Complete the following sentences.

1. Three commands used to filter are _____, _____, and _____.

2. The character _____ is used to link files together.

3. A _____ is used to take the output of one DOS command and use that output as the input for another DOS command.

4. The _____ sign is used to tell a DOS command to take its input from the file that follows that sign.

5. _____ is the option used to sort a file in reverse.

Matching Exercises

Choose the correct letter from the right-hand column.

1. FIND

a. Sends that contents of a directory or a file to the screen a screenful at a time and waits until you instruct it to continue

2. SORT

b. Used to take the output of one DOS command and use that output as the input for another command

3. MORE

c. Used with FIND to display each line and its line number where a string of characters is found

4. Pipe

d. Places the contents of a directory or file in alphabetical and numerical order

5. /+n

e. Used with FIND to display only the number of lines that contain a certain string of characters

6. /V

f. Used with FIND to display the lines that do not match the criterion

7. /C

g. Sorts a file beginning with a particular column

8. /N

h. Locates a specific string of characters within a directory or the contents of a file

Glossary

Application Software Software designed to perform a certain type of task such as word processing, spreadsheet, or database applications.

ASSIGN The DOS command that makes programs think a disk drive is actually a different drive.

ATTRIB The DOS command used to change the read-only status of a file.

AUTOEXEC.BAT The batch file that, when placed on the boot disk, is automatically executed when the computer is booted.

Backup A copy of stored data made to protect against data loss.

BACKUP The DOS command that lets DOS copy a specified group of files to a series of floppy disks.

Batch files Special files that contain DOS commands that are executed in sequence when the file is executed.

Booting the System The process of loading the operating system into a computer.

Buffer A small storage area set up to store DOS commands as they are entered. Only the most recent file is retained.

Byte A storage location that can hold one character.

Central Processing Unit The "brains" of a computer. It carries out instructions stored in RAM and directs all the components of the computer system.

CD The DOS command that allows you to change to another subdirectory.

CHKDSK The DOS command used to allow the user to check the status of a disk.

CLS The command to clear the screen and place the cursor in the upper left-hand corner.

CGA Stands for Color Graphics Adapter. One of the first color monitors used on the IBM personal computer. It allows the use of 16 colors in text and four in graphics.

Cold boot The process of initially starting the machine by turning it on.

Commands Instructions to the computer.

Concatenate The process of combining two or more files into one. This process uses the COPY command.

COPY The DOS command to duplicate one or more files.

CPU See Central Processing Unit.

Ctrl-S The combination of keys pressed to stop the scrolling of information on a monitor screen.

Cursor The position indicator on a monitor screen. It appears as either a flashing hyphen or a small bright rectangle.

DATE The DOS command that allows the user to enter the current date.

Default disk drive The currently active disk drive that DOS automatically directs its commands to unless they are directed elsewhere.

DEL The DOS command used to delete a single file or group of files.

DIR The DOS command used to display the disk directory.

Directory tree The list of all the subdirectories found on a disk and how those subdirectories are connected.

DISKCOMP The DOS command to compare the contents of one disk with the contents of another to find out if they are exactly the same.

DISKCOPY The DOS command to duplicate an entire disk.

Directory The special area of a disk where DOS keeps track of what files are stored on the disk, how big they are, and when they were created.

DOS An operating system used on personal computers. The term stands for Disk Operating System.

DOS editing keys The keys that allow the user to redisplay and edit the most recent DOS command.

Drive designator The single letter followed by a colon that is used to indicate the disk drive in use.

Echo The display on the monitor screen of data that has been input from the keyboard.

ECHO The DOS command that can be used to turn off or back on the display of DOS commands as they are executed. The command can also be used to display a message even when the echo is turned off.

EDLIN The DOS line editor.

EGA Stands for Enhanced Graphics Adapter. A more advanced color monitor that allows up to 64 text colors.

ERASE The DOS command used to delete a single file or group of files.

Extension The three characters that follow the period after the file-name.

External DOS commands DOS commands not loaded into RAM upon booting but loaded directly off the disk when needed.

FDISK The DOS command to allow you to set up one or more partitions on your hard disk.

File A collection of items stored on a disk, such as applications programs and data such as letters, spreadsheets, and lists.

File allocation table or FAT The special area on a disk where DOS keeps track of which disk areas are occupied and which are free to be used.

Filename A name, up to eight characters in length, used to identify a file's contents.

Filters The DOS commands that are used for piping.

FIND The filter that allows the command being used to display only lines of information that contain the search string.

Floppy disk The most commonly used storage device for microcomputers. The 5 1/4-inch and 3 1/2-inch disk drives are the two primary sizes.

FOR The DOS command that can use a list of parameters and execute a DOS command using each of the parameters in turn.

FORMAT The DOS command to set up a disk initially for use. It can also be used to erase from a disk contents that are no longer needed.

Fragmented What happens to a file when DOS begins storing it in an area on the disk that does not have sufficient room to store the entire file. The part of the file that does not fit in the first area is stored in another area, causing the file to be stored in separate locations.

Function keys Special keys on the keyboard that can be assigned specific functions by the current program.

GOTO The DOS command that can change the order of execution of the batch file commands.

Hard disk A storage device that allows the storage of large amounts of data. Hard disks store more information and are also faster than floppy disks.

Hardware The physical equipment that makes up the computer system.

Hidden files Files that are not listed when you use the DIR command. Two DOS files are hidden on a bootable disk.

High density disks The type of 5 1/4-inch disk that can store 1.2 megabytes of data.

IF The DOS command used to test a condition in a batch file.

Input devices Equipment used to enter data, text, or other information into the computer's memory.

Internal DOS commands DOS commands that are stored in RAM when the system is booted. To use these commands, you do not need to have a DOS disk in the computer.

Keyboard The primary input device used on microcomputers. The alphabetic and numeric keys are in the standard typewriter positions, with many other keys available.

LABEL The DOS command to allow the user to change the volume label on a disk.

Laser printer A type of printer that uses a print technology similar to a copy machine.

Lost allocation clusters One of the disk problems found by the CHKDSK command. It occurs when a program allocates space for a file but does not save the file information in the directory.

Magnetic tape A storage medium used to make backup copies of hard disks.

MD The DOS command used to create new subdirectories.

Megahertz The unit for measuring how fast the computer clock runs that processes data and instructions. A megahertz is one million cycles per second. The faster the clock runs, the more powerful the computer is because it can process data faster.

MODE The command that allows you to give instructions to the hardware attached to your computer.

Modem A communications device that lets one computer send information to another computer through the phone lines.

Monitor A display device used on a microcomputer.

Monochrome A type of monitor that uses a single color to display data.

Mouse A hand-held device that when rolled across the desk top sends cursor information to the computer.

Num lock A toggle key that changes the function of certain keys from cursor movement keys to the numeric keypad.

Operating System The interface program between the application programs and the hardware.

Partitions The areas of the disk that are set up for the various operating systems.

PATH The DOS command to tell the system which tree paths to follow to find executable files.

Path name The subdirectory where the file can be found.

PAUSE The DOS command that allows the batch file operation to be suspended while the user reads the screen, switches disk drives, and so on.

Piping The process of using the output of one command as input to another command.

PRINT The DOS command that allows you to print files while the computer is executing another program.

Printer A device to allow a computer to create a permanent record of information by printing it on paper.

Programs Instructions written to carry out certain activities on a computer.

PROMPT The DOS command that can be used to change the DOS prompt.

RAM Stands for Random Access Memory. The temporary storage area in a computer where programs and data are stored during processing. When the computer is turned off, the contents of RAM are lost.

RD The DOS command to remove an unwanted subdirectory. It must be empty to be removed.

Redirection The process of sending output to a disk file or the printer instead of to the screen. Input can also be redirected.

REM The DOS command that allows comments to be placed in a batch file so they can be printed on the screen as the batch file executes.

RENAME The DOS command to allow a filename to be changed.

Reset key A special key found on some computers that can be used to perform a warm boot.

RESTORE The DOS command used to copy to the hard disk the files copied from the hard disk using the BACKUP command.

Resolution The clarity of the image displayed on the monitor screen.

Root directory The original directory on the disk.

Scrolling When the top line on the screen is pushed off the screen by additional lines being displayed.

Sectors Small sections of a track on a disk.

Software Instructions written to direct the computer to carry out certain tasks.

SORT The DOS filter command used to sort directories or files.

Subdirectory A list of files found on a disk that are stored under a sub-directory name.

SYS The DOS command that can be used to copy the system files to a previously formatted disk.

System software Instructions to the computer to operate the system.

TIME The command that allows the user to enter the current time.

Tracks Concentric circles of magnetic storage on a disk surface.

TREE The DOS command that prints all the subdirectories and, if specified, the files found there.

TYPE The DOS command that allows the data in a text file to be displayed on the screen.

VER The command to find the DOS version number currently in use.

VOL The DOS command used to display the volume name.

VGA Stands for Video Graphics Array. A type of monitor that allows up to 256 text colors and better resolution than other standard color monitors.

Warm boot Clearing the memory and restarting the computer by pressing and holding down the Ctrl followed by the Alt and Del keys.

Wildcard characters The asterisk and question mark, which can be used in many DOS commands to modify the command to use more than one of the files on the disk.

Word A unit of data that is processed at one time. It does not correspond to a word in English.

Index

Quick Reference

DOS COMMANDS

APPEND	To set a directory search order for data files.
ASSIGN	To reassign disk drives.
ATTRIB	To change a file's attributes.
BACKUP	To back up hard drives to floppy disks.
CH *or* CHDIR	To change directories.
CHKDSK	To check a disk's status.
CLS	To clear the screen.
COMMAND	To load an additional copy of COMMAND.COM.
COMP	To compare files.
COPY	To copy files.
DATE	To display or change the system date.
DEL	To delete files.
DIR	To list the contents of a directory.
DISKCOMP	To compare floppy disks.
DISKCOPY	To copy floppy disks.
ERASE	To erase files.
FIND	To find a string of text.
FORMAT	To format a disk.
JOIN	To connect two disk drives into one.
LABEL	To add or change a disk's volume label.
MD *or* MKDIR	To make a subdirectory.
MODE	To set the controls for printers, video, and async communications ports.
MORE	To display one screen of information at a time.
PATH	To set a directory search order for COM, EXE, and BAT files.
PROMPT	To set or change the system prompt.
RECOVER	To recover a file from a disk with a bad directory.
RENAME (REN)	To rename a file.
REPLACE	To selectively replace files on one disk with files on another.
RESTORE	To restore backed up files from floppy disks to hard drives.
RD *or* RMDIR	To remove a subdirectory.

SELECT	To select a different country configuration.
SET	To display or set the system environment.
SETUP	To set your computer's parameters.
SHARE	To enable file and record locking.
SORT	To sort directories and/or the contents of a file.
SUBST	To substitute a hard disk subdirectory for a disk drive.
SYS	To transfer the DOS system files to a hard disk.
TIME	To display or set the system time.
TREE	To display the directory (and files) of a disk.
TYPE	To display the contents of a file.
VER	To display the DOS version being used.
VERIFY	To set or show verification of data written to a disk.
VOL	To display the volume label of a disk.
XCOPY	To selectively copy files from one or more subdirectories.

CONFIG.SYS COMMANDS

BREAK	To turn on/off the break (interrupt) function.
BUFFERS	To specify the number of buffers allocated to data transfers between RAM and disk drives.
DEVICE	To specify any additional device drivers.
FILES	To specify how many files can be open at one time.
LASTDRIVE	To specify how many disk drives your computer has.
SHELL	To specify another command processor other than COMMAND.COM.

BATCH FILE COMMANDS

CALL	Calls another batch file.
ECHO	Turns on/off the display of batch commands.
FOR... IN... DO...	Allows the use of the same batch command on multiple files.
GOTO	Jumps to a subroutine within a batch file.
IF	Allows conditional execution of a command.
PAUSE	Pauses a batch file until a key is pressed.
REM	Displays a message to the screen.
SHIFT	Shifts the command parameters one parameter to the right.